The Making of a Human Bomb

THE CULTURES AND PRACTICE OF VIOLENCE SERIES

Series Editors:

Neil L. Whitehead, University of Wisconsin, Madison

Jo Ellen Fair, University of Wisconsin, Madison

Leigh Payne, University of Wisconsin, Madison

The study of violence has often focused on the political and economic conditions under which violence is generated, the suffering of victims, and the psychology of its interpersonal dynamics. Less familiar are the role of perpetrators, their motivations, and the social conditions under which they are able to operate. In the context of postcolonial state building and more latterly the collapse and implosion of society, community violence, state repression, and the phenomena of judicial inquiries in the aftermath of civil conflict, there is a need to better comprehend the role of those who actually do the work of violence—torturers, assassins, and terrorists—as much as the role of those who suffer its consequences.

When atrocity and murder take place, they feed the world of the iconic imagination that transcends reality and its rational articulation; but in doing so imagination can bring further violent realities into being. This series encourages authors who build on traditional disciplines and break out of their constraints and boundaries, incorporating media and performance studies and literary and cultural studies as much as anthropology, sociology, and history.

NASSER ABUFARHA

The Making of a Human Bomb

AN ETHNOGRAPHY OF PALESTINIAN RESISTANCE

Duke University Press
Durham and London
2009

© 2009 Duke University Press
All rights reserved.
Printed in the United States of America on acid-free paper ⊗
Designed by C. H. Westmoreland
Typeset in Quadraat by Keystone Typesetting, Inc.
Library of Congress Cataloging-in-Publication Data appear on
the last printed page of this book.

TO MY FATHER,

Ahmed Abdelhadi Abufarha

CONTENTS

Acknowledgments ix

CHAPTER ONE Introduction 1

CHAPTER TWO Histories and Historicities in Palestine 25

CHAPTER THREE State Expansion and the Violence of
"Peace Making" in Palestine 62

CHAPTER FOUR The Carrier 97

CHAPTER FIVE Dying to Live 134

CHAPTER SIX The Strategies and Politics of Martyrdom
in Palestine 187

CHAPTER SEVEN Conclusion 222

Appendix 241

Notes 243

Bibliography 257

Index 267

ACKNOWLEDGMENTS

This project would not have been possible without the consistent support of a number of people. In particular, I wish to extend my deepest gratitude to the ongoing intellectual engagement of my advisor, Professor Neil Whitehead, with the theoretical and methodological approaches to the study of violence over the course of my doctoral studies, including his own extensive and enlightening scholarship on the subject. I also express my deep appreciation to Professor Larry Nesper, Professor Sharon Hutchinson, and Professor Flagg Miller from the Department of Anthropology at the University of Wisconsin, Madison, for careful reading, comments, and discussions which sharpened my analysis and provided me with multiple ways of thinking about the various aspects of my project. I also thank my committee members from outside the Department of Anthropology, Professor Lieh Payne from the Department of Political Science and Professor Heinz Klug from the Law School, for providing me with valuable insights from other disciplines which broadened the scope of my analysis.

Embarking on a project to write a book on this sensitive and complex topic has been both a challenging and a rewarding experience. I extend my thanks to my family in Palestine who hosted me and supported me during my fieldwork, to the numerous people I interviewed, and to those who assisted me in arranging interviews and obtaining data critical to my work. I would also like to express my great appreciation for the patience and support I received from my family as I conducted fieldwork overseas and spent long hours immersed in research and writing. My special thanks to my partner for her constant engagement with my work and critiques of my writing, and to my children for their enormous tolerance of long periods of work and for providing joyous breaks from the intensity of my research.

I also thank my friends in Madison, who helped me and supported me on multiple fronts and provided me with relentless encouragement. Furthermore, I wish to express my appreciation to Fair Trade Coffee House on State Street, Mother Fool's Coffee House on Willy Street, Company of Thieves Café on Johnson Street, and the Multicultural Student Center at the University of Wisconsin and their staff for providing me with a perfect environment in which to think through and write most of the pages of this book.

CHAPTER ONE

Introduction

I returned to Palestine on 1 October 2003 to conduct my field research after being away from the region for over four years. It was my first trip to Palestine after the outbreak of Al-Aqsa Intifada. I had for the first time experienced having to cross so many roadblocks and checkpoints. For the first time I experienced traveling in a taxi through gravel and dirt roads in the mountains and the fields, going around checkpoints and roadblocks. It was the first time that I arrived in my village from a major trip through the eastern village side road instead of the main road from the south. Jenin, my local town, and my village Al-Jalama, five kilometers apart, were isolated from each other. I had been on the road all day and arrived at dark. When I first arrived at home, one of my mother's first few comments to me—she is in her late seventies—was *shufet chaif akhathu et-tariq minna* (See how they took the road from us!!). She was referring to the Israeli blockades of movement and confinement of the village: all roads are "officially" blocked with mounds of soil, large concrete blocks, or deep ditches, while Israeli tanks and hummers roam, track, and chase blockade "violators," passers-by who are constantly trying to reopen the road or, by monitoring Israeli army movements, circumvent a roadblock so that they can go about their daily activities of farming, shopping, going to school, going to the doctor, or going to work. My mother's comment was striking to me at the moment. However, little did I know at the time that it would become profound and central to my research on the subject of suicide bombings. As I discovered, suicide bombings create cultural conceptions of accessibility and represent the breaking down of barriers, thus mediating issues of confinement, isolation, and fragmentation on the one hand and freedom and unity on the other.

I conducted my research on political violence in Palestine as carried out by Palestinian groups against Israeli targets. What are known in the West as suicide bombings are referred to by Palestinians as 'amaliyyat istishhadiyya (operations of martyrdom). Even though I examine suicide bombings in the Palestinian-Israeli conflict, my research provides a template for analyzing similar forms of violence in other political and ethnic conflicts, be they regional or global. This research seeks to present an understanding of the violence through historical and cultural lenses and demonstrates that violence can only be entirely understood against a backdrop of specific histories and cultures. The analyses that I apply here to the Palestinian-Israeli conflict will provide a template that can also be applied in other contexts, but the conclusions may differ.

My research explores three areas with respect to the martyrdom operations in Palestine that scholars on the subject of violence agree to be areas of theoretical importance: the cultural poetics of political violence in Palestine; the nature of state violence (by Israel) and the mimetic violence carried out by resistance groups; and the relevance of globalization, modernity, and the consequent resurgence of traditions in shaping this form of violence (Whitehead 2004). To that end I interviewed members of Palestinian resistance factions who set up suicide-bombing operations and other political activists who give political context to the act of suicide bombing, to get an understanding of the groups' political and military strategies in carrying out martyrdom operations. I talked with families of participants in these operations and looked into the participants' life histories to assess the logic of the suicide, martyrdom, or sacrifice missions. I also reviewed myriad ways of representing martyrdom violence and interviewed a number of cultural performers (songwriters, painters, dancers, etc.), producers of the poetics of resistance who shape the broader Palestinian cultural discourse within which the act of the martyr is given meaning. In addition, my research is situated in an ethnographic representation of Palestinian life that sees the Palestinians' encounter with Israel as the cosmological and ontological basis of the present cultural order in Palestine (see the discussion of methodology later in this chapter).

By examining the Palestinian encounter with Israel and the generative cultural schemes produced by the encounter, the aesthetics of the performance of Palestinian "suicide bombing" missions, their cultural representations, and the poetics that their performance and representations generate, I argue that the practice of sacrificing Palestinian bodies and applying violence against the "enemy" in the same act mediates cultural ideas of uprooting and rootedness, fragmentation and unity, confinement and freedom, domination and independence. These social processes are mediated through the cultural conceptions generated in the poetics of the performance that create unconfined life, unsegmented peoplehood, and unfragmented Palestine in the Palestinian cultural imaginary. This free and united life in the cultural imaginary is created in contrast to Palestinians' ontological conditions of fragmentation, confinement, displacement, and encapsulation. Similarly, these acts represent defiance to the international order and assert agency, self-reliance, control over life, and a long-sought independence against a backdrop of a history of political domination. These aesthetics create polarizations between the *ontological conditions* of encapsulation, fragmentation, physical confinement, displacement, and political domination and the *aspirations* of unity, freedom, and independence of Palestinians and their rootedness in Palestine. Through these cultural conceptions the participation in the sacrifice or martyrdom and the application of violence against Israeli publics become intelligible and meaningful acts and generate a process through which a system of motivation arises. The sacrifice creates the naturalized, free, pre-occupation Palestine; the violence against Israeli publics destabilizes the normalcy of the "enemy" in Palestine, challenging its presence and asserting Palestinian rootedness in contested places. Moreover, the participants' taking of their own lives in the performance asserts their independence and self-reliance. Within this discourse of sacrifice and martyrdom performed along mimetic violence, the death of the sacrificer is conceived as a form of life or a better life that makes death in sacrifice not something to be feared but rather an aspired form of living. In this view, death is about living, not dying. To die is to live through the iconic image of the martyr within the cultural poetics of the resistance and through the freedom and unity of Palestinian peoplehood and the land of Palestine that is created in the cultural imaginary.

These positive cultural conceptions associated with the performance of martyrdom in Palestine should not obscure the reality that these acts of martyrdom include acts of indiscriminate terror against Israeli publics in civil spaces. That my research does not focus on these victims is in no way an attempt to hide these aspects of the martyrdom performances or to lessen their cruelty. However, my research is focused on the perpetrators and the ways in which the performance of violence is constructed, motivated, and mediated from the perpetrators' perspective. And in this regard the killing of Israeli civilians in particular and the illegitimacy of these acts of violence in the global political discourse carries some of those potential meanings. I explore these constructions and conceptions in the discussion of the meanings and strategies of martyrdom in the following chapters.

Collective and group violence has long existed in the human experience. However, in the last decade there has been an alarming increase in the use of violence as a medium for cultural assertion and social and political mediation in regional ethnic conflicts such as those in Bosnia and Rwanda. Most recently, there has been a frightening use of "suicide" bombings in Palestine, Iraq, Chechnya, Afghanistan, and even Europe and North America. My research project seeks to understand the *making* of the *human bomb* through ethnographic study of their historical, cultural, and political constructions in Palestine. If we seek to understand these violent practices, we must move beyond condemning them and questioning their legitimacy and examine the social and political processes that make them meaningful in their local settings. If we were to limit our discussion of this form of violence to issues of legitimacy, we would not even begin to understand its production, much less be any better equipped to deal with it. And if we continue to think of violence as fueled by the inherent hatred of its perpetrators, we will be blinded to the social processes through which violence is constructed, and the only policy options we will have for dealing with violence will involve applying similar or greater violence, thus validating the acts of the perpetrators and leaving us hostage to cycles of violence and counter-violence. A better understanding of violent practices is a must if we seek to develop more appropriate and effective responses to it. The widespread use of suicide bombings makes clear that this form of violence is becoming more meaningful to more people around the world. And with this increase in popularity, the military response becomes increasingly invalid and ineffective. Pure military responses seem only to have contributed to the intensification of suicide bombing thus far.

The frightening rise in the use of suicide bombings and strategies of martyrdom by different groups with local agendas in Palestine, Sri Lanka, Iraq, Chechnya, and Afghanistan, and others with global agendas in the United States, Britain, Spain, Indonesia, and Morocco, has prompted an array of new research that seeks to understand suicide bombings and to investigate and explore responses to them. Several recent academic articles and books on suicide bombing have been published. These works have focused variously on the intensity of suicide bombings and their widespread application in the global context (Atran 2004; Bergen 2002; Gambil 1998; Reuter 2004; Saez 2000; Victor 2003), political motivations (Bloom 2005; Hafez 2003; Pape 2005), and psychological and socioeconomic dimensions (Andoni 1997; Davice 2003; El-Sarraj 2002; Merrari 1990; Reich 1990). Anthropological and sociological contributions include Dorraj on "Martyrdom in the Iranian Political Culture" (1997) and Andriolo's "Murder by Suicide: Episodes from Muslim History" (2002). Even some economists offer explanations, as in "Suicide-Bombings as Inter-generational Investment" (Azam 2005). The emerging field also includes discussions of terrorism and suicide bombings from a philosophical perspective (Margalite 2002; Walzer 2004), as well as contributions by state strategists like Shaul Shay, head of the history department of the Israeli army (*The Shahids*, 2004, with a foreword by the director of Israeli military intelligence, Major General Ahron Farakash), as well as Khosrokhavar's *Suicide Bombers: Allah's New Martyrs* (2005), sponsored by the French Ministry of Foreign Affairs. In addition, there are contributions by Palestinian academics (Khashan 2003), and works that explore the origins and political goals of suicide bombing, its gender dimensions, its legitimacy, and responses to it.

However, the literature on the subject thus far is still a long way from providing a full understanding of the various manifestations of violence through suicide, its cultural constructions, its motivations, and its role in political and military strategy. My research strives to provide a holistic approach: to gain a solid anthropological understanding of this form of violence so that we can develop effective responses to it. There is a need to move the analyses beyond the actions themselves and their political underpinnings. Without expanding the analysis to social and cultural realms at the level of individuals, groups, local communities, society at large, regional communities, the society of the enemy state and its support, global powers, and international observers, this form of violence cannot be entirely understood. A holistic approach, after Ferguson (2003), requires a lot of work to accomplish but is necessary if we are to do justice to the subject and provide comprehensive analyses that can afford us the tools to develop effective responses.

My research demonstrates that the political dimensions of these forms of violence cannot be separated from a broader cultural dynamic that underlies the motivation of groups and individual participants. Even the most careful political analyses of these forms of violence will fall short, precisely because martyrdom is mediated through cultural forms and local experiences. It is rather the cultural schemes as they are transformed across time—as well as the cultural representations of the performance of violence that illuminate the oppositions, analogies, and homologies integrated into the performance—that constitute a critical field of analysis. What are the political impact and cultural significance of engaging in violence through self-sacrifice and martyrdom? How are the acts of sacrifice and martyrdom constructed and culturally conceived? These are important questions in analyzing and understanding these forms of violence.

My background growing up in Palestine not only gives me a deep understanding and appreciation of the historical and cultural backdrop of this form of violence in the Palestinian context but also provides me with a level of comfort necessary to discuss sensitive issues with social and political actors. My research is first and foremost a project of providing an anthropological understanding of martyrdom and the violence of suicide bombings in Palestine by Palestinian groups and individuals. My position as a Palestinian ethnographer provides me with access to inside information for anthropological analysis. Second, growing up with the same experiences as the subjects of my research enables me to appreciate the cultural conceptions, histories, and ontological conditions to which my subjects refer when they articulate their thoughts. This position also gives me an insider lens with which to deconstruct the semiotics and poetics of the cultural representations associated with this particular form of violence.

On the other hand, being a Palestinian ethnographer, researching this highly sensitive topic, has presented challenges during my fieldwork and research. Some of these challenges are related to the fieldwork itself, others to the presentation of the research outcomes. Throughout this project I found myself walking a fine line between being viewed by my research subjects as a security threat or in one way or another as potentially undermining the resistance, and being considered as legitimizing what is characterized as a terrorist act in the West. My research recognizes the fact that these acts of violence are already legitimate and culturally appropriate forms of resistance in Palestine. The idea behind my anthropological research into violence is neither to condone it, nor legitimize it, nor condemn it. My research is aimed at understanding violence from the perpetrator's perspective, to illuminate the social processes through which the violence became legitimate from the perpetrator's perspective and thus, potentially, to open doors and possibilities for an alternative mediation of the social processes that are now being mediated through acts of violence.

Martyrdom in Palestine

The 'amaliyyat istishhadiyya (martyrdom operations) practiced today in Palestine are a fairly recent development in the Palestinian resistance discourse that started in 1994. This form of political violence in Palestine was introduced by the Palestinian nationalist-Islamic group Harakat al-Muqawama al-Islamiyya–Hamas (Islamic Resistance Movement–Hamas) as a form of protest against and opposition to the Oslo "peace process" of the 1990s. Later in 1995 the other Palestinian Islamic-nationalist group, Harakat al-Jihad al-Islami (Islamic Jihad movement), started carrying out such operations as well. These operations intensified after the beginning of the latest Palestinian uprising, Al-Aqsa Intifada, in the fall of 2000 and were adopted by other Palestinian groups, secular and leftist, such as Harakat al-Taharur al-Watani al-Filistini–Fatah (Palestinian National Liberation Movement–Fatah) and al-Jabha al-Shaa'biyya li Tahrir Filistin (Popular Front for the Liberation of Palestine, or PFLP).

The practice of self-sacrifice by Palestinian fighters is however nothing new to the Palestinian resistance. Self-sacrifice has been the core strategy for generations of Palestinian resistance groups. The practice was glorified in the al-Karameh battle,[1] in which Palestinian fida'iyeen members of

...ıc Palestinian resistance factions of the PLO scored a victory against the attacking Israeli army near the village Karameh in Jordan in 1969. Ever since the *fida'i* (the one who sacrifices self) became the icon of the Palestinian resistance, symbolizing bravery, honor, and sacrifice. After al-Karameh the Palestinian resistance throughout the 1970s rested on *'amaliyyat fida'iyya* (operations of self-sacrifice) as the main form of resistance. These operations were mainly cross-border operations from Jordan and Lebanon, in which most mission carriers engaged with their Israeli targets until their death.

Hamas first executed operations in the Israeli-inhabited towns of Afula and Khedara in the spring of 1994, in which the mission carrier strapped explosives to his or her body and then set them off. These operations were described as *'amaliyyat istishhadiyya* (martyrdom operations), or as *'amaliyyat fida'iyya* (self-sacrifice operations) by some of the local media. The *fida'i* (sacrificer) notion is more secular, the *istishhad* (martyrdom) notion more Islamic. Today istishhad is the most common term for acts of sacrifice in the Palestinian resistance and is used by Islamic, secular, and Marxist groups alike. Some of the regional media, however, like al-Jazeera, still refer to *istishhadi* operations as *'amaliyyat fida'iyya* (self-sacrifice operations).

The term *fida'i*, for the one who sacrifices self, is derived from *fida'*, which is paid in money or goods to free or rescue someone who became a prisoner of war or got in trouble with others. The term *fida'* is also used for the liberation of something or someone. For example, one would say: "*mata fida' al-watan*" (he died in sacrifice for the homeland). The notion of the *shahid* (martyr)[2] is also not new in Palestinian resistance discourse. The shahid is anyone who dies fighting in defense of the nation or the homeland. All the *fida'iyeen* who died in cross-border operations are considered *shuhada'* (martyrs). Also noncombatant victims of the *intifada*—ordinary people, women, and schoolchildren—are all considered *shuhada'*. The term *shahid* is used culturally to refer to anyone killed by the aggressor, whether a fighter or victim of aggression, whether a member of an Islamic, Christian, secular, or Marxist organization, whether targeted or untargeted. The term *istishhadi*, now used in particular for those who carry out the martyrdom operation or suicide bombing, is new and represents the equivalent of the *fida'i*: the one who performs the self-sacrifice.

The shahid (martyr) became the icon of the first intifada (1987–92).

The concept of the shahid, the victim who falls at the hands of oppressive occupation, was in line with the political dynamics of the time, when efforts were made to lobby the international community for support of Palestinians' quest for freedom. The first intifada primarily banked on the international community and global powers to place pressure on Israel to reverse its occupation of the West Bank and Gaza and to address other issues of conflict with Israel such as the fate of Palestinian refugees. In contrast to the first intifada, which had as its main intended audience the international community, the second intifada that broke out in September 2000 after the collapse of the peace process was a response to the failure of the international community to bring about a meaningful political change in Israel's occupation of the Palestinians. Thus, in the second intifada the international community was to be disregarded. In the second intifada Palestinians directed their actions primarily at Israel, the Israeli publics, and world Zionism. The second intifada emphasized self-reliance, as Palestinians abandoned hope for the international community's meaningful involvement in the Palestinian question at an official level. The collapse of the "peace process," the intensification of the Palestinians' fragmentation, and the consolidation of Israeli containment and occupation policies that were the outcomes of these "peace" processes, along with the expansion of the war in the region by the United States and Britain and the politics of the New World Order, all represent a collapse of the world system to which Palestinians could potentially look for help. The aim in the second intifada was to disregard the international community and further challenge the established international order and its rules. The international order is understood by Palestinians as merely curbing Palestinian resistance while ignoring the restoration of Palestinian rights and paying only lip service to the Palestinian being violated by Israel. These political dynamics resulted in a reconceptualization of the resistance: Israel in Palestine was now challenged through direct engagement with Israel and Israelis, with the Palestinians relying on their own resources to achieve their political aspirations.

While the notion of the shahid (martyr) implies victimization, the *istishhadi* (martyrous one) is an active notion that emphasizes the heroism in the act of sacrifice. And since the istishhadi is active, the new term also makes the image of the istishhadi contain more life than the shahid does. The act of *istishhad* (dying in martyrdom) has developed not only into a military and political strategy for groups and individuals but into a cultural act loaded with meanings. It is primarily those meanings that give the concept its political and military weight. In the second intifada a new discourse of *istishhadiyeen* (martyrous ones) has been articulated in ways that alleviate the intentionality of martyrdom as an act of heroism. In this new discourse of martyrdom Arab and Muslim solidarity is to be achieved through cultural references associated with the acts of martyrdom: the target audience lies within the Palestinian community and radiates outward toward Israel, Israeli publics, and Zionist supporters abroad. The international community is no longer a primary audience: its protest of violent actions that target civilians in defiance of international law is no longer a concern for the Palestinian resistance. To the contrary, part of the construction of martyrdom operations during the second intifada is to challenge this political international order.

The term *istishhadi* did not exist in the Arabic dictionary, nor does the concept of actively seeking martyrdom exist among traditional Islamic notions. The use of the term *istishhadiyeen* (plural, the ones who execute martyrdom operations) was introduced by Hamas and aims to attach religious meanings to the act of self-sacrifice, since Hamas conceives of Islam as the most solid ideology through which to achieve the goals of the Palestinian national struggle. The istishhadiyeen have captured the imagination of Palestinian youth and the general public in similar ways as the *fida'iyeen* of the 1960s and the 1970s. The istishhadi now carries new meanings and qualities above that of the shahid. The image of istishhadi is the icon of the Palestinian resistance, replacing the icon of the shahid of the first intifada and the notion of fida'i, which was the icon of the resistance in the 1960s and 1970s. These lexical differences and the rise of the discourse of the istishadiyeen in the resistance have created a new cultural space for the istishhadi in Palestine, one that occupies the highest, most noble ground, above that of the shahid. Hamas leaders have asserted as much. For example, one of the Izzideen al-Qassam Martyrs Brigades, Anwar, stated:[3] "The *istishhadi* is an advanced stage and above *shahada* because it comes with a desire and a persistence and a motivation with sincerity. The culture of *istishhad* has become domestic to the Palestinian people. It's become a natural thing, not strange. It has become a picture of the nationalist Islamic work. It has entered the Palestinian popular dictionary. The people see the ist-

ishhadi as he has gotten the highest degrees of nationalism and religion and sacrificed self and has gotten the biggest reward: paradise. Everyone who takes such a mission is considered a hero and maybe a neighborhood or a street or a square would be named after him." The process described here, of strapping oneself with explosives and blowing oneself up in a crowd of the "enemy," is referred to in Palestine as *al-'amal al-istishhadi* (the work of martyrdom), whether applied against military or civilian targets. It differs lexically as well as in its cultural contents and military and political impact from operations carried out by armed fighters against Israeli targets, military or civilian. The istishhadi operations represent a distinct kind of performance separate from conventional armed resistance in that they are mainly aimed at Israeli public life: buses, cafeterias, markets, nightclubs.

Operations of this sort have spread over most of the Israeli urban centers and reached rich and poor neighborhoods, including an operation in Tel Aviv only a couple of blocks from Prime Minister Ariel Sharon's residence and within one block of the Israeli Ministry of Defense. Those who carry out these operations are not necessarily members of political groups but rather volunteers who offer themselves to these groups. These operations in particular inflict an intense feeling of fear and horror on the Israelis, and while also instilling a sense of strength and assertion of identity among Palestinians. It is these operations of istishhad that are the subject of my inquiry.

Western scholars and media commentators generally refer to the istishhad operations as suicide bombings. President George W. Bush as well as British government officials are increasingly using "homicide bombing," a term introduced as part of the "Global War on Terror" and one that makes the act more obscure rather than accessible. The various terms used in the West tend to confuse our understanding of the acts by leading us to associate the acts with the terms' usual meanings. Hardly anyone in the western scholarly and media discourse would refer to "self-sacrifice operations" or "martyrdom operations," as is done in Palestine. The concept of "self-sacrifice" is at the core of the act of istishhad and it is totally missing from the English-language terms used by most commentators on the subject.

Over the past decade journalists and scholars have written extensively in an effort to explain the individual motivations and logic underlying

"suicide attacks." In this connection it is useful to recall Émile Durkheim's analysis of suicide in nineteenth-century Europe. Durkheim distinguished three kinds of suicide: egoistic, fatalistic, and altruistic
(Durkheim 1951). Egoistic suicide occurs under conditions of psychological trauma and social isolation from which death is seen as an escape.
Fatalistic suicide is committed by individuals who feel oppressively isolated from their social setting. Altruistic suicide, by contrast, occurs
under conditions of high social integration and strong social bonds: the
suicide is committed out of a sense of obligation toward the community.
Durkheim's three kinds of suicide help us to understand where the act of
martyrdom may or may not fit within the notion of suicide.

A recent anthropological inquiry by Dabbagh (2004) into suicide in
Palestine finds that in spite of the severe conditions of the Israeli occupation, suicide as a way to escape conditions of social isolation and psychological trauma is still infrequent in comparison with western societies.
Dabbagh conducted her research in the West Bank during the 1990s with
the focus of her data collection on Ramallah and Jenin. Although the
1990s are a social period totally different from that which followed the
outbreak of Al-Aqsa Intifada in September 2000, neither period demonstrates people in Palestine suffering from conditions of social isolation
from their own communities. What they do suffer from is geographic
isolation and fragmentation, which are normally compensated for by
various forms of conceptual integration and assertions of unity of the
land and unity of the people in the conceptual spheres, processes that I
will explore in the coming chapters. The one kind of suicide that is
relevant to this analysis is Durkheim's notion of altruistic suicide. The
sense of duty and obligation toward the community or the nation is
strong among most of the participants in martyrdom operations. However, that sense of duty and obligation is not limited to the community.
Those who carry out martyrdom missions can be motivated with a sense
of obligation toward the land, the homeland, the city or place to which
they are strongly connected, the nation, the Divine, or previous and
future generations. Hence even the notion of altruistic suicide does not
fully describe the logic of the individual act.

Sacrifice, on the other hand, which was originally implicit in the
Arabic-language discourse in Palestine, gets closer to communicating
the individual psychology and cultural meanings of the act, as well as

how the act gets transformed from the individual level to the colle
level through its poetics and cultural conceptions. Here Hubert's and
Mauss's notion of "objects of sacrifice," which could be any addressed
party, the land of Palestine, the Palestinian nation, or the Divine, is more
appropriate to describe the act than *altruistic* suicide. The "objects of
sacrifice" refer to "those kinds of things for whose sake the sacrifice
takes place" (Hubert and Mauss 1964, 10). Hubert and Mauss give the
name "sacrifier" to "the subject to whom the benefits of sacrifice thus
accrue, or who undergoes its effects," which in the fida'i or the istishhadi in this context is the social person who benefits from the effects
of the sacrifice. However, I apply the term *sacrificer* because the fida'i or
the istishhadi is both the one who undergoes the sacrifice effects and
acquires its benefits and at the same time the one whose body is the
sacrificed object or the *victim* in the act of sacrifice. The istishhadi represents the "moral person" who bears the cost of sacrifice. Hubert and
Mauss (1964) define sacrifice as a "religious act which, through concentration of a victim, modifies the condition of the moral person who
accomplishes it or that of certain objects with which he is concerned"
(13). The concentration of the istishhadi body produces an assertion of
the istishhadi social person. Through its cultural conception the concentration of the istishhadi becomes a sacrificial offering from the Palestinian people. Hence the Palestinian people gain the benefits of sacrifice
and undergo its effects.

The act of the istishhadi brings about twofold results. The sacrificer
gains moral qualities as the "person who accomplishes the sacrifice"
and the land of Palestine gains sacred qualities as the "object of sacrifice." Both processes of attaching meaning call for the regeneration of
the act. The more acts of sacrifice are committed, the more the istishhadi
gains moral qualities and becomes idealized. At the same time, the more
istishhadiyeen are sacrificed for the land, the more the land becomes
sacred, requiring more sacrifice to save it or honor it. The *victim*, who is
the istishhadi in the biological body, is the intermediary between the
sacrificer (the istishhadi as the social person or in his or her identity) and
those to whom the sacrifice is addressed, namely the land of Palestine,
the Palestinian place (Jerusalem, Haifa, Bissan, Safad, etc.),[4] the Palestinian nation, the Divine, or a combination of these based on the individual actor's or viewer's construction. The exchange of blood constitutes a

"blood covenant" (Hubert and Mauss 1964) that fuses human life with the addressed party, the land, the place, or divine life on the one hand and an exchange between the sacrificed body parts and the land of Palestine on the other. Furthermore, the concentration of the *victim*, the biological body, in the act of sacrifice concentrates or asserts the identity of the actor or sacrificer—here the istishhadi in the social person—and by extension concentrates the sacrificer as the Palestinian people.

This concept of sacrifice informs the dynamics of martyrdom in Palestine today. Human sacrifice in many forms is an ancient tradition in the Middle East (Green 1975). The concept further informs the relations of individuals to the community at micro and macro levels. Sacrifice is also conceived as it was at the time of its origins in ancient mythology: as that which creates life. The cultural conception of sacrifice is a ritual sequence connected to patterns of creation and exchange. Lincoln (1991) explores these concepts among the Persians, Indo-Europeans, Scythians, and Celts and demonstrates how sacrifices are acts that accompany transformations from the microcosm to the macrocosm. The dismembered parts of the sacrificed victims create the universe. These conceptions are achieved through correlations of different parts of the universe, which are seen as having been created by corresponding pieces of sacrificed human bodies. Thus the act of sacrifice represents a "homologic relation" between the human body and the environment.

In the Palestinian context the sacrificed Palestinian bodies in Palestine correlate alternative shapes to one another in a homologic relation; the dismembered body parts *create* the new universe within which *Palestine* is *alive*. In the Palestinian cultural representations of these acts of sacrifice and martyrdom, the blood is water that nourishes the fields where streams would flow and birds would sing. The human flesh is soil where flowers bloom. These meanings are conceived through the poetics of the performance, the sensory meanings polarized between realities and aspirations. The polarizations generate poetics within which a fusion in the *new* generated *life* in the cultural imaginary is achieved. The performance of every ritual of sacrifice by Palestinian martyrs in the land of Palestine repeats this process of transforming microcosm to macrocosm, shifting substance from the sacrificed body of the martyr to the "alloformic" parts of Palestine, to sustain *Palestinian* life with Palestinian characteristics and guard against the disappearance of Palestinian signs through reconfiguration. Thus the sacrifice creates a new ontology through metonymic re-constitutions. In the Palestinian context, the notion of *sacrifice* is a more appropriate way to describe the act of the human bomb than "suicide" in any of its forms, because it encompasses the transformations and exchanges that take place between the sacrificed human body, the *human bomb*, and the land of Palestine and the Palestinian people.

The martyrdom notion in the new formulation of istishhadiyeen, building on the concept of the fida'iyeen, communicates the same meanings of sacrifice, adding to them a new Islamic strategy within which the sacrifice is enacted. The fida'iyeen discourse of the 1960s and 1970s was formulated in a political dynamic similar to that of the istishhadiyeen discourse. It emerged in response to the Arab regimes' defeat in 1967 and the Israeli occupation of the remainder of Palestine. The fida'iyeen discourse was also one that asserted self-reliance, sacrifice, and heroism. The istishhadiyeen discourse builds on the history of the fida'iyeen, transforming it into a generation of resistance informed by local knowledge, traditions, and thought. The istishhadiyeen discourse emphasizes the Islamic characteristics of the resistance. Still, the istishhadiyeen discourse is fundamentally different from the fida'iyeen discourse, in that the istishhadiyeen take their life in their own hands while the fida'i fought and took on missions that most certainly would end their lives. The assertion of the Islamic characteristics in the acts of the resistance also comments on, and engages with, increasing globalization and its local effects. Nevertheless, the devotion to Islam or belief in the Divine is not a necessary condition for the construction of sacrifice to take place, even in this new discourse of martyrdom that emphasizes the Islamic character. The fusion of the human life with the land, the place, or the nation, or the assertion of agency in the absence of belief in the Divine, constitutes a logical individual motivation for performing the sacrifice ritual.

The sacrificial notion sits well with the theoretical understanding of the violence applied and performed in the act. The istishhadi mission contains two acts of violence. One is applied against the performer's biological body and the second against a set of victims from the community of the "enemy." The application of Whitehead's concept of violence as a "cultural performance" (2002) and Riches's definition of violence as

16

a "communicative vehicle" (1986) would help us understand that the violence included in the act of sacrifice is a cultural performance that expresses and communicates cultural ideas, mediates social processes, and at the same time communicates with the "enemy." The dual violence included in the act makes its performance suitable to the political strategies of the moment, directed inward at Palestinian society and outward at Israeli society. It focuses the political and cultural ideas expressed through acts of resistance to the Palestinian and Israeli societies who are the new audience of the Palestinian resistance. Through the bodily practice of sacrificing Palestinians' bodies in the land of Palestine, Palestinians are recreating the ontologically fragmented Palestine and segmented Palestinians; as the sacrifice is performed. The violence disturbs the normalcy of the cultural order in Palestine (Israeli society) that replaced the Palestinian order, created the current ontology, and represents the primary obstacle to the physical unity of Palestine and the connectedness of the Palestinian people. The intentionality of taking one's own life through an act of sacrifice in the mission of martyrdom asserts an agency and an independence that articulate Palestinian identity and peoplehood in the face of an ontological order imposed by Israel that denies recognition and entitlements to the Palestinians and subjects them to social fragmentation. Thus beyond the dynamic of the encounter with the "enemy," the act of the human bomb contains cultural assertions of identity and place, and rootedness of identities in places. The terms used to refer to the act are crucial to analysis, and the notion of sacrifice is the appropriate one with which to frame our analysis of the istishhadi operations.

Methodology

I started my field research by making ethnographic observations: listening to ordinary people's reactions to acts of martyrdom, reading commentaries, poetry, and obituaries about the acts published in local and regional media and on web sites. I examined materials produced by the organizing factions such as posters, videos, booklets, and statements claiming responsibility for martyrdom operations. I also interviewed some of the families of istishhadiyeen as well as active group members

early in the fieldwork. These initial readings, interviews, and observations in the field were a launching pad. Together, these initial research
assessments along with the literature review that I had conducted before
my travel to the field guided the rest of my research. The initial assessments gave me clues as to where the meanings are derived from and how
people relate to acts of martyrdom, which enabled me to focus my questions in subsequent interviews and guide the lens through which I
looked at various aspects of the act.

As I considered the literature on violence and reflected on my initial
field assessments, I noticed recurring themes and references in most
materials produced about these operations to ideas about land and place,
Israeli state violence, global systems and ideologies, and religion and
religious duty. Because of the repeated assertion of these ideas I developed a research strategy to investigate the multiple dimensions of acts of
martyrdom. These dimensions included the nature of Palestinians' encounter with Israel; the history of that encounter; Palestinian ideas about
land and the symbolic representation of Palestinian identity; the historical context of the rise of the istishhadi represented in Palestinian iconography and the ways the istishhadi has risen within the resistance
discourse; the cultural, political, and military dimensions of the istishhad in the Palestinian resistance; and the relevance of global ideas
and powers, and their impacts and practices, to the formulation of istishhad as a form of resistance.

To explore these dimensions my research consisted of multi-tiered ethnography examining the act of the human bomb and ideas about the act
in different cultural spheres and publics within Palestinian society. To
assess the ways the act of the human bomb was formulated, popu-
larized, and integrated into everyday social life in Palestine, the study
encompassed seven areas: (1) the martyrdom operations performed by
Palestinian groups; (2) the actors as groups and individuals; (3) the
organizing groups' literature and cultural production; (4) Palestinian
cultural representations of the encounter and resistance; (5) the local
and regional communities' commentaries and literary productions concerning the martyrdom operations and their carriers; (6) the dynamics
and history of the Palestinian encounter with the state of Israel; and (7)
Palestinian rootedness in place and ideas about land.

With respect to operations performed by Palestinian groups I collected data on 213 Palestinian operations carried out by Palestinian groups during al-Aqsa Intifada between 2001 and 2004. Among these 213 operations were 80 that are considered 'amaliyat istishhadiyya (martyrdom operations), in which mission carriers exploded themselves along with their targets by using explosive belts or detonating a car while driving it. The other 133 operations were 'amaliyyat fida'iyya (self-sacrifice operations) carried out by Palestinian fighters through armed attacks on Israeli targets, military and civilian, where the chances of surviving were close to zero or the carrier went on the mission with the express purpose of fighting until death. I have also studied 14 martyrdom operations executed by Hamas and Islamic Jihad against Israeli targets between 1994 and 2000. I studied data on Palestinian attacks on Israeli targets published by the Israeli Ministry of Defense as well as several books by Palestinians documenting the Palestinian istishhadiyeen. My analyses of the data on martyrdom operations performed by Palestinians against Israeli targets examined the individual actors, their geographic distribution, age, gender, education, and profession; the organizing groups; the aesthetics of the performance with regard to the place of application, targets, timing, and political dynamics of the time period; and the number of fatalities caused by the operation.

In studying the actors as groups and individuals, I considered the life histories of nine of the istishhadiyeen from the Jenin area. My inquiries into these life histories included interviewing their families (fathers, mothers, siblings), reviewing materials and booklets published about them by groups that sponsored their operations, as well as gathering information about them from activist interviews. On the organizational side, my inquiries included interviews with four kinds of agents involved in constructing the act: (1) the organizing leaders (leaders of the military wings of the factions that set up martyrdom operations); (2) the organizing members (general members of military wings that carried out the operations); (3) political leaders (leaders of political groups that sponsored the operations); and (4) political activists (the meaning makers of the act, or the mid-level activists that normally give meaning to martyrdom operations and were an interface between the militarized resistance and the wider community). These four types of players exist in all five of the active political groups, and my interviews included three of them: Hamas (Islamist), Fatah (secular), and the PFLP (Marxist).

The study of the organizing groups' literature and cultural production consisted of closely examining posters of martyrs, booklets published about martyrs and martyrdom operations, video- and audiotapes of martyrs' messages made and released by groups, statements of responsibility issued by the organizing groups, and threats by the groups to carry out further operations in response to Israeli state violence. My analyses took into account how these cultural products were disseminated among the Palestinian publics, as well as how organizing groups produced the image of the istishhadi in song, art, and revolutionary language or speeches at parades, demonstrations, and political chants. My own participation in marches, parades, and demonstrations were sites of data collection and opportunities to analyze these productions. During my participation in these events I wrote ethnographic details of how they unfolded, recorded chants and slogans, talked with participants and organizers, and took photos.

In the fourth tier of my research I correlated the material I had gathered with a study of Palestinian cultural representations of the encounter with Israel and resistance. Here I examined Palestinian cultural expressions outside the organized factions: art productions, theater performances, posters, and songs by artists and groups that expressed ideas about the encounter with Israel and resistance. I based my choice of materials on their popularity, their level of dissemination, and the cultural impact that they seemed to generate. To supplement my analyses, I conducted interviews with artists, dancers, conductors, painters, singers, and songwriters.

In my study of the local and regional communities' commentaries and literary productions of the martyrdom operations and the istishhadiyeen, I closely examined commentaries in the printed media in reaction to the martyrdom operations, especially those that took place while I was in the field. I also included literature from local Palestinian newspapers, magazines, and web sites by Palestinian writers, as well as regional Arabic-language writings republished or circulated in Palestine. These writings are mainly political commentaries, poetry, and obituaries of martyrs.

In the sixth tier of my research I examined the dynamics and history of the Palestinians' encounter with the state of Israel. Here I took a close look at the ethnographic present in Palestine to see how Palestinians encounter Israel in their daily lives. Their experiences include Israeli restrictions of Palestinians' movements; confinements and the walling off of Palestinian communities; the dynamics of contact at the checkpoints; and Israeli raids on Palestinian towns and targeted assassinations. I examined the micro impacts of these encounters on the daily lives of Palestinians as well as their macro impacts on social transformations, group formation, the alteration of groups and localized leaderships, and shifts in the political and military strategies of groups. I also explored the state of Israel's direct and indirect involvement in producing Palestinian violence. Specifically, I looked at Israeli state violence in its various forms—raids into Palestinian towns, targeted assassinations, home demolitions, sonic terror and violence in the imaginary, population confinement and encirclement—and how these forms of state violence affect the intensity, frequency, and forms of violence carried out by resistance groups. I also analyzed the Israeli state's involvement in the Palestinian groups' formation, operations, and armament by researching the Palestinian groups themselves rather than the Israeli state agencies involved. I have included a historical overview of Israeli state expansion in Palestine through secondary sources, as well as analysis of the Oslo "peace processes" during which the Palestinian martyrdom operations were first formulated, relying on original material. Here I provide a review of the agreements of Oslo and the formation of the Palestinian Authority (PA) and its obligations under the terms of these agreements. To extend the ethnographic representation of the encounter with the state and give the analysis further depth beyond the historical material, I bring in some of my own experiences of encounters while growing up under Israeli occupation.

I then move on to the study of Palestinian rootedness and ideas about land. It became evident during the course of my research that land and ideas about land and identity were prominent components in the framing of the martyrdom operations by various sets of viewers. In this phase of my research I consider Palestinian symbols in relation to land, how these symbols were formulated and transformed across time, and the use of these symbols and their performances in Palestinian cultural production. The details of this research have been published in a separate article (Abufarha 2008). I apply the insights produced by my research into symbols and symbolic representation in my analysis of the representations of martyrdom operations. Moreover, I have deepened the analysis by looking at traditional Palestinian land tenure and how Palestinians have negotiated tenure rights with expanding states in modern history. In this part of the research I conducted interviews with Palestinian farmers and reviewed secondary sources.

In all, I have spent three years conducting this research, supplementing a lifelong personal engagement with topics related to Palestine. My research included one year in the field conducting ethnographies and collecting data, plus two additional visits back to the field during the course of writing in the following year. My research was situated in Jenin and surrounding villages, since this area has been the most active in carrying out martyrdom operations. Furthermore, Jenin is the area of Palestine with which I am most familiar and connected: I grew up in Jenin and graduated from its high school. My research followed a strategy of "purposive sampling" (Bernard 1988). In particular, it was based on following the act of the human bomb in diverse cultural and political spaces in Palestine. Within each of these spaces the act engaged different sets of cultural and political agents. My goal was to get a close understanding of those sites and the ways these cultural spaces are constructed by the agents active in them.

I conducted forty-three interviews during the course of my research, broken down as shown in the accompanying table.

I conducted most of the interviews in a semi-structured format, though some were unstructured. Subjects participated in informal discussions with me regarding the resistance, their understanding of it, and how their actions aligned with their ideas. I took handwritten notes in Arabic during these discussions and translated them into English afterward. I chose not to tape any of the interviews, to avoid posing any security or legal risks for the people I interviewed as well as to make my interviewees comfortable to carry on frank discussions of sensitive subjects.

In my analyses of the data I situate the ethnographic present in the historical context. I analyze the collected data using "focused coding" (Emerson 1995) of information from the interviews, ethnographic observations, and identified collective meanings among communities. My approach encompasses identifying analytically relevant themes by connecting data from the various individuals in the study, the narratives, the group culture, the popular culture, and the observations, to draw out the meanings and ideas expressed through violence and to relate these

Interviewees	Number of Interviews
Families of istishhadiyeen[5]	9
Active groups' military wing leaders and brigade members[6]	6
Active groups' political activists or meaning makers[7]	4
Active groups' political leadership[8]	1
Intifada general activists[9]	5
Women activists[10]	3
Refugee issue activists[11]	2
Families affected by Israeli raids and intrusions into Palestinian towns[12]	2
Cultural performers (conductors, dancers, painters, and singers)[13]	5
Traditional village farmers[14]	5
Scholars[15]	1
Total	43

expressions to the actors and their communities. I further relate these cultural ideas to the political dynamics of the encounter with Israel and its histories. Through this approach I have been able to produce a historical ethnography of martyrdom in Palestine.

Overview

My research is presented in a way that reflects the tiers of the study. In chapter 2 I explore the junctures of histories and historicities in Palestine. I provide a lens for seeing how the Palestinian present was formed through the history of the colonial encounter and further illustrate how the histories are shaped by the political dynamics and attitudes of the present and how through these dynamics the land has emerged as an object of sacrifice in the Palestinian cultural discourse. The chapter also illuminates the image of pre-Israel Palestine that is vivid in the Palestinian cultural imaginary. In chapter 3 I analyze the history of Israeli state expansion schemes in Palestine, of which the Oslo "peace process" is the most intensified phase. In this chapter I deconstruct the "peace process" of the 1990s, exploring global powers, the involvement of "development" agencies in the process, and how the martyrdom operations were formulated by Palestinian groups in resistance to the process. I further explore the nature of Israeli state expansion and its wider impact on Palestinian society, militarization, rebellion, and group formations and transformations.

In chapter 4 I describe Palestinians' daily lives, focusing on the many ways Palestinians encounter Israel and Israeli agents. In this chapter I demonstrate the multifaceted ways in which the encounter with Israel is a daily subject in Palestinians' thinking and conversations, and how it influences their decision-making processes in everyday life. This chapter offers a window for seeing the Palestinian ontological conditions and their social impact. Making these ontological conditions visible is necessary to realize the extent of polarization created between these conditions and the cultural conceptions that are generated by the performance of martyrdom and their cultural representations. In chapter 5 I present the cultural discourse of martyrdom in Palestine. Through an analysis of the life histories of three martyrs and the wider impact of their operations in Palestinian society and beyond, I illustrate the cultural life of the martyr. I explore the image of the life of the martyr as imagined by mission carriers before their martyrdom and as constructed and represented by the community. I further illustrate how the wider Palestinian society relates to martyrdom operations. Moreover, I illustrate how violent acts of martyrdom in Palestine are cultural performances that assert rootedness and identity among Palestinians, and resolve questions of denial and existence as well as uprooting and rootedness. I further demonstrate how these cultural conceptions create an unconfined and united Palestine, its implied accessibility and freedom illuminating the stark contrast between the ontological conditions demonstrated in chapter 4 and the aspirations of freedom, independence, and the ability to live in Palestine.

In chapter 6 I examine the various forces that actively construct the acts of martyrdom and their military and political strategies. I explore and demonstrate how the violent acts of the human bombs fit into the political and military strategies of Palestinian resistance factions. I demonstrate how violence as a cultural expression that mediates social pro-

cesses is integrated into military and political strategies. I further discuss
how these performances of violence in the public places of the "enemy"
and the cultural meanings that they carry move the battlegrounds from
the physical fields to the conceptual fields. I point out that martyrdom
strategies rest on moving the battle to levels of identity and conceptual
rootedness, thereby altering the power configurations of the encounter.

Finally, in chapter 7 I discuss the implications of my research for the
anthropology of violence and for a comprehensive analysis of the various historical, cultural, political, and military dimensions of the human
bomb at the local, regional, and global levels. I further crystallize the
development of this form of violence in the historical context and the
space that it occupies in Palestine today. I also provide insights into
future research on possible appropriate responses to the strategies of
martyrdom in Palestine.

CHAPTER TWO

Histories and Historicities in Palestine

WHOSE HISTORY

Historians have written extensively on Palestine from different perspectives: history of Palestine, history of the Holy Land, history of Israel, and so on. Although I am aware of the various perspectives and narratives, and recognize that these various histories are histories of the same landscape, I am particularly interested in how Palestinians view their own history. The history of Palestinian social dynamics in the landscape of Palestine over the period of my inquiry is the history that I seek to understand. Some understand history as a narrative and say that Palestine has a contested history with multiple competing narratives. However, what is relevant to my analysis is history as lived by the Palestinians. The histories that the Palestinians relate to and how they relate to the Palestinian sense of self, or historicity, is the history that has a bearing on the story of the Palestinians and relevance to my inquiry into the making of a human bomb. Historicity as it "reflects both the historical experiences . . . and the cultural significance of recalling the past" constitutes the most relevant history to the present (Whitehead 2003, xi). Thus narratives that are not part of the Palestinian construction of their history have little or no bearing on this story. My interest in the past focuses on how the past is intertwined in the construction and constant transformation of the Palestinian cultural identity and representations. I am looking particularly at the historical narratives (histories) that are modes of consciousness for the Palestinians. Through them Palestinians define and represent themselves and relate to the rest of the world and, more importantly, to Israel and Israelis. Only through exploring the junctures of histories and historicities in Palestine can we historicize the Palestinian cultural present.

Making sense of history goes beyond the record and the event. As important as the event itself is, how the event is remembered, how it is narrated, presented, and told and by whom are critical to understanding the impact of the event. Historical anthropology offers an avenue for using multilayered historical sources that go beyond the text to include the story, the oral narrative, the landscape, and the present, giving depth to a historical analysis that strives to present solid grounds on which to assess the development of social processes and the motivations and causes of present-day social phenomena as well as the historical construction of ideas and thoughts that inform decision making (White 2000). An anthropological approach to history does not confine history to the written text and archives, which mostly represent the state's account of history and often fail to include the historical narratives of nonstate peoples (Abercrombie 1998). In my consideration of history I take into consideration the multiple sources of history: the text, the event, the stories of individuals, the cultural representations, and the landscape, as well as the dynamics of current social processes, to historicize our understanding of social phenomena in present-day Palestine. If we seek to present history in order to understand the social processes of the present, then any fact, event, reality, perceived reality, story, tale, or even myth that has generated related social processes composes a historical reality that is part and parcel of the historical record.

The history of Palestine is grounded in oral narrative transmitted from one generation to the next or narrated through what Herzfeld (1997) calls "social poetics" in song, play, or art. Oral history is concerned with "how, what, and why people remember and narrate the past" (Ritchie 2003, 12). Palestinians have not lived under their own governance, so their historical narrative was not institutionalized and taught in the formal education system administered successively by Britain, Jordan, and Israel. The Palestinian education system did not teach any Palestinian history under Israeli occupation. The mere mention of the word "Palestine" was not allowed. In my middle school we were asked to buy an atlas for our geography class. The atlas was printed in Beirut. Unlike European and American atlases, Arab atlases put Palestine on the map, but not Israel. Throughout the atlas that we bought, the word "Palestine" was covered with a thick black marker. When we found two occurrences of the word

"Palestine" that had been left uncovered in the text, it was an amazing thing for us, and we went around the class showing the word "Palestine" in print. Boys started looking through the pages to see if the *eraser* had missed the word "Palestine" in their atlases too. The word "Palestine" was not strange to us, nor was the map of Palestine. We had always written "Palestine" on every canvas, from the trunks of the trees, to the walls of the village, to the streets and in the soil of the sidewalk, to the palm of our hands, to every notebook we had. We wrote "Palestine" as much as we wrote our names and even more. We carried the carved wooden map of Palestine as a keychain, and most Palestinian youth still do the same. The denial of Palestine in the "official" cartography of the occupier did not remove it from our conceptions. Nor did the placement of "Israel" on the official cartographical records make it real to us. We related to our own spatial conceptions and representations through "indigenous cartography" (Vidal 2003), the many representations of Palestine in calligraphy, painting, carving, songs, stories, and similar cultural forms. But it was a big deal to see "Palestine" printed—that rarely happened. It looked "official" all of a sudden. In the environment where I grew up, "Palestine" was not part of the official record; that is why it was so amazing to me then to see it in print and why it is important for me now *not* to limit my sources to the official records. Even though "Palestine" was not part of the record, it pervaded the life of my classroom. It was a central part of everyday life. In fact, the reason I am writing this history now is that Palestine persists with tenacity. Perhaps the denial of Palestine as a space in the "official" record is itself part of the construction of Palestinians' tenacity that I reflect on in the following pages.

With an official education system that did not teach Palestinian history, Palestinians mainly turned to informal education to learn about their history from their parents and grandparents, fellow inhabitants of their villages, and local and national cultural representations to learn and understand their history and make sense of their present. These cultural representations and popular historiographies are the primary source of Palestinian historical constructions. To understand this history in relation to the present Palestinian social setting, in this chapter I offer a chronology of the Palestinian-Israel conflict as seen, lived, remembered, and told by Palestinians. I highlight historical events and histories that had a significant impact on social and cultural transformations. Marshall

Sahlins (1985) uses the notion of "prescriptive events" to describe events that start whole chains of cultural schemes. Similarly, Veena Das (1995) uses the notion of the "critical event" to refer to events that call for action. I use these notions to mark the cultural significance of "prescriptive" and "critical" events in Palestinian history. I further expand on the presentation to include the development of a symbolic cultural representation that has been transformed along with Palestinians' encounters with foreign powers. Together the historical events and the cultural representations, or "social poetics," of these events, and the cultural processes that these events and their poetics have set in motion, are the historical backdrop against which we can base our analysis of today's cultural dynamics in Palestine in general, and the historical and cultural production of violence in particular. The political dynamics in Palestine today are the products of a century of active encounters between Palestinians and foreign powers. To understand the present, we need a solid understanding of the history that generated it.

Pre-Israel Palestine

Palestinian society in the nineteenth century consisted mainly of small communities of farmers who cultivated grains and vegetation as well as orchards of fruits and olives on the hillsides; semi-nomadic communities that raised mainly sheep and goats were scattered throughout the landscape but concentrated near Hebron, the Negev area, the Jordan valley, and the upper Galilee region. Urban centers were small and dominated by merchants and craftsmen, with the exception of the coastal cities of Jaffa and Akka (Acre), which had regional economic significance through trade. These urban centers also became cultural centers, along with the historically significant city of Jerusalem, a destination for world travelers and Christian pilgrims (Gray 1876).

When European Jewish nationalists (Zionists) developed an interest in Palestine, they sought to acquire land in Palestine by immigrating individually or through the organized attempts of the Jewish National Fund. The early Zionist attempts to acquire land from the Palestinian *fellahin* (rural Palestinian communities) were mostly unsuccessful because of the Palestinian traditions of collective land ownership and the social dimension of land transfer in the fellahin culture. Although there have been many discussions of land ownership and land expropriation in Palestine (Abu Saad 2002; Al-Dabbagh 1970; Atran 1985; Falah 1983; Jiryis 1973; Khalidi 1991; Kimberling and Migdal 2003; Marx and Avschalom 1984), none gave us a plausible explanation of how this traditional collective land ownership was managed and governed and how it related to Palestinian social life and cultural constructions. Some made reference to the collective land ownership in rural Palestine, but without explaining the systems the fellahin used to organize this ownership within the individual hamula[1] and village and across several hamulas and villages. Growing up in one of the villages of the Marj Ibin Amer[2] plains, I have heard many stories of land division and allocation by the elderly of the village over the years, and have further investigated the understandings of these traditions among the older generations in the region.

In Palestinian culture and especially among the fellahin, land is treated more as a homestead rather than as real estate. It is passed down through the family, and to a certain extent it is still considered a disgrace to sell land outside the family or the village. The majority of the lands in Palestine were the properties of the Palestinian rural population, the fellahin, and the Bedouins (semi-nomadic tribes). Understanding the culture of the fellahin and the Bedouins and their relation to the land is key to understanding the pre-state system of land tenure in Palestine and the present Palestinians' relation to the land. Referring to the fellahin of Palestine as peasants, as they are often referred to in the English-language scholarship, even by Palestinian scholars, misrepresents the cultural life of the Palestinian fellahin society, because peasantry has European connotations. A peasant in European culture is understood as a farming worker with little or no land ownership. The fellahin of Palestine are rural farming communities with communal, shared ownership of the land, cultivated according to communal traditions. They owned the land and the means of production (working animals and tools). The Bedouin communities were semi-nomadic communities that also had shared ownership of land as grazing grounds and shared ownership of the herds that they raised on these lands.

To understand the land ownership system in the society of the fellahin, one also needs to understand the concept of the feddan, a measurement of land area that may vary from one region to the next. The size of the

feddan is related to the area that a man with one 'ammal (working animal)[3] can plow in the wafer period, a period of three to four weeks[4]
between the wasem (when there has been sufficient rain for seeding but
the land has dried enough to allow for plowing) and the al-marba'aniyya
(the winter period, when there is consistent rain).[5] The size of the feddan
will vary because some soils are easier to plow than others. For example,
the feddan in the village of Al-Jalama where I grew up was sixty dunums
(six hectares), whereas in the village of Zer'in,[6] only five kilometers
north, it was eighty dunums (eight hectares).

   The land in the villages was owned collectively by the village residents
or by the hamula. Boundaries in the plains were marked by al-qaq,[7] a plant
that bursts out of the ground with the first grass right after the first rain
in the fall, when the land is ready to be plowed, and remains for most of
the year as long as there is moisture in the soil. Some people place a large
stone or a stack of flat stones called qa'qur to mark the corners of par-
cels.[8] In the plowing and seeding season, lands were divided between
village residents every fall based on ability to cultivate. A household
would receive half a feddan share annually for each male member and half
a feddan for each 'ammal (working animal) that it owned and was available for work. Thus zalameh wa 'ammal (a man and a working animal)
would get one feddan share, and a household with a father and three
mature sons and four 'ammal would get four feddan. An absentee man
from the community would not receive a share of land for that year. A
working animal is costly to keep throughout the year and is therefore
counted like a man in the distribution process.[9]

   This system of land ownership was used by the villages to distribute
ardh as-sahil (the lands of the fields) for cultivation, which ensured that
the land would be allocated efficiently. In the mountains or on the hill-
side, aside from areas and hills designated as collective grazing grounds,
people had individual or family ownership of orchards or land with trees
(ardh mushajjara). Ownership was vested in those who planted and maintained trees, or who inherited land. Orchard owners marked boundaries
mainly by planting prickly cactus trees along the boundaries or erecting
sinsileh (stone walls). Women were not allocated shares in ardh as-sahil
even though they participated in the harvest, since the concept of feddan
distribution was based on the ability to plow, an activity normally carried
out by men. However, some women gained land ownership through

maher (dowry). In some cases families were financially unable to send a major gift with their bride daughter when she was to be married to a man from a different hamula. In such cases they would give their daughter one feddan or more as a gift, and the groom's family would gain ownership of additional land in another village where the bride's family had a *nasab* (family relations through marriage). Women could also gain ownership of orchard lands through inheritance or traditions of plantation and maintenance. Among the Bedouin communities, concepts of land ownership were also communal and collective for the tribe as a whole. Boundaries for grazing grounds were respected by other tribes and the neighboring villages through tradition and the tribe's protection. Tribal lands were referred to by association with the tribe's name (Falah 1983).

Communal land ownership did not prevent land sales or transfer of ownership, but the sales were more complicated than a simple exchange of land for money. Land exchange entailed a process of negotiating social relations between buyer and seller, since the buyer would be incorporated socially into the seller's village or at the least become a neighbor. So whether to sell or not always depended on the nature of the party's interest in the land and the social relation sought from the family approached. Marriages across families often facilitated land exchange, in that a social bond would be established that would allow for the exchange to take place. The buyer would then no longer be an outsider, providing an element of continuity of the land in the family holdings through the children of the new marriage.[10] Understanding indigenous systems of land ownership is important to assessing communities' relations to the land and the importance that land has in the social context beyond its materiality. An awareness of these systems is vital to our analysis of state land inscriptions and registrations, land sales, conflicts over land, and the role that land plays in the cultural construction of nationhood among Palestinians. In particular, it is important to understand Palestinians' conceptions of space and place and the image of the pre-state or pre-occupation Palestine.

In 1858 the Ottoman Authority introduced the land registry law called *tabu* to inscribe rights of land ownership. Landowners were instructed to have their property inscribed in the land register. For the most part, people continued their tradition of communal land ownership, and the attempt to inscribe land entitlement into individuals' names did not succeed in documenting or fully changing the state of land ownership in Palestine (Falah 1983). However, some families or individuals from the local and regional urban population who were prominent in the state structure took advantage of the loose manner in which the tabu registered lands. They registered large pieces of land in their names that were not necessarily theirs. The Turkish authorities were not as concerned about documenting communities' rights to lands as they were in attaching each plot of land to the name of an individual or family that would then be responsible for paying property tax. This is typical of states' practices around the world: "seeing like a state" entails uniformity and transparency in land tenure, and entitlement is seen through the lens of obligations for tax revenue (Scott 1998). The Turkish land register did not require a physical survey before registration. As a result, other urban families bought lands from the state, which assumed ownership of nonregistered lands (Khalidi 1997).

The local residents of villages whose lands were registered to urban landlords thus became like serfs on their own land, as their rightful ownership of the land was no longer recognized by the Turkish authorities. Yet the farmer still maintained and cultivated his land and lived off it. Whether the taxes were paid by the new landlord who collected his share of the crop or directly by those who registered their lands, the fellahin recognized little difference economically, because the land did not have much economic value beyond the harvest. Either way the state now had an interest in a share of the harvest (in the form of property taxes). This was the main reason that fellahin did not bother to challenge the legal entitlement of those who registered their lands to themselves. The registrants would have to pay taxes anyway, and the process of registration gave the authorities more data, strengthening their hand in the case of an inquiry and making it more likely that the children of those who registered could be conscripted. For this reason some fellahin preferred to have their land registered in the names of others.[11] Even after the Turkish land registry was introduced, people continued to make property transactions through the traditional agreements of sale signed by witnesses. The number of witnesses to a land sale contract would average about ten.[12] Still, the traditional norm of land transfer was always tied to the social life and its relation to the land. People sold lands to people they knew from the community or neighboring communities. Because the material value of the land was limited to the harvest, it was tied directly to life over the land.

When European Jewish nationalists sought to acquire land in Palestine the dynamic was completely different form that which characterized acquisitions by Turkish government officials and absentee urban families. Jewish land buyers sought actual possession of the land and had a political agenda. For the Palestinians, the land was the only means of survival for its owners. Land and the working of the land were the main sources of the social organization of the village. The lives of the Palestinians depended on having land to work economically and socially. Jewish immigrants were unsuccessful in securing land purchases from the Palestinian fellahin, but the Jewish National Fund approached the absentee landlords who had acquired land entitlements through the Turkish land registry (Jiryis 1973). The absentee landlords looked at land as strictly real estate and were therefore willing to entertain offers, and because the Jewish agencies were well funded the offers were attractive. Once the Jewish agencies acquired legal entitlement to land by purchase from the absentee landlords, local residents were evicted from their lands so that the new owners could settle the land themselves (Khalidi 1997; Kimberling and Migdal 2003).

The loss of Palestinian land through these purchases marks the beginnings of the confrontations between the Palestinian natives and the Jewish nationalist project from Europe. The Palestinian farmers, rightful owners of the land according to tradition, were unwilling to leave their land and met the evictions with resistance. Leaving the land would mean leaving the village as a whole, and some villages were completely evacuated when the lands were taken away. This occurred in several villages in the Bissan and Tabaria areas in north central Palestine. The processes of land dispossession persisted through the end of Turkish[13] rule and during the British[14] rule of Palestine after 1917. Many tales of land dispossession remain vivid in Palestinian memory, as they are narrated through cultural production and passed on through the generations. To this day confrontations over land are at the heart of the conflict between native Arab Palestinians and the immigrant Jewish population.

Early confrontations with Jewish settlers became what Sahlins (1985) refers to as "prescriptive events," in that they produced whole schemes

⎪ltural processes among Palestinians and Jewish immigrant commu-
⋯⋯s. These events upset the tradition of communal life in Palestine and
set in motion new social processes in Palestinian society, centered on the
articulation of identity and rootedness in the land. The land, the environment, and home were no longer to be taken for granted by Palestinians.
Their rootedness, attachment to the land, and exemplifications of self
and community in the landscape became subjects of cultural dominance.
The Palestinians narrated early episodes of confrontation and refusal to
surrender lands to new foreign buyers as examples of resistance and
defiance. Through these narrations the Palestinian farmer, the fellah,
defiant and rooted in his land, became the symbol of Palestinian nation
making. The *kuffiyya* or *hatta*, the *fellah* headdress, later symbolized the
association with this image of the rooted farmer by the Palestinian resistance and its supporters (Khalidi 1997).

The forced dispossession of land by absentee landlords, supported
by the state's legal system of land entitlement, was regarded as an attack on the community life and its social fabric. Against this backdrop
emerged the notion of *al-ardh 'ardh* (the land is honor), which persists
with strength among Palestinian fellahin communities to this day. The
'ardh is one's own honor as kept and protected through women's honor
and sexuality. Selling the land to strangers is like selling one's wife or
daughter for prostitution. The forceful dispossession of land is not regarded as a mere loss of land: it is a blow to one's sense of self, community, and honor. But selling land in a socially sanctioned manner is more
like arranging a marriage for the land. This understanding of the relationship to the land led to the Palestinian characterization of the forceful
establishment of Israel in Palestine in 1948 as *ightisab filistin* (the rape of
Palestine). The notion that Palestine has been raped and is being raped is
narrated in songs, poems, and paintings that depict Palestine as dis-
gusted with those who have forcefully occupied her and as resisting
them and seeking liberation from the rapists. In a recent statement by
Hamas's military wing (Izzideen Al-Qassam Brigades) the word *mughta-
sabah* "raped" (referring to various Israeli towns and settlement sites)
appeared twenty-one times.[15] This representation has transcended Palestinian cultural production, extending to the Arab region as a whole. The
famous Iraqi exiled poet Muzaffer Al-Nawwab uses the metaphor of
raped Palestine in his criticism of Arab officials' silence on the conquest

of Palestine and their pressures to quiet Palestinian resistance. He addressed Arab leaders in the mid-1970s:[16]

Jerusalem is the bride of your Arabhood
Why did you let in all the fuckers of the night into her bedroom
And you pulled out all of your daggers
And pumped up yourselves with honor
And you shouted at her, to be quiet in order to keep the grace honor
How honorable you are sons of a bitch
QUIET RAPE!
. . . .
You, Jerusalem is the bride of your Arabhood
Why did you let in all the syphilis into her bedroom
And you stood up to her, to be quiet in order to keep the grace honor
What horns are you[17]
Sons of a bitch suffice you yelling
She will tighten her braids and return the load on you
She will return the load on your integrity
She will return the load on you house after house
And she will poke her fingers into your eyes
YOU ARE MY RAPISTS . . .
Be infertile, Oh land of Palestine
Be infertile, Oh mother of martyrs
From now on this pregnancy is from the enemy
Disgraceful . . . frightening
This land will not pollinate with other than the Arabic language
Hey princes of conquest, die . . .

For members of the Palestinian resistance, the voices of the resistance in its multiple forms, as we will explore over the following chapters, are the *screams* over the rape of Palestine.

After the British took control of Palestine in 1917, the British Administration in Palestine quickly moved to reorganize the status of land tenure in Palestine and prepare the Palestinian landscape for the creation of the Jewish national homeland. One of the first ordinances introduced by the British was the Woods and Forest Ordinance in 1920, which was designed to confiscate lands that were largely used as grazing

grounds by the Palestinian rural population, the fellahin, and the Bedouins. These lands were classified as state forest owned by the state, and
the British sought to register the land as land plots in individuals'
names, not in the name of the village or the family (Falah 1983). Given
that the declared British political agenda was the establishment of a
Jewish homeland in Palestine, the underlying rationale went beyond
facilitating the state's management system and taxation and extended to
the practicality of making the land salable as real estate so that the newly
recruited population, the European Jews, could acquire land. The fellahin and Bedouin society resisted the British Land Settlement Ordinance, mainly because it did not allow for their tradition of collective
ownership.

The process of land confiscation and land division also affected Palestine in that the British authority sought to advance its project of modernization and urbanization (Lerner 2000; Inkeles and Smith 1974) by
recruiting young men for jobs in the city and enlistment in the police and
the army. The British placed many industrial centers in the city of Haifa,
most notably the oil refinery that was fed through a pipeline from northern Iraq. The economic boom in Haifa attracted many workers and
entrepreneurial opportunities. The city of Haifa witnessed rapid growth
and emerged as a new cultural center and one of the dynamic Arab cities of the region. Artists from Beirut, Cairo, and Damascus gathered
and performed in Haifa. Similar developments were taking place in the
coastal city of Jaffa during the 1930s and 1940s. Local Palestinian in-
dustries boomed, from textile and cosmetics, to heavy machinery, to
regional trade (Khalidi 1984).

By the time they were taken over by Jewish militias in 1948, Haifa and
Jaffa had become Palestinian national symbols. Tales of prosperous life
in the cities later became the image of modern Palestine thriving. The
lively city life of cinemas, theater, festivals, and Egyptian stars performing in concerts; the famous Lebanese, Syrian, and Palestinian poets in a
munazara;[18] cultural and economic exchanges with other Arab centers
like Cairo, Beirut, and Damascus; and the fellahin of Marj Ibn Amer
selling their watermelon and cantaloupe in Beirut and Damascus—all
combined to create the image of a Palestine that had been ruined by the
Jewish nationalist project. To this day the image is continually constructed in tales told by members of the older generations in Palestinian

villages and refugee camps. To them the stories are the object gia; to the young they are a vision of the future.

The Rise of the Resistance

The acceleration of land confiscation and the mass Jewish immigration facilitated by the British authorities led to widespread awareness among Palestinians of the Jewish nationalist threat and the need to organize to resist it. This awareness of the Zionist project in the 1930s coupled with frustrations about the local leadership of the Palestinian notables and their lack of effectiveness in confronting colonialism led to the formation of new initiatives of resistance (Al-Kayyali 1978).[19] In 1935 Palestine underwent a general strike in protest against the smuggling of a weapons shipment to Jewish immigrants and the British authorities' complicity. Young Palestinian activists called for a conference to organize a popular resistance to the authorities and the Jewish threats. Amid the charged political dynamics of the strike, on 20 November 1935 the British police assassinated Sheikh Izzideen Al-Qassam, the vocal imam at Haifa's largest mosque, Masjid Al-Istiqlal (the Mosque of Independence), and head of the Moslem Youth Association. Several of his friends were killed along with him, and their funeral gathered thousands of Palestinians in Haifa, who carried the shahid (martyr) through the streets, chanting Allahu Akbar ("God is Greater"). Demonstrators clashed with British police, stoned their cars and stations, and walked with the martyrs' bodies for three and a half hours before they laid them to rest, buried with their clothes soaked in blood according to the Islamic tradition of burying a shahid in the state of his or her martyrdom (Za'iter 1980). This scene was to be repeated thousands of times in the days, years, and decades to come throughout the Palestinian cities. Today Hamas's military wing Izzideen Al-Qassam Martyrs Brigades is named after Sheikh Izzideen Al-Qassam.

These political developments and the martyrdom of Sheikh Izzideen Al-Qassam became what Das calls "critical events" that called for new forms of action (Das 1995). They set in motion confrontations between Palestinians and British police, which extended the strike to full-fledged civil disobedience that brought economic life in the country to a near-halt (Pappe 2004). The period is known as the Revolution of 1936. The prominent call of the revolution was a demand to cease Jewish immigration to Palestine and bring about Palestine's independence. Palestinian countrymen armed themselves and engaged in raids on British police forces. Thousands of Palestinians died in clashes with police, tens of thousands were arrested by the British authorities, and hundreds were sentenced to death by the English courts and executed (Za'iter 1980).

The events of the Revolution of 1936 became a dominant feature of Palestinian popular memory and conceptions of history. Ted Swedenburg's "Memories of Revolt" (1995b) is an excellent ethnography of this period that demonstrates how popular memory is the main source of the Palestinian conception of history and how this memory becomes a form of resistance. These historical events were recounted by Palestinian historians in the 1960s and 1970s and came to define the revolutionary context of the Palestinians in these periods. Examples of the histories are those of Abdel Wahhab al-Kayyali, Mustafa al-Dabbagh, Akram Z'aiter, and Naji 'Alloush, as well as the writings of Ghassan Kanafani. The Palestinian-American historian Rashid Khalidi criticized these historical writings for their reliance on oral narrative and local historical sources and discredited their authors, in particular Abdel Wahhab al-Kayyali, Naji 'Alloush and Ghassan Kanafani, as "activist-historians" (Khalidi 1997, 195–98). Regardless of the historical and analytical shortcomings identified by Khalidi, these histories were the main historical materials through which the Palestinian factions taught their membership the modern history of Palestine.[20] They are the histories to which Palestinians related and with which they formed bonds. They were drawn on by Palestinian singers and actors, and formed the basis for historical narratives to Palestinian story writing. El-Funoun ash-Shaa'biya (Popular Dance Troop) performed the dance plays Wadi at-Tufah (The Apple Valley) and Misha'al[21] in the early and mid-1980s, which narrate Palestinian battles with British forces. These histories had a greater impact on Palestinian consciousness than the scholarly, documented, archive-based history of Khalidi, since Palestinians had little exposure to his historical narrative and his sources. However, Palestinians had wide awareness of the "activist-historians" histories. These historical records, taught in the inner cells of PLO factions in the 1970s and 1980s, were also narrated by activist revolutionary poetics. Cultural productions and repre-

sentations of the events of resistance to the British rule, land confiscations, and Jewish immigration gave the Palestinians a historical context
for their present mediums of consciousness, and a call for action.
Khalidi criticizes these histories for their failure "to mention the appall-
ing losses suffered by the Palestinians during the course of the revolt, or
to assess the uprising's slim possibilities of success from the very beginning, or to ask what the Palestinians might have done differently and
more successfully in the same historical circumstances" (1997, 196).
But Khalidi fails to consider why these histories are so widely accepted
and adopted by Palestinians to make sense of their present and history.
His own brand of history—"failure narrated as triumph" or "defeat as
victory"—has no popularity, resonance, or relevance to Palestinians'
sense of their history. R. Khalidi is right to point out that "what was at
work . . . was a perfectly normal rewriting of history to fit the circumstances of the time it was written, providing a narrative appropriate for
the 1960s, when the Palestinians were again being told by these same
historian-activists, and the PLO, to take their fate in their hands and
launch armed struggle against heavy odds" (197). Yet the same applies to
Khalidi's own "rewriting" of history. His rewriting of Palestinian history
also fits the "circumstances of the time it was written," providing a
narrative that was suitable for facilitating the Oslo peace process—at a
time when Palestinians were being asked to provide concessions on a
range of core issues such as recognition of Israel in Palestine, Palestinians' rights to historic Palestine, and the Palestinian right of return,
without anything real being offered by Israel in return. Several Palestinian scholars have made calls for concessions to Israel: Khalil Shiqaqi and
Sarri Nusseibeh of Al-Quds University in Jerusalem, for example, often
make pragmatic arguments in the mainstream media. Yet the public is
more favorably disposed toward the works of people like Salman Abu
Sitta,[22] who would also fit Khalidi's description of "activist-historians."
Khalidi overlooks the extent to which people's attitudes toward and
views of the present shaped their historical constructions and historical
consciousness. The interplays between historical narratives and present
consciousness are important junctures that enable us to assess the cultural processes of the present and their historical backdrops. These interplays are the historicities described as "the historical experiences"
and "the significance of recalling the past" (Whitehead 2003).

As I walked the streets of Jenin during my field research in 2003 and 2004, music shops played a tape of Palestinian folkloric and revolutionary songs describing what was reported by Palestinian human rights groups as the Jenin Camp massacre of April 2002. The Israeli army attack on the camp destroyed a whole neighborhood in the center of the camp, killing over sixty people and wounding many others. In spite of the disastrous outcome of the attack, the Palestinian resistance marked a historic episode of steadfastness and standing up to the Israelis. The songs in the tape bring the battle to life and make heroes of the fighters, invoking their names and using folksinging to describe the battlegrounds, the attack, and the defense. I interviewed the songwriter and singer at a blacksmith shop in Jenin where he was working on a stove. After he washed his hands and sat for the interview, he was at first caught off guard when I asked about phrases he used in the song. Then he seemed to acknowledge that his songwriting was a form of history making:[23] "This event should not be for nothing. This needs to be there for the future generations. I believe that the Jenin battle was special. It's our right to take pride in the exceptional performance of the camp. We must assert the heroism [of their resistance] over the catastrophe [the death of the fighters and the extensive destruction in the camp]. We take pride in this struggle." There is a monumental difference between recalling the event as a catastrophe and recalling it as an episode of collective heroism. This consciousness of the cultural significance of recalling and recoding the past is the historicity. The Palestinians consistently seem to recall history in ways to sustain their struggle and empower it toward the restoration of their rights.

The way histories of the "activist-historians" are narrated and the widespread consciousness of these histories among Palestinians make them more relevant than their critics in the Palestinian context. People's current consciousness of their entitlement to the right of return, for example, and of how that consciousness is related to present circumstances and future aspirations, has a profound impact on what history the people find meaningful. It is not as simple as constructing a historical narrative that would lead the people to abandon their aspirations toward restoring their rights and recognizing their entitlements. The important question to ask is why Palestinians relate more to "heroic" histories that lead them to take challenges "against great odds" and less to *defeatist, pragmatic,* or *rational* histories that would lead them to resign themselves to the will of "great powers" imposed on them.

The central event in Palestinian modern history is the loss of Palestine in 1948 and the establishment of the state of Israel in it. During the Jewish militia war that year for the establishment of Israel and its aftermath, Israel had erased approximately 418 Palestinian villages from the six hundred Palestinian villages that fell under its control. The new state moved Jewish populations to occupy Palestinian homes in urban towns. Eleven Palestinian cities were settled by Jews and became Jewish cities after most of their Palestinian residents were evacuated, and in some cities all of the Palestinian residents were displaced.[24] Over 800,000 Palestinians were displaced and exiled. Displaced Palestinians were and still *are* denied reentry into Palestine by Israel. The events of 1948 were followed by systematic Israeli reconfiguration of Palestine into Israel directly after its takeover. The Israeli ethnic cleansing campaign against the Palestinian population that fell under the control of new Israel continued through the 1950s.[25] Jewish Kibbutzim with Jewish names were erected on the sites of 121 Palestinian villages (PASSIA 2002; W. Khalidi 1992). The UN erected refugee camps for displaced Palestinians as temporary shelters awaiting resolution in the neighboring Arab states of Jordan, Syria, and Lebanon. The exodus referred to by Palestinians as *al-Nakba* (the catastrophe) represents the main "prescriptive event" in modern Palestinian history. The schemes of cultural processes generated by these events and their narrations redefined and continue to redefine Palestinians' sense of identity, sense of homeland and rootedness, and perceptions of the future.

The Birth of the Fida'iyeen

The exiled Palestinian population eventually gave up hope that the Arab governments and the international community would restore their right to return home. In 1965, seventeen years after the beginning of their exile, Palestinians formed their own organizations to mobilize for a Palestinian armed struggle to liberate Palestine. In 1967 Israel moved and took control of the remaining Palestinian territories of the West Bank and Gaza Strip in what it characterized as a "preemptive" military campaign against Egypt, Jordan, and Syria. After the war the Palestinian population that was annexed to Jordan, and those lands administered by Egypt fell under Israeli military rule. The city of Jerusalem also fell under Israeli control and Israel directly annexed the city (Morris 1987; Pappe 2004).

Newly organized Palestinian organizations in exile carried out raids on Israeli military targets and Israeli settlements through the Lebanese, Syrian, and Jordanian borders. These groups established bases in Jordan and carried out most of their attacks across the Jordan River. The Palestinian guerrilla members of the resistance movement were called the *fida'iyeen* (those who sacrificed themselves), since most cross-border operations would result in being killed in action. After the defeat of the Arab regimes in the 1967 war, the fida'iyeen stepped up their attacks against Israeli targets. On 18 March 1968 the fida'iyeen planted a mine in the Jordan Valley that blew up a bus and killed thirty Israelis. This prompted an Israel military offensive on the Palestinian resistance based in Jordan near Al-Karameh camp on 21 March 1968. The word *al-Karameh* in Arabic means "dignity," and the Al-Karameh battle turned out to be the battle of dignity for the Palestinians. The Palestinian resistance was led mainly by the Palestine National Liberation Movement (Fatah), founded and organized by a nucleus of Palestinian student groups at the University of Cairo led by Yasser Arafat, and the Popular Front for the Liberation of Palestine (PFLP), founded by George Habash, a medical student at the American University of Beirut. In the Al-Karameh battle Israel suffered an unexpected level of casualties, with twenty-eight dead and sixty-nine injured, and thirty-four tanks damaged or destroyed. The attacking Israeli army was forced to withdraw. Although the Palestinian resistance suffered ninety-eight deaths and casualties were higher than those of the Israelis, it was seen as a victory that the Palestinian fighters were able to repel an Israeli army that had just inflicted a humiliating defeat against the armies of Egypt, Syria, Jordan, and Lebanon. The Palestinian resistance was aided by one Jordanian army brigade, but the victory was narrated as a purely fida'iyeen victory, one that restored Arab dignity (Gowers and Walker 1991).

Reports from the Al-Karameh battle described Palestinian fighters strapping themselves with explosives and throwing themselves at Israeli tanks, and firing rocket-propelled grenades from point-blank range at

Israeli army units. Interviews with the fida'iyeen and media reports described fierce Palestinian fighters ready to sacrifice themselves, running to take on the enemy. The wreckage of Israeli tanks and the remains of an Israeli soldier were used by the fida'iyeen to show their victory and break the image of an invincible Israeli army (Gowers and Walker 1991). After Al-Karameh the *fida'i* emerged as a Palestinian icon.

Al-Karameh was another "prescriptive event" in Palestinian history. The battle changed the perceptions of Israel among Palestinians, set new Palestinian cultural processes in motion, and created a new dynamic in regional politics from which the Palestine Liberation Organization (PLO) eventually emerged as a major power player in the region. The fida'iyeen numbered only a few hundred when they were attacked in Al-Karameh. However, in the first two days that followed the battle, the Fatah group alone received over five thousand applications from Palestinian and Arab youths seeking to enlist in its ranks (Gowers and Walker 1991). Many revolutionary songs celebrated the fida'iyeen. The Palestinian national anthem that began as *Biladi, Biladi, Biladi* (My country, my country, my country) was changed by the resistance singers and chanters to *Fida'i, Fida'i, Fida'i* (sacrificer, sacrificer, sacrificer). This version of the Palestinian national anthem remains the official anthem today, sung by Palestinian schools every morning and at all official ceremonies.

All eyes were on the resistance, such that the rise in popularity of the Palestinian resistance movement threatened the stability of the monarchy in Jordan. The Palestinian resistance factions escalated their campaign and began operations designed to draw international attention to the Palestinian plight. The PFLP hijacked four European passenger planes in September 1970, forced them to land in an abandoned airfield in Jordan, and blew them up after their evacuation. The hijacking brought the tension with the Jordanian government to a climax. The Jordanian Royal Guard units conducted an all-out military campaign against the Palestinian armed groups in Jordan by the end of 1971, which officially drove all organized Palestinian factions out of Jordan (Cubert 1997). The Palestinian factions regrouped in the Palestinian refugee camps in Lebanon and set up their offices and base of operations in Beirut. By the mid-1970s the Palestinian organizations that united under the umbrella of the PLO gained Arab and international recognition as the "sole representative of the Palestinian people."

Palestinian cultural productions in the years to come idealized the fida'i and the act of sacrifice as the ultimate honor and act of giving. Palestinian groups used many forms of "social poetics" to narrate the victory of Al-Karameh and the "heroic" fida'iyeen raids on Israel that made the fida'i a Palestinian icon. The klashin (Kalashnikov), the weapon of the fida'iyeen, became a symbol of pride in the Palestinian revolutionary culture like the sword in classical Arab poetry. In the fida'iyeen camps and in Palestinian refugee camps people danced with the klashin to the accompaniment of revolutionary songs. Palestinian revolutionary songs dominated the airwaves throughout the 1970s. Palestinian youth sang and memorized songs of sacrifice, the fida'iyeen, and the klashin.

Recent scholarship on Palestine has begun to consider popular culture as a source of political analysis (Stein and Swedenburg 2005), but how popular culture is employed in political and military strategies and used in mediating social processes is still largely overlooked. During the 1970s and early 1980s revolutionary statements and songs broadcast by the PLO's mobile radio station, Sawtu Filistin (Voice of Palestine) was a medium for mobilizing youth in the West Bank and Gaza. Al-'Ashiqin (The Lovers) was the main Palestinian singing group adopted by the PLO and became the primary source of Palestinian expression for Palestinian communities through the constant broadcast of its songs on PLO radio. These songs attached meanings to the act of sacrifice. They provided cultural representation to the acts of resistance that could be lived by non-participant Palestinians in the cultural imaginary and hence serve as a recruiting and mobilizing force. They became popular songs among Palestinian youth. The themes prevalent in the songs of al-'Ashiqin included revolution, resistance, sacrifice, return, and self-reliance. An example of a song with the theme of sacrifice:

> Wa ja'altu min jurhi wa dima' lil anhari jadwal, aoh aoh aoh
> I have made from my wounds and blood a stream for the rivers [of
>   Palestine], Aoh, Aoh, Aoh
> Wa hamaltu rashashi, aoh aoh aoh, litahmila ba'adiya al-ajyalu minjal, aoh aoh
> And I have carried my machine gun so the generations after me would carry
>   the sickle, Aoh, Aoh, Aoh

Making streams for Palestine's rivers resonated with people at the time when Israel was just implementing water diversion projects that dramatically decreased the flow of the Jordan River. These images of the sacrifice created in the songs are very much in line with the understanding of sacrifice in a cross-cultural context. The sacrifice is a medium for exchange between the human body and the universe. And here the sacrifice is a medium of exchange between the fida'i body and the land of Palestine. This exchange is achieved by situating the sacrificed body and the land of Palestine in a "homologic relation" (Lincoln 1991), in which the blood of the sacrificed Palestinian body corresponds to the water feeding the streams and rivers of Palestine. Through the performance of sacrifice for the land of Palestine offered in the raid against the occupiers of Palestine, homologies are fused through the cultural conception of the sacrifice, with the life of the sacrificed Palestinian transformed to give life to Palestine and hence to Palestinian peoplehood. The sacrifice is also presented for the benefit of future generations: "so the generations after me would carry the sickle."

Other songs also connected the sacrifice as a performance that asserted presence in the face of political processes that denied the very existence of Palestinians. Segments of these songs that I recall include:

darbi mur, darbak mur, ida'as foq idlu'i u mur, qaddesh hath ish-sha'b itha'ir dhahha
     ibdamu ta-ya'ish hur?
My road is bitter, your road is bitter.
I die, you step over my ribs and pass.
How much did this revolutionizing people sacrifice its blood so it lives free?
Fida'iyeh wel-aakher had fida'iyeh, fidai'yeh ew inna ar-rad fida'iyeh
Sacrificers and to the last end we are sacrificers.
Sacrificers and we've got the response, sacrificers
Hiz el-baroud ya sha'abina hiz el-baroud
Shake the guns, our people, shake the guns
Sammi' ed-donya hatha sowt rassassina
Let the world hear this is the sound of our bullets
Ayi 'ibara sha'abina shal el-baroud
What is the lesson of our people carrying the arms?
Rafadh el-waraq, rafadh el-haki, rafadh el-woa'oud?
They rejected the paper, they rejected the talks, they rejected the promises
Qassaman ma nirmi slahina min yaddina
We pledge the oath that we will not let go of the arms from our hand

illa ba'ed man-nharirik ya ardhina

Not until we liberate you, our land

Ya raba'ina ya shaba'ina el-dami wahhad darbina

Oh, our pals, our people, the blood has unified our path

law mit tayyara min fougi

law mit dababeh gudami

laa'mal silah min sidri wa-ahmi rfigi

If there were a hundred aircrafts above me

If there were a hundred tanks in front of me

I will make a weapon from my chest and save my comrade

In these songs and many others "sacrifice" is a "response" to a collective "bitter" reality. In addition to being an act to the people and the land, sacrifice is presented as a "performance" for the "world to hear," a performative and communicative act (Whitehead 2004; Riches 1986).

The sacrifice as presented in these songs involves negating oneself for the birth of the greater good, or to modify the conditions for the greater good. Here the "objects of sacrifice," which in this case was for the land of Palestine and its people, are the parties for whom the sacrifice take place (Hubert and Mauss 1964). The fida'i is both the one who undergoes the sacrifice and acquires its benefits and at the same time the sacrificed object or *victim* in the act of sacrifice, the "moral person" who bears the cost of sacrifice. The sacrifice became the foundation of the Palestinian resistance. The act of the fida'i in the Palestinian context brings about twofold results. The sacrificer gains moral qualities as the "person who accomplishes it" and the land of Palestine gains sacred qualities as the "object of sacrifice." Both processes of attaching meaning call for the regeneration of the act. The more acts of sacrifice are committed, the more the fida'i gains moral qualities and hence becomes idealized. At the same time, the more fida'iyeen are sacrificed for the land, the more it becomes sacred, calling for more sacrifices to save it or honor it.

Many assume that the act of sacrificing oneself must have a strong religious dimension, but belief in the Divine is not a necessary condition for these constructions to take place. The fusion of the human life with the land in the absence of the Divine constitutes a cultural performance that has the capacity to address multiple sets of witnesses.

Graffiti in Wadi Berqin, home town of Shadi Al-Toubasi, who carried out a mission in Haifa. The graffiti read: "Haifa will not forget you, Shadi. Enjoy the paradise." Photo by author, November 2004.

These witnesses could be the Divine, the community, the "enemy," international observers, or the land itself. These constructions still inform today's sacrifices in the Palestinian resistance. Shadi Al-Toubasi is a Palestinian boy from the village of Wadi Berqin who carried out a martyrdom mission, or "suicide bombing," in Haifa on 31 March 2002. The graffiti on a wall in Shadi's village reads *Haifa len tansak ya shadi* (Haifa will not forget you, Shadi). Whether Shadi's sacrifice was addressed to Haifa or other witnesses, Haifa was assumed to be the addressed witness in the perception of some of Shadi's fellow villagers, an assumption which informs others' constructions of the act and possible future actors. In the Palestinian context the perception of fusion between the human sacrificer and the land is more prevalent than fusion with divine life, especially in cultural representations, although the latter also exists.

Those early acts of sacrifice by the fida'iyeen and many of today's similar acts make reference to these conceptions in the poetics of the resistance and the symbolic representation of the martyrs' fusion with

Shadi's memorial in the nearby Martyr's Graveyard Jenin Camp being visited by
one of his friends. Photo by author, November 2004.

the land as exemplified in the *shaqiq* (the poppy), also known as *hannoun*.
The poppy is believed to have acquired its red color from the blood of
martyrs, of those who died for the land. The land honors them by turning their blood into flowers. The more flowers there are in the spring,
the more reminders exist of how sacred the land has become, which
further intensifies the attachment to it in the view of living Palestinians.
Through these histories the land of Palestine has emerged as an object of
sacrifice in Palestinian cultural representation and practices.

The West Bank and Gaza as Centers of Palestinian Resistance

The PLO power base in Lebanon has grown into that of an organized
army. The PLO has managed to stockpile weapons, rocket launchers,
armored vehicles, and tanks, aided at first by countries from the Soviet
bloc and financed by Arab donations and Arab governments, who saw in

their support for the PLO a relief from the pressure of their people to engage on the Palestinian question. The shelling of Israeli settlements in northern Palestine and the Israeli shelling of Palestinian refugee camps and military bases in southern Lebanon were regular activities in the late 1970s (Gowers and Walker 1991).

In June 1982 Israel waged a military campaign against the bases of the PLO to destroy its organizational presence in Lebanon. Israel invaded southern Lebanon with overwhelming force, occupying much of the south in the first few days of the fighting. Although the fighting continued in the south, Israeli forces advanced to Beirut and encircled the city, enforcing a siege on Palestinian forces there. Palestinian factions fought Israeli forces on the outskirts of Beirut throughout the summer of 1982. The Israeli forces devastated Beirut with air, sea, and land bombardment for eighty days. Rounds of international diplomacy led to an arrangement for Palestinian fighters to evacuate the city; they were moved mostly to Yemen and Tunisia, with some factions going to Syria.

The defeat of the PLO and the disengagement of the Arab regimes from the struggle, particularly Egypt after it signed a peace treaty with Israel in 1979, had two significant outcomes. First, the defeat of the PLO as a secular nationalist movement gave rise to political Islam as an alternative form of nationalism. Political Islamist groups like the Islamic Brotherhood that were active in Palestine, especially in the Gaza Strip, used the political and cultural vacuum created by the defeat of the PLO and pointed to its failures. New Palestinian Islamic organizations emerged in the late 1980s during the intifada, such as Harakat Al-Muqawama Al-Islamiya-Hamas (Islamic Resistance Movement–Hamas), which represents the Palestinian wing of the Muslim Brotherhood Society (MBS), and Harakat Al-Jihad Al-Islami (Islamic Jihad Movement, known as al-Jihad). I would argue that these organizations remained nationalist in their political programs, as we will see in the coming chapters. The second outcome of the invasion of Lebanon and the defeat of the PLO was the return of the resistance to Palestine. After the defeat of the PLO in Lebanon there was no meaningful challenge to Israel from the exiled Palestinians, since their fighters no longer operated in any of the bordering states. Thus the Palestinians in the West Bank and Gaza realized that they had to take matters into their own hands to respond to the Israeli occupation. This development represented a major shift in the Palestinian resistance, in the sense that for the first time since 1948, the resistance movement, the leadership, and the main theater of operation were inside Palestine again. In the 1970s Palestinian youth who wanted to join the armed struggle against Israel used to go to Lebanon. This trend was ironic: the Israeli target was right there in Palestine, and going to Lebanon made it that much harder to penetrate Israeli border security to reach targets. Little did the Israelis know that by destroying the PLO bases in Lebanon they brought the revolution home, also resulting in a more radical shift within the resistance.

Supporters of the Palestinian factions on Palestinian university campuses in the West Bank and Gaza were already articulating a Palestinian national consciousness (Bruhn 2004). Resistance to Israeli politics and practices of control were already under way across Palestinian cities in the West Bank and Gaza in the form of demonstrations and protests against Israeli military rule. Palestinian factions in exile organized grassroots organizations that aimed at mobilizing youth into the resistance and at raising their awareness and consciousness of the occupation and its practices. This is the period during which I grew up in Palestine. Many political processes were at work: the raising of awareness to current political dynamics, the teaching of history, symbolic exemplification in the land and history through expressions of attachment to the olive trees, and iconic historical narratives. A rise in political awareness and historical consciousness intensified resistance to Israeli rule. Moreover, Israeli attempts at "state expansion" seeking to incorporate Palestinian communities in the West Bank through what was called *idara madaniya* (civil administration) in the late 1970s prompted further articulation of Palestinian identity. A common chant of Palestinian youth during demonstrations of this period was *la idara madaniya* ("no to the civil administration"). The discussions of why one should resist "Israeli civil administration" and rather stay under "military rule" until a national liberation was achieved became a medium through which the resistance faction could articulate Palestinian identity and what it meant to be Palestinian.

During this period Israel started its projects of settlement building in the West Bank and Gaza, which entailed expropriating land from Palestinians—not only those in the West Bank and Gaza, but also those who had fallen under Israel in 1948 but had not been displaced. On

30 March 1976 six Palestinian farmers in a village in the Galilee were killed by the Israeli army for refusing to evacuate their land after the Israeli court issued confiscation orders for their lands. This event recalled the early confrontations over land dispossession and became a "critical event" that called for action. The killings of the farmers were widely protested by the Palestinians in Israel and in the West Bank and Gaza alike. The day became memorialized on the Palestinian calendar as Land Day, a day for demonstrating commitment to the land and intensifying the resistance, as Palestinian group statements called for action. Land Day became such an important occasion that Israel started closing schools and universities on that day in the early 1980s and extended the closings to two weeks by the mid-1980s. To this day Israel seals off the West Bank and Gaza as Land Day approaches, fearing that Palestinian operations will intensify in the days leading up to it.

Growing Up under Israeli Occupation

Understanding the dynamics of Palestinians' youth encounter with Israeli soldiers is important to gaining a grasp of the internal social processes that these encounters generate in Palestinian youth culture. Although it means breaking away from conventional ethnography, I wish to share some of my experiences growing up under Israeli occupation, to give a close view of how these experiences shape consciousness and social processes. Sharing these personal accounts will also give historical depth to this ethnography and thus enhance my analysis of the present political and cultural dynamics in Palestine. I will also show how current dynamics of encounters in Palestine between youths and soldiers are the outgrowth of the social process and meaning making that started in that period, generating experiences similar to my own.

I recall one experience when I was in the twelfth grade at the Jenin Secondary School in April 1982. We were placed under siege by the Israeli army in my school in Jenin for a whole day. One boy started singing a song that he had heard on the Voice of Palestine, and I was surprised that everyone knew the whole song by heart, as well as every other song we sang that day. We started the day with a small demonstration before classes while waiting for the bell to ring. As was typical for any demonstration at the time, the students threw stones at the two Israeli soldiers who constantly monitored our school from their post on the rooftop of the building next to it. These soldiers called for help, and the students stormed the few Israeli army jeeps that came to the rescue. The army pulled back and surrounded the school. They later announced on their loudspeakers that no one was allowed to leave. Under siege at the school, we spent the day throwing stones until there were no more stones on the school grounds, and singing the songs of the Voice of Palestine. Some students started breaking bricks from the school's landscaping in the front yard, which was upsetting to the principal. Later in the afternoon the Israelis brought about twenty army vehicles full of soldiers. After taking positions around all sides of the school the army started shooting and stormed the school with teargas bombs. We were forced to go back to our classrooms. The school had about five hundred students in the tenth through twelfth grades. After we were forced back to the classrooms and the teargas cleared up, the army broke into the school in terrifying numbers.

My classroom was on the second floor, so the soldiers did not get to us for a while. In the meantime we looked out the windows to see them dragging the students from the first-floor classrooms and beating them in the school's front yard. Waiting to be beaten was as terrifying as the beating itself. Eventually about six or seven soldiers walked into my classroom and started hitting us hard in the face with thick, wooden clubs and the backs of their M-16 rifles, while shouting at us to get out. I made my way to the door where my fellow students were jammed, managing to suffer only one hit. At the door I hesitated and tried to go back. There was a row of soldiers about twenty meters long, standing in the veranda corridor to the staircase and hitting students with their sticks when they passed. As I hesitated at the door the soldiers inside jumped toward me and I dashed into the row of torture outside. In the corridor I passed through the soldiers with a speed I did not know I had. I suffered a few hits, as there was no way to escape. I could not stop at the end of the corridor or turn down the stairs where I was supposed to go. Instead I jumped onto the metal pole of the staircase and hung on there for a moment. Then a soldier ran at me, so I threw myself down to the center of the staircase. I got up and ran down the second half of the stairs, where at the exit of the staircase a soldier tried to hit me with his stick on my lower legs. I jumped over his stick and came down flat on the ground.

I got up and ran away after getting a kick from the soldier that ran at me. I ran around the front yard of the school, screaming like everyone else, and two soldiers were chasing me and saying 'ala batnak (on your stomach). I ran around in circles until I could not run any more, then went down on my stomach like the rest of the students. A few soldiers gathered over me, kicking me and hitting me with their sticks and the back of their M-16s. I fell as prey; all I could do was watch myself get beaten. Moments after the crowd of soldiers left me and went to chase other students who were running around screaming, a full-figured soldier came running toward me and kicked me in the chest with his steel-toed boots while I was down on my stomach, face down as instructed. For a while I could hardly breath. I felt as if I was about to totally collapse. As the soldier directed his killer kick to my chest, he said, "falast-tizi huh"—"Palestinian—my ass, huh."

After the Israeli soldiers got the whole student body to lie on their stomachs in the front yard, they released the teachers, all being held in one room, and sent them home. As for us, they collected our ID cards,[26] assembled us in groups of about twenty each, and ordered each group to run in front of an army vehicle. During the run, the vehicle was speeding up behind us to push us to go faster and kept scaring us by coming close enough to almost hit us and actually knocked some students down. We were being taken to the Israeli military headquarters in town, which is about three kilometers from our school. I did not have enough energy left in me to run that far in front of their truck, so I threw myself down at the side of the road. The truck stopped and two soldiers came down on me, kicking me all over my body. I pulled myself up and ran again for a short distance and threw myself down at the side of the road again. The soldiers stopped, cursed at me, told me to follow quickly, and they went on with the rest of the students.

I watched the students pass by as they ran in front of the army trucks and waited for a suitable opportunity to sneak to one of the side roads. I went to town and rested at a shop that belongs to a relative from the village. There I rested for a while, then went and had a falafel sandwich. I was aching all over my body and had a fever. I had to then follow to the military headquarters about two hours later to retrieve my ID. Otherwise

I would become wanted. There students were still being checked at the main gates of the compound. I stood in line with the rest of the students who were being checked in. Standing in that line was one of the most terrifying experiences of my life. The boys were being searched by an athletic soldier, who after searching the student would start talking to him and wait for the right moment to direct one of two terrifying hits by surprise. One was a head-butt to the forehead, which left most students with blood streaming down their faces; the other was a strong punch in the stomach. With the condition I was in, the pain left me barely able to stand the breeze in the air. I was seeing tens of these hits, one after the other, and waiting for mine as we advanced a couple of steps in the line after every scream of the next student in line. Moving forward was moving closer to torture. The torture built up as time passed; those who were toward the end of the line and waiting for their hits, like me, lived the experience of the hits dozens of times by seeing them applied to those in the front of the line. One wanted to jump out of the line to take the hit right away, in order to be freed from waiting for it. The soldier was called on his walkie-talkie just as only two students remained before it was my turn to take a hit. It felt as if I was drowning and someone had pulled me out. No matter who was going to take the place of the soldier being called, there was no way he could be as terrifying. We were then checked by the normal gatekeeper soldier, who quickly searched us and let us in.

Inside, all the students were sitting on the ground in one large circle. I was one of the last few students, so I would sit at the edge. I knew from experience that those who sit at the edge get most of the beatings, as the soldiers fear walking inside the bunch. I asked the students to make room for me in the middle, because I was getting really sick. My condition was showing on my face and my fellow students quickly made room for me. We spent the day undergoing harassment and beatings. The students at the edges got most of the beatings, with the exception of those whom the soldiers picked on by asking them to come out and taking them to the side, where they beat them one by one in front of the crowd. We spent the rest of the evening watching someone getting beaten, overcome by the fear of being the next victim. We were made to chant "*yasqut Arafat*" ("Down with Arafat") and "*ya'ish Begin*" ("Long live Begin").²⁷ My fever and chest pain increased as the evening passed. About 11:00 p.m. *al-hakem al-'askari* (the head Israeli military officer of Jenin) came out and addressed us with a megaphone. He told us that this was just a lesson, and he would not mind repeating it again and again if we did not behave. After his speech the soldiers called our names one by one from the stacks of ID cards. Once a name was called, the student took his ID card and was released.

People were gathering nearby in town and we got assistance in transportation. I got home around midnight. My parents went through the bruises and marks I had. Apparently I had two major breakages in the ribs in addition to many bruises and sore spots. My parents ruled out taking me to the hospital because, like schools required to report absent students, hospitals were required to report injuries to the military. The Israeli army made arrests and investigations based on these reports. Fearing that I would get arrested, my parents just wrapped my chest with a cloth. I was unable to lie down on my back or either of my sides. I was experiencing so much pain from all over my body. I spent the night exhausted, unable to sleep from the pain, my mom next to me with her eyes watering all night long because she could not find a spot on my body free of pain on which she could rest her arm to comfort me. All she could do was suffer and watch me suffering. The next morning I had to go to school, so I would not be recorded as absent and subject to arrest. The army was at the gates of the school as my father dropped me off in the morning.

Victims of violence may use their experience to reconfigure their social context in ways that would empower the body politic of the community rather than weaken it or drive it toward social trauma. In what follows, I recall and analyze the social dynamic at my high school and how the student body reacted to the physical trauma of the violence and made sense of it. The student conversations at school the day after the beating were an attempt to make sense of the events of the day before. During this period the battle between the Israeli occupation authority and the Palestinian resistance factions was about how to influence the youth. To control the young, the Israeli army was using practices of domination like those I have described, intimidation, and threats against students and fathers. The violence performed by the Israeli state army—an Israeli soldier picking up a student, taking him to the side, and beating him in view of five hundred other students gathered in a circle—presents Riches's three components of violence: perpetrators, victims, and witnesses (Riches 1986). Positioned as such, violence is a performance that seeks to influence the target audience (Whitehead 2004), in this case the

Palestinian youth. On the other hand, Palestinian factions were articulating symbols of nationhood, attachment to the land, and concepts of heroism and sacrifice for the land and its people. The few students at the school who were considered supporters of certain political groups were among those who were more comfortable talking about the events and making sense of them. Those students were not necessarily members of the groups but mostly siblings of prisoners and activists. At lunch break on the next day of school, most students were making jokes about the collective abuse that the student body had suffered. Students were recalling, describing, and commenting on what happened with this guy and the other guy. We made jokes about each other's beatings. Everyone had suffered the same abuse—the cool guys, the activists, the smart students, the quiet students, the city boy, the camp boy, the village boy, the rich, the poor—though all wanted to maintain their social stature in their group of friends and in the classroom as a whole. Hence it was desirable to transform the abuse suffered at the hands of the army into something brave and heroic, something "cool." This was not a strategy consciously developed by the resistance factions as much as something that satisfied a need among the youth to deal with the humiliation suffered in front of their peers. The interests of the resistance factions and the general youth coincided here. The process of turning the endurance of abuse into cool and hip acts of bravery and heroism became both an adolescent trend and a mobilizing strategy for the factions. With the passage of time and so much abuse by the Israeli army, many heroes among Palestinian youth were and are being made.

Children of the Stones

These processes of making heroic youth culminated in the intifada in 1987 and were fully developed during it, as the youth led the daily activities of the intifada and gained a prominent social status, one reported by other ethnographies of this period (Jean-Klien 2000; Joseph 1994; Peteet 1994). Women also played a role in supporting the elevation of the youth status in the intifada period (Peteet 1994). Women as mothers or sisters would have more leverage over their sons or siblings than they would over their husbands or fathers. Women saw an opportunity to have more access to the decision-making process and improve their position in the power structure of the family and the community at large by shifting the center of power toward the youth and away from the elderly and the notables. This shift persists to varying degrees among Palestinian communities, depending on how closely involved the community was in the intifada and how much the hierarchy of power was transformed.

I was just returning from the United States after the completion of my undergraduate studies in the summer of 1989, during the height of the first intifada, when I was awakened early in the morning by about a dozen Israeli soldiers in my room. They asked for my ID, took it, took me outside, and had me stand by the outside wall. My brother, who lived next door, was also held there. The soldiers were going through the village, house by house. They were taking youths and men outside and sending them in different directions. My brother and I, after being held standing at the wall for a couple of hours, were ordered to paint over the graffiti on the walls of the girls' school nearby and not to leave the school before the soldiers came back. My first reaction was: "I don't have paint." The soldier came at me to hit me for daring to respond when my brother directly intervened and said, "We have paint, we'll do it." My brother explained to me that because he and his family lived next to the school, they were used to this. So they were prepared, with brushes and some white paint. We went to his house, where we each got a bucket of paint and a brush, and started painting. It took us about an hour to paint over all the graffiti on the school, but the problem was that we kept waiting and the soldiers were not coming back to check our work. Slowly the graffiti was starting to show through again as the paint was drying. By the time the soldiers came back to check on us the paint was dry and the job was obviously not satisfactory for the Israeli army, so we were ordered to do it all over again. We went on painting again, but fortunately this time the soldiers stayed around and we were able to show them the paint while it was still wet, so we got our IDs back before the soldiers returned to the center of the village. We learned after their departure from the village as a whole that they had gathered all the men between fifteen and fifty years of age, divided the streets of the village among them, and made them sweep the streets. When the job was done the soldiers gathered the men at the village square in the center of the village and had them sit on the ground in rows, with their hands above their heads.

In the village gatherings after the departure of the Israeli army harassment squad, I seemed to be the only young person who was upset by the experience. The rest were all joking about what had happened to them. I was disturbed, and my disturbance seemed out of context. Older people made fun of me, saying, "They even dragged the American," in reference to my being a recent graduate from America. By now the process of turning enduring abuse into acts of heroism was fully developed in occupied Palestine, and most youth were not humiliated by the experience of abuse by the Israelis. To the contrary, there was a sense of pride that the Israelis had picked on our village because it was an active village. The targeting of communities and individuals by the Israelis became a source of pride, to be narrated and cultivated in social order and social setting.

Similarly, in January 2005 I was traveling in a taxi from Jenin to Ramallah. We were stopped by what the Palestinians call an Israeli *makhsum tayyar* (flying checkpoint).[28] The Israeli soldiers dragged out of the car a young guy who was among the passengers. One soldier twisted his arm, pushed forward, and had him sit on a stone nearby while investigating him. After his release and our departure from the checkpoint, he told us how he was used to "much more than this." "This was nothing this time," he asserted. In contrast, I witnessed a similar incident in 1980 when an Israeli soldier slapped a young passenger twice after checking his ID at a checkpoint near Jenin. After getting back in the taxi the guy was so angry and embarrassed that he said, "I swear had he hit the third slap . . ." Today's youth have turned the embarrassment and humiliation suffered at the hands of the Israeli army, who actively intend to humiliate the youth, into a cool thing to endure. This incident also brings to the fore the position of the ethnographer and his or her relation to the power structure in the field and research subjects. As a Palestinian ethnographer sitting in that taxi, I could have been subject to the same harassment by the Israeli soldiers. I experienced the stress that every other Palestinian experiences every time we pull up to a checkpoint. As a Palestinian researcher in Palestine, I knew that at any moment I could be pulled into the context and become a subject. In fact, that happened several times during my research, and I bring in some of those experiences in the next chapters. This would not be so for a foreign or Israeli ethnographer doing research in Palestine. Similarly, the reaction of the victim and the response he expressed to the viewers of his abuse in the taxi was seen as the act of communicating freely and without awkwardness to a fellow Palestinian peer, which might not have been possible with a foreign reporter.

Transforming the endurance of violence and abuse into heroism had an impact on a whole range of social conceptions in the dynamics of Palestinians' encounter with Israel. Beyond the beatings, the arrest, injury with a bullet, or ultimate fate as a shahid (martyr) emerged a cool, hip experience among the group. In the presence of his parents I interviewed Madi, a fifteen-year-old boy from Nablus, who narrated climbing on top of an Israeli tank while it was patrolling the streets of Nablus. Madi is a cool-looking kid with a sleek hairdo, clean-cut on the side and curled and spiked on top, stiffened with hair mousse. With much excitement and energy, he described how he was on top of the tank when "the soldier opened up the cap, the son of a bitch was gonna shoot. I kicked his gun with my foot and threw myself off the tank and banged on my ass against the street. I got up and ran away like a missile before the next tank reaches me."[29] Madi's younger brother went on to tell how daring his brother was. To Madi and his brother, climbing up the tank and surviving was a very cool thing, especially the act of getting close to the tank and stoning it from close range. Engaging in these activities and narrating the engagements was a source of prestige. The Israeli army is the game in town. For the youth, tackling the Israeli army is the way to define oneself within the group and to compete between groups.

Majdi from the Jenin Refugee Camp described to me how when his group got hold of a tank and climbed on top of it, it did not allow members of other groups to come near it: "Once we are on top of it, the tank is ours. If other boys not from our group try to climb up, we kick them off and hit them with the sticks or metal rods we usually have."[30] Once the kids are on top of the tank, they usually take everything they can possibly disassemble while the tank is still in the camp. The youth in Jenin area are more at ease: they say that the soldiers riding in tanks fear Jenin and will not dare open the tank and come out while in town. Majdi explains how the members of his group get on top of the last tank in the column of tanks coming into town so there are no tanks behind it to shoot at them. Their normal capture is one 250mm or 300mm machine gun on top of the tank, two boxes of ammunition, metal water jugs, and tools. The boys that chase the Israeli soldiers and climb the tanks are the shabiha, the jocks of the camp, the cool dudes. The more daring one is, the more popular one gets. The group that captures the most out of the invading Israeli army is the coolest in the eyes of the youth and to the members of the resistance factions who are the recipients of the ghanimeh (spoils of war). Injuries suffered in the process are badges of heroism and pride. Withstanding a hit from the Israelis is as much an act of heroism as scoring a hit against them. Falling dead in the process and becoming a shahid is the ultimate act of heroism and sacrifice. Thus competition for prestige within and between groups in the dynamic of engagement between the occupied and the occupiers contributes to the generation of the shahid.

For seven years the Palestinians in the West Bank and Gaza sustained the activities of the first intifada, which mobilized all sectors of Palestinian society in civil disobedience against the Israeli occupation. Sustained, intense, and close confrontations of Palestinian youth with the Israeli army made up the landscape of everyday life in the West Bank and Gaza. Palestinian factions organized Al-Qiyada Al-Wattaniyya Al-Muwahada lil-Intifada (Unified National Leadership of the Uprising), which issued weekly leaflets that outlined the daily activities of the intifada. In addition to daily confrontations with the Israeli military, the Unified Leadership engaged in acts of civil disobedience that enforced strikes, boycotts, and the nonpayment of taxes, and threw away the ID cards issued by the Israelis in some villages (Gordon, Gordon, and Shriteh 2003). Israel responded with beatings, teargas, rubber bullets, live ammunition, curfews, the closure of schools and universities, deportations of activists into exile, and tens of thousands of arrests. The Israeli minister of defense at the time, Yitzhak Rabin, gave instructions to his soldiers to "break their arms," referring to the Palestinian youths throwing stones. A long wave of violence followed, as the Israeli army chased Palestinian kids and youth and broke the arms of those they could catch. The experiences of the first intifada broke much of the barrier of fear among Palestinian youth. Sustained Israeli harassment and abuse meant sustained processes of hero making and martyr making for Palestinian youth culture.

At the political level, the first intifada mounted enough pressure on the state of Israel from within Israeli society and the international community to bring about negotiations with the Palestinians for the first time since the establishment of Israel in 1948. These negotiations commenced in 1991 at a conference sponsored by the United States in Madrid. Palestinian representatives in the negotiations were mainly civic institutional leaders and members of the faculty at Palestinian universities in the West Bank and Gaza. These leaders were not necessarily members of any particular faction, but the Palestinian factions were in agreement on their representation. The next decade of exchange between Palestinians and Israelis became characterized as the "peace process." It was during this "peace process" that the 'amaliyyat istishhadiyya (martyrdom operations) began in the mid-1990s. At first the martyrdom operations were mainly organized by Hamas, the new Islamic Resistance Movement. Today they are carried out by many Islamic and secular groups. In the next chapter I present the political and cultural dynamics of the emergence of these operations and explore the complexities of this "peace process" and its relation to the articulation of martyrdom discourse in Palestine.

CHAPTER THREE

State Expansion and the Violence of "Peace Making" in Palestine

The Palestinian issue and the Palestinian-Israeli conflict have been a site of active international diplomacy for nearly a century. This diplomacy calmed down after the establishment of Israel in Palestine in 1948 and was activated again after Israel's territorial expansion into the remainder of Palestinian territories and the neighboring Arab states in 1967. After the Six-Day War in 1967 Israel put forward several plans to its neighboring Arab states, all of which were presented as "peace" proposals. After the first Palestinian intifada in 1987–93 the Palestinian-Israeli conflict took front seat in international politics and became the focus of international diplomacy throughout the 1990s. Much has been written about the flaws of the "peace process" of the 1990s and its "obstruction of peace" rather than the promised peace (Aruri 1995; Guyatt 1998; Klieman 2000; Said 2000; Wright Jr. 2002). But what I am interested in here is how these "peace" processes fit into the history of the colonial state expansion and how these expansions configure in the production of violence.

In this chapter, I provide a historical assessment of the cultural impact that the contact with colonial state expansion has had on Palestinian indigenous communities and their inter-community relations as well as their reactions to this expansion. I apply Ferguson's and Whitehead's concept of the "tribal zone" (2001), representing the "physical and conceptual space" that is shaped by the cultural contact through state expansion. I am particularly interested in the social transformations associated with the colonial contact and the reconfiguration of political and spatial boundaries as well as processes of militarization, resistance, and rebellion. I explore the wider consequences of the encounter with colonial

expansion and the changes in sociopolitical formations
it—how the contact creates and modifies political groupi
forms cultural practices.

The Oslo "Peace" Process

Before the first Palestinian intifada, and during the Israeli occupation of
the West Bank and Gaza, Israel made repeated attempts to incorporate
Palestinian communities in these territories into the state system, all of
which were vehemently and successfully resisted by Palestinians. Some
of these attempts at incorporation include the rawabet al-qura (Village
League) project in the 1970s,[1] the Israel-Egypt peace treaty in 1979 and
its proposal for al-hukm al-thati (Palestinian self-governance—the term
"self-autonomy" was used in English),[2] the al-idara al-madaniyya (Civil
Administration) project in the early 1980s,[3] and the al-taqasum al-wazifi
(division of duty)[4] project that Israel tried to establish in cooperation with
King Hussein of Jordan over the Palestinian population in the West Bank
and Gaza in 1985. Each of these attempts at incorporation failed, either
because of mass Palestinian mobilization against it (as with al-idara al-
madaniyya), or because a Palestinian faction assassinated a key Palestinian participant (the PFLP's assassination of Zafer al-Masri put an end
to the al-taqasum al-wazifi project in 1986). Israel was faced with the outbreak of the first intifada in the West Bank and Gaza in 1987. The intifada
was a popular Palestinian uprising that demanded self-determination, an
end to the Israeli occupation, and Palestinian statehood.

The intifada led to international pressure on the United States to induce Israel to engage in dialogue with the Palestinians and neighboring
Arab states. This process was initiated in the Middle East Peace Conference in Madrid in 1991, sponsored by the United States and orchestrated
by James Baker, secretary of state in George H. W. Bush's administration.
In that process the United States insisted on excluding the PLO leadership from the process, instead including only local representation of the
Palestinians from the occupied territories of the West Bank and Gaza.
Consequently Palestinians were represented by a delegation of fifteen
leaders of civic institutions and university faculty, headed by Dr. Haidar
Abdelshafi, director of the Palestinian Red Crescent Society in Gaza.

Israel, in an effort to sabotage a political process that it was engaged in under duress, took advantage of the weakness of an isolated PLO leadership, excluded from the process, by initiating secret talks with this leadership in Oslo, separate from the Madrid process. Israel and the PLO leadership announced what seemed like a sudden agreement in 1993 after President Clinton's administration was newly in place. The shared declaration of an agreement between Israel and the PLO leadership put an end to the Madrid process and started a new one, orchestrated mainly by Israel, which came to be known as the Oslo Middle East peace process. The Oslo process represents another Israeli attempt at encapsulation and incorporation of the Palestinians in the West Bank and Gaza, however, this time using a traditional Palestinian leadership that had been in crisis and had become increasingly isolated and obsolete. In the Oslo process Israel mapped out the geographic encapsulation and handed over the management of administrative affairs to its new Palestinian partners, whom it chose in select numbers from the Palestinian factions in exile.

In the Oslo process Israel divided the West Bank territories into areas A, B, and C. "A" areas were placed under the control of the Palestinian Authority (PA), "B" areas were under the joint control of Israel and the Palestinian Authority, and "C" areas were to remain under direct Israeli control. This demarcation was the first cartography of Israeli encapsulation presented to the Palestinian public and was matched on the ground by a network of checkpoints and roadblocks. Within "A" areas Israel transferred civil administrative powers to the Palestinian Authority in accordance with article VI of the Oslo Declaration of Principles: "authority will be transferred to the Palestinians on the following spheres: education and culture, health, social welfare, direct taxation, and tourism, the Palestinian side will commence in building the Palestinian police, as agreed upon." According to these "agreements" Israel would maintain "external security" and "foreign affairs": the jurisdiction of the Palestinian Authority with regard to power transferred would not apply to Jerusalem, settlements, Israeli military locations, and Israelis. The term "Israeli" is defined in the agreement to include "Israeli statutory agencies and corporations registered in Israel."[5] In other words, the PA had no authority over Israeli military or civil activities in Palestinian areas.

Furthermore, the Oslo process envisioned that the Palestinian Authority would enforce Israeli law in areas under its control during the "interim" period of power transfer. The agreement included an annex concerning power transfer for each of the following spheres: education and culture; health; social welfare; tourism; and taxation, including Value Added Tax (VAT) on local production. In each annex Israel provided a list of all Israeli and Jordanian laws,[6] as well as Israeli administrative regulations and Israeli military orders to remain in effect during Palestinian governance. The agreement authorized the establishment of a Palestinian legislative council that would be permitted to legislate within the confines of the agreement: "The Council will be empowered to legislate, in accordance with the Interim Agreement, within all authorities transferred to it."[7] Furthermore, the Agreement on Preparatory Transfer of Powers and Responsibilities between Israel and the PLO of 29 August 1994 gives Israel the power to approve or disapprove legislation passed by the Palestinian Legislative Council based on whether the legislation "exceeds powers transferred" to Palestinians, is "inconsistent with the provisions" of the agreement, or affects "powers and responsibilities which were not transferred to the Palestinians."[8] The agreement also gives Israel the freedom to pursue groups and individuals wanted by Israel in areas controlled by the PA.

In addition to confining the PA to implementing and executing Israeli laws, policies, and military orders as described in detailed annexes, the agreement relieved Israel of any liabilities and obligations arising from its occupation of the territories and threw these obligations on the shoulders of the Palestinian Authority. Point 1 of Article IX, Rights, Liabilities and Obligations:[9]

a) The transfer of powers and responsibilities to the Palestinian Authority under this agreement will include all related rights, liabilities, and obligations arising with regard to acts or omissions which occurred prior to the transfer [emphasis added]. Israel and the Civil Administration will cease to bear any financial responsibility regarding such acts or omissions and the Palestinian Authority will bear all financial responsibility for these and for its own functioning.

. . . .

e) In the event that an award is made against Israel or the Civil Administration by any court or tribunal in respect of such a claim, the Palestinian Authority shall, once the award has been paid by Israel, reimburse Israel the full amount of the award.

Thus all liabilities and obligations arising from three decades of Israeli military occupation, decades filled with killings, torture, destruction, human rights violations, and land confiscations, would be transferred to the new Palestinian agency. In the Oslo process Israel far exceeded what it had hoped to accomplish in the previous incorporation projects, which were vehemently resisted by Palestinians. The key to Israel's initial successes in this regard was that it worked directly with a traditional Palestinian leadership that was losing ground. The media also played a major role in celebrating Israel's colonial expansion scheme as a historic peace accomplishment and covered up the details of the injustices being done to the Palestinians. Palestinians were unaware of all these details. The Declaration of Principles, released in 1993, referred to annexes that were never released until much later in the process. These annexes were attached to the 1994 agreement, but it is not clear how widely they were released in Arabic to the Palestinian public. Many of the PA administrative personnel whom I talked to still deny that the agreement includes the annexes.

On the ground, however, before handing administrative "control" over to the Palestinian Authority, Israel took aerial photos of every Palestinian village that would fall in areas A and B, and developed something called al-kharita al-haykaliyya (the skeleton map). They gave copies of this map to the PA land management authority to be the basis for land use and development that the PA was authorized to approve. Al-kharita al-haykaliyya mapped each village to the limits of the built-up area at the time these maps were drawn, between 1993 and 1996, allowing little or no room for village growth. The cities that fall in area A as well were drawn in the al-kharita al-haykaliyya format, and while some were given a little room to grow in surrounding lands, priority for growth was given to nearby Israeli settlements or settlement access roads. The Israeli process of controlling land through urban and regional planning schemes is very complex, whether in the West Bank and Gaza or in Galilee, where there is a concentration of Arab villages. Falah (2005) presents a detailed analysis of what he calls the geopolitics of "enclavisation" schemes that Israel implements in the West Bank and Gaza. A detailed review of these maneuvers is beyond the scope of this research. However, it is important to demonstrate the extent of the state of Israel's encapsulation of Palestinian communities through the "peace process."

The PA is authorized to grant building permits only within the confines of the al-kharita al-haykaliyya. Houses built outside of al-kharita al-
haykaliyya are subject to demolition by the Israeli army, and most do get
demolished by Israel. The PA land use department is the same department that managed land use under Israel, keeping its Palestinian staff
from the Israeli administration according to the "agreement"[10] and adding additional staffing from the PA to replace the departing Israeli staff.
The PA land use department grants permits concerning A areas and gets
final authorization from Bet Eil[11] for any plans in B areas. Palestinians
seeking land registration, transfer of ownership, or permits concerning
their properties in C areas have to deal directly with the Israeli regional
command center. The regional command center is an Israeli army base
for each region in the West Bank that directs Israeli army activities. The
regional command center has a corresponding regional office in the PA
body called al-irtibat al-madani[12] (administration of civil coordination
department).

The Birth of Al-Istishhadiyeen (The Martyrous Ones)

In essence the Oslo process intensified the encapsulation process and
the state's expansion. The lines of al-kharita al-haykaliyya defining areas
A, B, and C dramatically altered property values and people's access to
and conceptions of their spaces. Because of restrictions on movement,
between the different A zones, intensified by the network of checkpoints
and areas B and C, Palestinian urban areas came to be regarded as areas
from which Palestinians were excluded or where their presence was
challenged. This separation of people from their spaces both physically
and conceptually is the primary factor in the construction of violence
performed in contested places, where violence becomes a medium with
which to challenge the identity of those seeking to occupy these spaces
(Friedman 2003). During the formulation and implementation of the
Oslo process the Islamic Resistance Movement Hamas executed the
first two suicide operations in the Israeli inhabited towns of Afula
and Khedara in 1994.[13] The first operation was carried out in Afula by
Ra'id Zakarneh on 6 April 1994: nine Israelis were killed and fifty others
injured. The second was carried out in Khedara (Hedera) by Ammar

Amarneh on 13 April 1994: five Israelis were killed and 130 injured (Al-Nawati 2002). Both operations' carriers were from the Jenin area.

Hamas's objective was to bring the "peace process" to an end. Yet Palestinian groups opposed to Yasser Arafat's leadership within the PLO were not successful in mobilizing popular opposition to the Oslo process for several reasons: many of the details of the agreements were kept secret; traditional opposition groups in the Palestinian "left" were experiencing their own internal crises after the collapse of the Soviet Union; and Palestinians, exhausted after seven years of intifada, were more amenable to giving the process a chance and having room to breathe. In this environment Hamas did emerge as the primary opposition to the Oslo process in Palestinian politics. Still, Hamas was not able to rally enough popular opposition to the process to bring it to a halt or derail it through political mobilization campaigns.

After the first two suicide operations in Afula and Khedara, Hamas's political bureau issued a statement making a direct link between the operations and Hamas's objectives to topple the Oslo process. The statement read: "Rabin's measures failed to stop our heroic operations, carried out amidst his efforts to implement the Oslo Agreement with all the shameful concessions on the part of the PLO leadership that it entails, and failed to fulfill the longing of the Zionist masses for peace and security. In the face of the sharpening Likud opposition to the agreement, this devastating failure caused Rabin to feel deep frustration and frightful floundering."[14] Hamas made clear its strategy of achieving a political goal, collapsing the "peace" process by diminishing Israeli support for it through the performance of violence. Hamas hoped to strengthen Likud's opposition to the process, to bring Rabin's government down, and to bring the Oslo process down with it. In fact Hamas executed the second wave of operations in February and March 1996, during the Israeli prime ministerial election campaign, which forced Shimon Peres, then prime minister, to halt final negotiation talks and helped bring Likud to power with the election of Benjamin Netanyahu in May 1996 (Hroub 2000).

Hamas's statement continued:

Rabin's government outdid itself in its repressive measures, which reached a crescendo when Rabin's troops conspired with settlers in the criminal massacre of Al-Khalil (Hebron) that targeted worshippers at the Al-Ibrahimi

Mosque as they knelt down for the dawn prayers. Likewise, the troops fired at pregnant Palestinian women while in their homes or balconies. These excesses have compelled all our people to rise up and intensify their resistance to occupation and to seek vengeance for the martyrs of the Hebron massacre.

In loyalty to the blood of martyrs, the Izzidin al-Qassam Brigades, which operate throughout the homeland, vowed to avenge the blood of martyrs. Accordingly, two of our heroic warriors carried out two martyrdom operations at Afula and Khedara, targeting centers of troop and settler concentrations, despite Rabin's heightened security measures that were especially strict during their celebration of the anniversary of the usurpation of our country.[15]

Here Hamas gives meanings to the act beyond its immediate political objectives. First, a direct link was made between the operations and the massacre committed earlier that year when an Israeli settler at Al-Ibrahimi Mosque in Hebron shot dead twenty-nine Palestinians during prayers. This connection shows that Hamas linked Palestinian violence against Israeli civilians to Israeli violence against Palestinian civilians, presenting Palestinian violence as a form of retaliation.

The second meaning of the statement is implied in the aesthetics of the acts: when, where, and how. The meaning is formulated and communicated through the timing of the executions and their settings and locations. The acts were carried out during the celebration of Israeli independence, or Palestine's "usurpation" as seen by Palestinians, and the locations of the performances were the Palestinian towns that are now cities inhabited by Israelis after the displacement of their Palestinian inhabitants. These aesthetics, along with the act of sacrifice by the actor (the mission carrier), insinuate the meanings of sacrifice for dispossessed land and relate them to local knowledge and semiotics and the history of sacrifice in the Palestinian struggle. They also reaffirm the link between Palestinians and the spaces from which they were displaced and excluded, and the spaces in which they are isolated, giving an identity to these "contested" spaces.

In local Palestinian knowledge and in the Palestinian system of meaning, the tradition of sacrifice is already well articulated through the history of confrontation with foreign intruders and in particular Israel, as explored in chapter 2. It is especially revealing that Hamas executed another operation in Ashdod on 7 April 1994, in which it killed thirteen Israelis in a shooting attack. This attack was carried out at the time between the Afula and Khedara operations but was not mentioned in the statement issued by Hamas's political bureau on 16 April 1994. Only the two operations that included the actor's self-sacrifice had a specific reference in the document. Hence the meanings that Hamas was trying to construct were for these types of operations in particular. Hamas is aware that operations involving self-sacrifice have a greater capacity to enter the imagination of Palestinians and Israelis. These two operations marked the beginnings of the formulation of the istishhadiyeen discourse, Hamas's new resistance tactics in the form of self-sacrifice.

Hamas categorized the operations as 'amaliyyat istishhadiyya (martyrdom operations), in contrast to 'a maliyat fida'iya (self-sacrifice operations), a term used earlier in Palestinian resistance discourse to refer to operations where the carrier had little or no chance of returning, making the execution of the mission a commitment to self-sacrifice. The notion of martyrdom, in particular the notion of the istishhadi (the martyrous one, who goes on a martyrdom operation, or seeks and is ready for martyrdom), makes the concept of fida'i (self-sacrificer, the one who goes on mission of self-sacrifice, or seeks and is ready for self-sacrifice) lexically more suitable to Hamas's religious ideology in its confrontation with Israel. These semantics are also more suitable for constructing a culture of martyrdom. Since its establishment Hamas has framed its political goals of liberating Palestine in religious terms, with Islam as the base for its ideological and political strategies. Hamas has viewed the struggle against the foreign intruders and occupiers of Palestine (the Israelis) as a jihad (fight against a threat to the nation). In Islamic teachings jihad is a fardh (religious duty) as long as the threat persists. The person who dies carrying out the duty of jihad is a shahid (martyr) in Islam. The "istishhadi" is a term coined by Hamas that builds on the Palestinian concept of the fida'i that developed in Palestinian resistance discourse, giving it new religious qualities while maintaining the associated meanings of sacrifice. That different Palestinian publics and media outlets variously use 'amaliyyat fida'iyya and 'amaliyyat istishhadiyya to refer to acts of martyrdom gives the acts both religious qualities and a broader cultural meaning of sacrifice that goes beyond religion and extends to land, homeland, nation, family, community, or group.

As Hinton (2004) points out, the "poetics" of violence is conceived of through what Turner (1964) calls symbolic polarization between ideological and sensory meanings. From the beginnings of the performances of these acts, the ideological goals and meanings as well as the sensory and cultural meanings were given in the performance of the acts, as explored in Hamas's statement. As the act gets melded into myriad cultural poetics of the resistance and articulated in the discourse of popular culture, it carries its own meanings, separate from the political goals of the organizing groups. It is precisely the process of constructing meaning over time, "poetics," that explains how these violent acts are then woven into the social life of society at large and motivate individuals to carry them through (Whitehead 2002). These poetics include both instrumental and ideological goals as well as local knowledge and sensory meanings, personal experiences, social grouping, and mimetic encounters and oppositions. Through these constructions of meanings associated with the performance of violence, ideas about identity that have been denied recognition, conceptions of space that have been isolated, and constructions of places that have been reconfigured get sensory mediation, and the performance of the act becomes intelligent and meaningful. The cultural poetics of the violent acts that are performed and enacted construct a cultural discourse within which a pattern of motivation arises.

In interviews, Hamas activists stated that their organization recruited participants for these operations until the Al-Aqsa Intifada of 2000. During the Al-Aqsa Intifada the number of volunteers for these operations more than satisfied the needs of the organization.[16] These realities were also communicated to me by leaders of other groups, like the Al-Aqsa Martyrs Brigades, who are sometimes overwhelmed by youths who volunteer for martyrdom operations.[17] When the Oslo process failed in the summer of 2000, it became apparent to the Palestinian public that the isolated geographic spaces delineated in the accords that were supposed to be "interim" were in reality the extent of Israel's "offer," making Hamas's enactment of these violent acts a meaningful act with which society at large started connecting.

It was not until the outbreak of Al-Aqsa Intifada that martyrdom operations took on their popular dimension in Palestine and that other secular groups like Al-Aqsa Martyrs Brigades (an offshoot of Fatah) and Abu

Ali Mustafa's Brigades (an offshoot of the PFLP) joined in planning and executing these operations. As the state's encapsulation process intensified and affected all spheres of individual and community life, which became apparent during the Al-Aqsa Intifada, the encounter became the main motivator and generator of these acts. Martyrdom operations provided a medium for mimetic practice to the Israeli state violence through a performance of violence and sacrifice within an articulated system of meanings. Thus the construction of these operations became a distinct pattern of motivation and mobilization, to the point where factions that did not participate in their performances lost credibility and popularity. I will now explore the details of these dynamics.

The Failure of Oslo

The Oslo process failed at the incorporation stage, just like the previous attempts at incorporation. Aside from active opposition to the process on the part of Islamic factions of Hamas and Islamic Jihad, two issues were underestimated by the planners and orchestrators of this incorporation scheme. The first was the complexity of maintaining the community's identity while incorporating it into a state system that insisted on defining itself along "ethnic" lines with the "Jewish" state. The state of Israel, Israeli society, and their extended support system of Jewish nationalism abroad (Zionism) insist on maintaining the "Jewish character" of the state. The second issue was the magnitude of the Palestinian right of return in political terms and the extent of Palestinians' connections to historic Palestine.

In the Oslo process Israel made one significant concession: for the first time, it recognized the existence of a distinct Palestinian identity. Israel had previously insisted on dealing with the Palestinian issue only through Arab governments and maintained that Palestinians were Arabs, making the conflict a conflict of borders with its neighboring Arab states. Israel continued to ignore any references to unresolved issues from 1948, like the right of return of Palestinian refugees, insisting that because it had taken control of the West Bank and Gaza territories from the neighboring Arab countries of Jordan and Egypt, any negotiation concerning the territories would have to be made with these coun-

tries. All these points of reference changed after the international pressure created by the first intifada brought about Israel's participation in
the Madrid conference, where Palestinians represented themselves and
were fully recognized as the party solely concerned with the Palestinian
issue. The Palestinian team included representatives of Palestinian civil
institutions that functioned according to agreed-upon processes; its various members handled different aspects of the negotiations. By maneuvering its way out of the Madrid process and making a "peace deal" with
the PLO leadership, Israel succeeded in making a kind of tribal chiefs'
pact with the PLO leadership through which it planned to complete the
incorporation phase, banking on the PLO chiefs to carry out the scheme
and quiet the opposition. Thus Israel bypassed the process and Palestinian society as a whole and made its pact with individuals who were
charged with selling the "agreement" to their organization (the PLO)
and the Palestinian people.

It is interesting to point out the differences between Oslo I (the first
agreement, signed in Oslo in September 1993), which was the first result
of secret talks between the PLO chiefs and Israel, and Oslo II (the agreement signed in Washington on 29 August 1994). Oslo I, presented as an
agreement between Israel and a "Palestinian team," begins: "The Government of the state of Israel and the Palestinian team representing the
Palestinian people agree."[18] The agreement makes no mention of who
the "Palestinian team" is or which body or organization it represented.
Nor is there any mention of the peace process in which the Palestinians
were being represented by a defined team from the West Bank and Gaza.
The release of the first agreement of 1993 was like a trial balloon. PLO
chiefs that made the pact with Israel kept open the option to dissociate
themselves from it should they fail to get it approved by the PLO and the
Palestinian publics. The agreement had no mention of the PLO or any
Palestinian authority other than a "Palestinian team." It spoke of trans-
ferring authority from the Israeli military in Gaza and Jericho to "authorized Palestinians." Oslo II was between "the Government of the State of
Israel and the Palestine Liberation Organization (hereinafter the 'PLO'),
the representative of the Palestinian people," and the parties to the
agreement claimed it to be "within the framework of the Middle East
peace process initiated at Madrid in October 1991."[19] By the time of the
Oslo II agreement in 1994, Israel and the new Palestinian partners had

hijacked "the Middle East peace process initiated at Madrid in October 1991." The PLO leadership incorporated some members of the Palestinian negotiating team at Madrid into the newly formed Palestinian Authority, whereas those who were critical of the Oslo agreements and their processes were pushed aside, including the head of the negotiating team, Dr. Haidar Abdelshafi.

While pursuing a strategy of coopting and deforming Palestinian representation through the process, Israel at the same time recognized the Palestinian identity of the communities that it was attempting to incorporate and that were seeking independence. In constructing the PA on the ground, the PLO employed many intifada activists into the Palestinian police and other security apparatuses, much as other colonial powers have sought to incorporate the armies of conquered territories into their expanding armies (Ferguson and Whitehead 1992). However, the PLO leaders presented themselves to the Palestinians as liberators. The movement among elements of Palestinian society at large, including the Palestinian police and security forces at the general membership level, was one of (Palestinian) state building. Consequently, these forces continued to clash with Israeli forces, which spread into an all-out confrontation in the fall of 1996 between the Palestinian police and the Israeli army when Israeli Prime Minister Benjamin Netanyahu attempted to open the tunnel that runs under Al-Aqsa Mosque in Jerusalem. This was a "critical event," which generated protest throughout Palestinian society, including the newly formed police force. The PLO (by now the PA) leadership managed to control the situation quickly and demonstrate to Israel its control over these forces. But the confrontation struck the first blow to the incorporation process, and Oslo as a whole became subject to increased scrutiny from the Palestinians as they began to question the extent to which it was carrying Palestinians toward a meaningful independence from Israel.

The second factor that contributed to the failure of the Oslo process was Israel's attempt to finalize Palestinians' exclusion from the territories over which it established itself in 1948. Often these territories of historic Palestine are referred to by western media as "Israel proper," distinguishing them from the territories occupied by Israel in 1967. As I explored in chapter 2, Palestinian refugees were exiled in 1948 from the territories that fell under the control of Jewish militias when the state of

Israel was founded. These territories included eleven Palestinian cities that were depopulated and settled by new Jewish immigrants to the newly established state, and over 418 Palestinian villages that were depopulated and later demolished by Israel. Toward the final phase of the Oslo negotiation process Israel attempted to end all Palestinian demands and claims for rights in these spaces; it insisted that the agreement on control over territory in the West Bank and Gaza that Palestinians would have to sign would constitute a declaration of the "end of conflict," one that would be enshrined in a UN resolution nullifying all previous UN resolutions pertaining to the Palestinian-Israeli issue, a number of which called for Israel to restore Palestinians' right to return to their homes in the territories that became Israel. Here was another killer factor for Oslo.

In the years leading up to the "final status" negotiations at Camp David in the summer of 2000, dozens of new Palestinian groups had been formed, mainly between 1998 and 2000 in Palestine, Jordan, Lebanon, Syria, Europe, and North America, whose main stated objectives and activism were centered on the Palestinian right of return.[20] Palestinian discontent has been prevalent since early in the Oslo "peace process," which has been perceived as ignoring the right of return and effectively turning its back to Palestinian refugees. This movement intensified and spread widely after the fiftieth anniversary of Al-Nakba and Israeli independence in May 1998. The events of 1948, recalled by Palestinians and Israelis with totally opposite meanings (catastrophe for Palestinians and independence for Israelis), became a "critical event" for Palestinians, a call for action. Palestinian refugees for the first time organized symbolic walks of return to sites of destroyed Palestinian villages. Several events were staged in the West Bank and elsewhere by Palestinians in Israel, like the walk from the village of Kabul to the site of the destroyed village of Damun. Other events included meetings of refugee youths at the Lebanese border fence, where youth from Sabra and Shatila Palestinian refugee camps in Lebanon met youths from Dhaisha and Aida camps near Bethlehem. Major conferences on the right of return took place in 1998, commemorating the fiftieth anniversary of Al-Nakba and discussing strategies to prevent the Palestinian leadership from "liquidating" (the term that was often used) the right of return. Examples include an al-Far'a refugee camp conference in the West Bank and conferences in Gaza, Jordan, Lebanon, the United Kingdom, and the

United States. In fact, by this time the whole Palestinian activist movement had moved to focus primarily on the right of return issue. This movement organized subsequent events and sparked a heated debate among Palestinians throughout the world about the right of return. Popular pressure on the Palestinian leadership put it in a position where it was no longer capable of signing a "deal" that did not address Palestinian refugee rights without delegitimizing its leadership. Consequently the Oslo process collapsed when the parties failed to reach a final agreement at Camp David in the summer of 2000.

The Palestinian leadership at the time failed to issue a document explaining why the "peace process" had failed; rather, in communicating with the Palestinian and Arab media it attributed the collapse to the issue of Jerusalem, even though according to most reports from Palestinian, Israeli, and foreign sources interim agreements on Jerusalem had been reached. But pointing a finger at Jerusalem was more convenient for the political leadership for two reasons. First, it amounted to a denial that the process from the outset had ignored the refugee right of return, which proved to be a primary Palestinian issue. Second, attributing collapse of the process to Jerusalem brought to the Palestinian leadership more sympathy from the Arab states than acknowledging the importance of the right of return would have done.

The Rise of the Istishhadiyeen

During the "peace process" of the 1990s Hamas and Islamic Jihad orchestrated fourteen suicide bombings performed as martyrdom operations in Israeli towns. These operations were executed in the period between 1994 and September 2000 and contributed to the collapse of the "peace process" and the beginning of the second intifada. Since the traditional PLO factions were all engaged in the Oslo process in some capacity, the only factions that were involved in armed resistance against Israel during that period were the Islamic groups, Hamas and Jihad. The operations were new and spectacular and had a shocking impact in Israel and beyond. Yet Hamas and Jihad were having difficulties in achieving popular Palestinian acceptance of this form of violence, as indicated in several statements that argued for their "legitimacy." These operations did not gain wide support at the beginning because they mainly targeted Israeli civilians at a time when Palestinians were hopeful that the "peace process" would lead to political arrangements with Israel that might respond to the Palestinian call for political independence. As a number of members of Hamas and Jihad indicated to me during interviews, these organizations recruited volunteers for martyrdom operations by training them to accept death and making promises with regard to the afterlife.

After the collapse of the Oslo "peace process" and the beginning of Al-Aqsa Intifada, however, popular interest in these operations rose. A new popular uprising was sparked by Ariel Sharon's visit to Al-Aqsa Mosque in Jerusalem in September 2000, and when the large-scale Israeli military response to this uprising destroyed much of the infrastructure that Palestinians had built during the "peace process" years in preparation for having a Palestinian state, there was a popular call to return to armed struggle and resistance. Palestinians now questioned Israel's intentions and its seriousness about reaching a political settlement. The loss of hope for a political settlement also affected the form of resistance and its political goals. Once Palestinians began to lose hope in negotiating a settlement with Israel, the resistance was no longer conceived of in the context of the political process and how it might advance Palestinian positions, but rather reconceptualized back to its origins, and was again seen as a means of challenging the Zionist project in Palestine as a whole. This reconceptualization of the resistance gave prominence to the martyrdom operations, which were recognized as the most effective means of challenging and destabilizing the Zionist project in Palestine. Martyrdom operations had been the most spectacular, painful, and visible form of resistance over the last six years and consequently became the pinnacle of the new Palestinian resistance against Israel.

In this new period of the Palestinian struggle, Al-Aqsa Intifada martyrdom operations gained their popular dimension, and the istishhadi became the new Palestinian icon, replacing the shahid and building on its predecessor the fida'i. During this new period the concept of the istishhadi got further articulation and began to enter the Palestinian imaginary. The istishhadi not only builds on the image of the fida'i, the icon of the PLO resistance of the 1960s and 1970s, but also moves the icon of the first intifada, the shahid, from victimization to heroism by asserting the intentionality of the sacrifice. The istishhadi, the hero who *carries out* a sacrifice mission, is active, whereas the shahid of the first intifada was a *victim* at the hands of the Israelis. This lexical difference corresponds to the political mood of a Palestinian public that had given up on the so-called peace process: no longer did the Palestinians rely on the international community as a supporter that would be swayed by the victimization narrative of the shahid discourse. To the contrary: demonstrating strength and self-reliance after the international community failed the Palestinians had become all the more important and more meaningful. Hence the istishhadi was now a higher icon than the shahid.

The new cultural representations of the resistance idealized in the istishhadiyeen build on and mirror the armed resistance by the fida'iyeen of the PLO in the 1960s and 1970s. This new cultural discourse is materialized through various cultural productions for every martyrdom operation that are widely disseminated, especially in the martyr's city, village, or camp. Posters of the martyr are affixed to walls, and hundreds of photos and postcards are distributed at his or her funeral. Activist groups produce booklets about their istishhadiyeen and brief summaries of their lives and distribute them through networks of supporters in the youth and activist communities. Some youth activist groups produce school notebooks with iconic photos of istishhadiyeen from a specific town, area, or group printed on the covers, and pass them on as gifts to students at the schools. Many of the materials produced about martyrdom operations and istishhadi videotapes also become available on web sites, memorializing the new life of the martyr in the wider community.

Group Formations and Transformations

The Palestinian resistance has experienced continual transformation and reconfiguration, along with changes in the dynamics of the confrontation with Israel. As some groups transform from violent resistance to political action after they gain political recognition, others move toward intensified resistance, and new political formations are born. As long as state expansion persists, there are processes of militarization, resistance, and rebellion among Palestinians, although the roles that a particular group plays will change over time. The casts of players in the groups change, as do the group formations and the groups themselves. Even so, one constant has been the practice of resistance, even as it too has been transforming in form, ideology, and strategy.

The traditional Palestinian resistance factions of the PLO of Fatah and the Popular Front for the Liberation of Palestine (PFLP) dramatically reduced their participation in armed resistance during the Oslo process. This decline created a vacuum in the Palestinian cultural spheres for means of expressing resistance to the continued Israeli state expansion policies—land confiscations, settlement building, confining and restricting the movement of Palestinians, arresting Palestinian activists—all of which coincided with the beginnings of active participation by Islamic groups in the resistance. During the first intifada two new resistance groups were organized, both guided by Islamic religion as an ideology and political strategy. These groups were the Harakat al-Muqawama al-Islamiyya (Islamic Resistance Movement), known by the Arabic acronym Hamas ("enticement") and Harakat al-Jihad al-Islami (Islamic Jihad Movement), otherwise known as Jihad. Hamas was formed as a military wing of Jama'at al-Ukhwan al-Muslimeen (Muslim Brotherhood Society, or MBS), originally an Egyptian organization that had been active in Palestine since the 1930s. Both groups were primarily active in spreading Islamic da'awa and rarely participated in Palestinian resistance, except at the time of their beginnings in Palestine during the revolution of 1936 against the British occupation (Abu-Amr 1994; Hroub 2000; Mishal and Sela 2000). Jihad was inspired mainly by MBS affiliates and filled its ranks by recruiting Fatah activists, with the aim of achieving national liberation goals through Islamic means. This option became more appealing to activists as the PLO became intensely engaged in the Oslo process. Islamic groups used as their primary recruitment grounds a pool of activists serving sentences in Israeli jails for resistance activities under the banners of the PLO factions of Fatah and PFLP.

The Islamic groups' main appeal to Palestinian youth was that they became the new medium for expressing resistance in practice when the PLO was being transformed into a state apparatus through the construction of the Palestinian Authority. These Islamic groups are nationalist in practice, and it is primarily their nationalist programs that are the platform connecting them to the Palestinian general public. The rising support that Islamic groups are generating in Palestine is not necessarily support for the MBS political goals to "transform society into an Islamic one, modeled after the first Islamic society, established by the prophet Muhammed and his companions" (Abu-Amr 1994, xiv) but rather a commitment to resisting Israeli occupation—not support for an Islamic society per se but for an Islamic platform for the liberation of Palestine. Any analysis that separates the sociopolitical goals of these groups from their nationalist programs and active participation in national liberation resistance, as Abu-Amr does, will make an inaccurate assessment of the "rise of Islamic fundamentalism" in Palestine. The stated goals of the Islamic groups Hamas and Jihad—establishing an Islamic society—have been the goals of the Muslim Brotherhood Society since its foundation. The group was present and active in Palestine for over fifty years and failed to achieve a significant popular dimension until the 1980s, when it established Hamas as a resistance group to the Israeli occupation. Furthermore, Hizb al-Tahrir al-Islami (Islamic Liberation Party, or ILM), which still does not engage in the resistance, has the same goals of establishing an Islamic society and has been active in Palestine for as long as the MBS but does not have any significant following. Both Islamic groups, Hamas and Jihad, draw their popular support and activists in the resistance based on a nationalist liberation program guided with Islamic thought as a political strategy. Thus it is their platform of resistance that brings them support, not their ideological goals.

Still, we cannot see the Islamic transformation in the resistance separately from the regional and global dynamics. The Islamization of the Palestinian resistance may be understood as part of the resistance to global hegemony, with Islam having become a medium to express difference, attachment to tradition, and the distinctiveness of local identities. The success of the Islamic revolution in Iran became relevant and an example to follow precisely because it was seen as freeing Iran from the grip of the United States and not necessarily because the success meant social and economic advancement. What is seen as attractive in Islamic strategies is liberation from local control by Israel and a global hegemonic discourse that measures "modernity" and "development" in terms of a willingness to be in alliance with western societies. In addition, the failure of the PLO to achieve nationalist objectives and its transformation into the PA—along with the collapse of the Soviet Union, which had been the main international supporter of national liberation

struggles in the region—helped Islamic groups to present themselves as
the viable medium for carrying out the resistance program and seeing it
through. Iyad Barghouthi, a Palestinian scholar who has been following
the development of the Islamic movement in Palestine and published
many books on the subject, explained to me that Palestinians would
rather see these groups applying their energy to the confrontation with
Israel than toward social change.[21] Palestinians are interested in the
resistance that the Islamic groups pose to Israel and not necessarily in
building an Islamic society governed by the shari'a (Islamic law). This
distinction is true, but no one can deny that having Islamic groups lead
the resistance would lead to social changes that coincide with the ideological and political goals of these groups.

Group Formations and the Perpetuation of Israel's "Security Threats"

After the outbreak of Al-Aqsa Intifada, and the shift that this outbreak
represented in moving popular political attitudes toward resistance and
away from political engagement with Israel, the traditional PLO factions
of Fatah and the PFLP established new wings that engaged in the resistance as well. The grassroots base of these organizations is nationalist
and is taking part in these groups precisely to be engaged in the resistance. The political engagement of their leadership in the political
process did not stop the groups from participating in the resistance
when there was a popular cry for doing so again after the peace process
collapsed. As Kamal, one of the leaders of the Al-Aqsa Martyrs Brigades
in Jenin, explained:

> The Authority [PA] had the best of the organizations' guys held in jails. The
> Authority was not concerned with supporting the resistance. To the contrary,
> they see the resistance as a stumbling stone to their program. At the begin-
> ning of the intifada, there was a popular rise, a movement in the nationalist
> feeling. We were concerned with distinguishing the honorable committed
> members of [Fatah] and naming those people. We started our work depend-
> ing on our own personal resources. There were some who sold their belong-
> ings to finance our activities. Until this moment there is not an official
> Palestinian side that supports something called military resistance.
>
> There were an increasing number of people falling as martyrs that gave an
> incentive to seek retaliation for these crimes. At the beginning it was just

demonstrations, we used to go to the Jalama checkpoint to demonstrate and we would come back with two or three martyrs. We sought to retaliate in similar terms as far as the size of losses and killing we suffer. We arranged for carrying out shooting raids at [Israeli] military vehicles from a distance. From a military standpoint this was not successful. When we started ambushing settlers' cars, this was a phenomenon that received enormous support. There was a distinct state where all wanted to express their anger and outrage. This was a personal local initiative separate from the Authority and in some cases separate of the *tanzim* [Fatah organization or its leadership] itself. Then we had a following in the West Bank as a whole. Then there was an agreement to name the people who are engaged separately [from the main organization, Fatah] and we agreed on al-Aqsa Martyrs Brigades. [22]

This narrative points to a disagreement between the grassroots membership of the PLO factions and their leadership. The birth of al-Aqsa Martyrs Brigades could have created a split in Fatah if the Fatah leadership had shown no interest in the group, or denounced it. But the Fatah leaders realized that the presence of the Brigades gave them credibility and maintained their connection to the grassroots who were demanding resistance. The PA leadership as well saw in al-Aqsa Martyrs Brigades a way to regain credibility after the total failure of Oslo and its promises. The PA uses al-Aqsa Martyrs Brigades in two ways, emphasizing to Israeli and American negotiators that the PA is connected to a Palestinian resistance faction and therefore has leverage over Palestinian resistance, and to Palestinians that there is a resistance group in favor of the PA's political engagement with Israel. Al-Aqsa Martyrs Brigades itself is not a united front. In the Jenin area there are four factions of al-Aqsa Brigades, from the Jenin Camp, the East Jenin neighborhood, Qabatiya village, and Yamoun and the villages of western Jenin. Each faction has its own leadership, although there are two main leaders: Zakariya Zbaidi of the Camp and Abu 'Arraj of East Jenin.

In the Jenin area and the West Bank in general only the al-Aqsa Martyrs Brigades have a militarized presence in the city streets. Some members of al-Aqsa Martyrs Brigades walk through the streets carrying guns. Other groups like Hamas, Jihad, and the PFLP keep their military cells secret and do not display their weapons openly. These groups may display their weapons when masked men carry them in a nationalist parade or demonstration, but Fatah allows overt militarized display daily in the

community. The overt display of weapons is a source of po\
prestige for the youth within the community and attracts peopl
groups for purposes other than resistance. Such open displays c
ons encourages formations as smaller groups vie for local control. In
Jenin these groups decide which taxis can park where. They protect taxi
drivers driving stolen cars, which upsets licensed taxi drivers who pay
taxes and licensing fees.[23] The groups also decide which pushcarts can
be or cannot be used in certain streets; this has important political
ramifications, since many camp residents grew up as refugees without
resources and became pushcart vendors out of economic necessity, and
since under today's conditions the pushcarts are no longer confined to a
designated square but rather are jammed into every street in front of
shops, which puts the pushcart owners and shop owners in direct conflict. The groups also dominate the political structure of the city and take
charge of dealing with criminals. Today no political official would dare
come to Jenin without prior arrangement with al-Aqsa Martyrs Brigades.
Anyone who did could count on a beating.

This reality of course threatens the social structures of the local community, not only the local political structure and its relation to the national structure. People are generally frustrated with the behavior of the
local groups, but their choices are limited. Cultic rule by local bands
that include corrupt in addition to well-intentioned people can be chaotic and lawless, but at least the groups are engaged in resistance to
the occupation; the agencies of the PA are not in control, and they
tamper with issues that impinge on the core of one's identity and liveli-
hood in Palestine. The encapsulation and fragmentation enforced by the
Israeli army impedes Palestinian capacities for national mobilization
and reinforces the localized formation processes. Beyond the impact
of geographic encapsulation and isolation, Israel seems to play a direct
role in facilitating localized formations. Most of the weapons they carry
are American-made, mainly M-16s originating from Israel. Some carry
the Kalashnikov, the weapon of the PA personnel. Bullets for the Kalashnikov sell for 28–32 NIS ($5.60–$6.40) each, while bullets for the
M-16 sell for 2–3NIS ($0.40–$0.60) each. The variation in the prices
between the two types of ammunition shows that the Israeli originated
weapon is by far more available than the Palestinian originated weapon.
Members of al-Aqsa Martyrs Brigades say that sometimes the suppliers

send them malfunctioning, exploding bullets, a defect that they attribute to Israel's involvement in supplying localized groups with weapons and ammunitions.[24]

The spread of small groups and the chaotic situation that they produce are cited by Israel as a "security threat" that must be eliminated. Their elimination is seen as particularly important in a state based on "ideological nationalism" (Ohnuki-Tierneny 2002), which requires constant reinforcement. Unlike states based on "ethno-nationalism" (Tambaih 1996), ideologically nationalist states lack a source of political unity like a common language, history, territory, or set of traditions. The force that will most effectively unify different publics from disparate backgrounds in Israel is the persistence of a common threat. The whole idea of the Jewish state was formulated by the Zionist movement in response to threats of anti-Semitism in Europe. To sustain the reasons for its own existence and to maintain the national unity permeated into a state, Israel must maintain the threat—that is, if it remains unwilling to change the ideas underlying its formation, which thus far it seems to be. In other words, subgroup formation and its accompanying threats create a rationale for sustaining the state. Whitehead (2002) describes this process in state expansion as "states make tribes and tribes make states": the deformation of society and the formation of subgroups create threats to the colonial state that are necessary for its unity.

Other investigations by Israeli scholars of Israeli army tactics find that Israel engages in provocative policies that lead to intensified Israeli encapsulation of Palestinian populations and more frequent suicide bombings. Zeev Ma'oz, cited in Bloom (2005), states: "Israel used targeted killing during times of relative tranquility in order to provoke escalation. The cases involved conscious and deliberate provocations through the use of limited operations. . . . In each of the cases, the Palestinian response was a series of suicide bombings which brought about increased Israeli pressure on Palestinians in the form of encirclement of the major population centers, entry into the Palestinian cities and refugee camps, mass arrests, and long curfews of the Palestinian population in the West Bank" (23–24). This and similar analyses demonstrate that Israel is active in perpetuating its own "security threats," which provide the tools of Israel's unity needed to counter and eliminate them. Maintaining unity requires maintaining the threat.

Tribal Democracy

In the months leading up to the Palestinian election for prime minister after the death of Yasser Arafat, the leading candidate at the time, Mahmoud Abbas, came to Jenin on 26 December 2004 and met with the factional leaders of the al-Aqsa Martyrs Brigades in Jenin, where they represent the strongest presence in the West Bank. Abbas came for photo opportunities with the Brigades leader Zakariya Zbaideh and some of its members so that he could present himself as being in harmony with the resistance. Two days after his visit, al-Aqsa Martyrs Brigades held a parade and rally in Jenin. More than two hundred armed men fired hundreds of rounds of bullets in the air. They marched through town and gathered at the rally, where speakers from the tanzim ("the organization," Fatah's local leadership) and al-kata'ib (the brigades) spoke. The Brigades' speaker was the top leader Zakariya Zbaideh. The message from the rally was the unity of the Brigades' subfactions and their unity with the tanzim and the political leadership. The head of the tanzim stressed Fatah's unity and its support for the PA political leadership, calling for support of the Palestinian struggle for freedom and statehood with Jerusalem as the capital, thus reiterating the typical official Palestinian political line. Zbaideh, however, called for unity and support for the struggle until Palestinian rights were restored, topped by their right of return. Shortly after Zbaideh's speech the armed men started leaving in different directions. There were still other speakers on the program of the rally, but after the armed Brigades members left, most of the crowd, approximately a thousand people, left. The major attraction was the armed resistance members, and the main reason to stay was to hear what they had to say. The crowd was not as interested in what the tanzim had to say. But the whole parade and rally served to show unity of Fatah or, more accurately, the results of the recent meeting between the PA leadership (the prime minister candidate Mahmoud Abbas), the local leadership of the tanzim (Fatah's leadership), and the leaders of the various subfactions of al-Aqsa Martyrs Brigades in the area. It was a demonstration of unity that was needed for the upcoming election.

This process is a classic example of Fatah's politics. Palestinian activists refer to Fatah's unity as the unity of the tribe. Fatah historically included subfactions and regional leadership that led localized forma-

The leader of Al-Aqsa Brigades delivering a speech at a rally in Jenin, December 2004. Photo by author.

tions like the subfactions of al-Aqsa Martyrs Brigades in the Jenin area. They unify in the face of threat to the mother organization. The unity is often achieved by building temporary alliances that reflect a range of common interests and exchanged demands, but not a unity in vision or political programs. One member of al-Aqsa Martyrs Brigades who took part in the Fatah unifying meeting in preparation for the election told me in the interview what members of his group told Abbas: *Itha bithayed 'an al-khat al-watani ihna bin qawwumek* ("Should you deviate from the nationalist program we will straighten you up"). These subfactions can be rallied when there is an overarching threat like competition with another faction. Hamzi, whom I interviewed about a year before the parade, was directing the parade activities. In his interview he stated: "The PA hangs on a straw. My suggestion to the PA is to resign and for us to go back to the days of the first intifada. The PA cannot provide for anything. From Oslo to this day, the PA has been a project to protect Israel. Our position is that Al-Aqsa Martyrs Brigades is the main hurdle in front of the PA. So, we will become the main tool to affect the PA."[25] Many members of al-Aqsa Martyrs Brigades share this view of the PA. But the PA often makes generous promises of positions in the leadership of the secret service or the police, promotion in the tanzim (Fatah's structure), or a guarantee of safety from assassination by Israel. The al-Aqsa Martyrs Brigades are the group most vulnerable to cult formation and tribalization schemes because their political organization, Fatah, is intertwined with the PA. In the absence of harmony with the political organization they lack the capacity for national coordination, especially in the face of Israel's tight encapsulation and confinement procedures. Most groupings of the al-Aqsa Martyrs Brigades are localized and operate independently. Hamzi explained: "The Brigades are small groups. We don't have an overall general strategy. What's common is our legitimate rights and those rights become the link between us. Our understanding of the current stage is that it's going to depend on personal initiatives, to retaliate on the Israeli depth as a way to deter Israeli practices." This view is shared by Reda: "Fatah or the military wing of Fatah, al-Aqsa, is still tied to the Palestinian Authority and Arafat. The period that Fatah was engaged in this form of resistance and sending these [martyrdom] operations was a period of chaos. They were organized as personal initiatives from field leaders. These field operators to this day, if they could [logistically] send operations they would. The political leadership is different."[26] These localized operations, especially when not coordinated through a political organization analogous to Hamas, threaten communities' social order and unleash destructive forces. In the absence of civil order, of a decision-making process, of national authority, or of adherence to a national political group, these subgroups create conditions of disorder in which charismatic leaders thrive. In September 2003 members of al-Aqsa Martyrs Brigades in the camp held the governor of Jenin district, who serves in the PA administration, beat him up, and threw him in the street dumpster. It was reported that the beating was due to the governor's allegedly having tapped into funds intended to support the camp. The governor fled the city and later the country after the incident. One member of al-Aqsa, Reda, saw different reasons behind the beating: "From the moment the new financial trustee of the tanzim [Fatah-Jenin] . . . took his post they hit Haidar Ershaid [Jenin's muhafez, or

governor]. Allegedly he had stolen the support money that was sent to
Jenin's Camp. The whole game of the *Muhafez* is that these guys knew
there are some talks of resolution, it is a relatively calm period. [The
Fatah financial trustee] is aiming at the *Muhafez's* position and that is
what really is behind the defamation of Haidar Ershaid. Now they say
that [——] was offered the *Muhafez* position. That is not true, he wanted
to burn the *Muhafez* so his position becomes available and he promotes
himself to it."[27]

These plotting, maneuvering, charismatic, and ritual forms of power
and leadership are exactly what the state seeks to achieve from its fragmentation and encapsulation policies. These processes are what ultimately limit societies' capacity to unite across geographic locales and
across charismatic individuals and personalities. The lack of unity keeps
the society affected by the expansion under state domination. They produce uncoordinated resistance from the fragmented groups without a direct link to a political program or coordinated political process to achieve
a political agenda. Such disordered resistance becomes only a source of
unity for the expanding state. This precisely describes the relation of
Fatah to the resistance, in that it is now motivated mainly by reaction to
Israeli practices. Ferguson and Whitehead (2002) call this a process of
tribalization. As Shalabi has stated: "The national struggle is not a consistent sequence. It is a matter of reaction, especially in Fatah. If they hurt us,
we hurt them. We reply to their practices. But the concept of the *istishhadi*
with al-Jihad and Hamas is different."[28] Even Fatah members observe
difference in the Islamic groups' practices as stated by Shalabi here.

Resistance to Tribalization Schemes

This policy of tribalization, cult formation, fragmentation, and corruption of Palestinian society is not working completely to Israel's advantage. As Shalabi notes, the reaction to these strategies is different in
other Palestinian groups. The tribalization processes that take place with
the encounter are most pronounced within Fatah. Other organizations
like Hamas, and to a lesser extent the PFLP, function according to a clear
set of procedures and decision-making processes. But they too are subject to the same cosmological and ontological conditions of the encounter: they cannot escape the effects of encapsulation and fragmentation,

which leads local cells in cities and villages to take local initiatives. time, this structure leads to the development of localized formations leadership. In other words, even the well-organized group most lil will suffer some of the tribalization effects of the encounter. Islamic Jihad, on the other hand, is not engaged in local Palestinian politics, nor does it engage much in the infrastructure of social institutions. On the contrary, they are primarily active in the resistance. The group can hardly develop a local leader before the Israelis assassinate him or arrest him.

Hamas in particular seems to be conscious of the discursive effects of factional politics. Hamas is the best-organized Palestinian group and has the most disciplined membership among the factions. In the West Bank Hamas does not allow its armed members to disclose or show off their weapons. Their members mostly blend in with the community, adhering to the social order of the community and making no effort to position themselves above it. The organization has a policy of retaliating against Israeli targets when it is violated by the PA. Hamas alleges that the PA killed eight of its members in Palestine Mosque in Gaza and that the PA provided information to Israel that led to the arrest of a number of members of its cells. Yet Hamas followed a strategy of retaliating against Israeli targets and *not* the PA for the PA's attacks on its memberships and its cells. This practice in turn helps to counter the tribalization processes. Had Hamas retaliated in kind against the PA and its security apparatuses, the tribalization process would have intensified. On the other hand, Hamas activists see that their policy of not retaliating against the PA is costly. As Anwar explained:

> In spite of [the PA's violations and killings of Hamas members] Hamas did not fire against these people. Dr. Abdel Aziz al-Rantisi's position was clear: "The Palestinian weapon will remain clean of the Palestinian blood and will remain pointed towards the enemy and not at the Palestinian chest." This policy served us at the popular level. But at the military level it cost us 130 operations that were [caused to fail] by the PA during the last four years. Retaliating against Israel redirects the attention away from the [internal] disputes. The disputes lead to splits in the Palestinian [unity]. Even if Hamas had the justification [to retaliate against the PA] this would lead the movement to lose credibility with the people. With an operation against Israel we kill two birds with one stone. We end the problem without the loss of credibility and the operation increases the people's trust in us.[29]

Salim stresses the point in a similar fashion, which indicates agreement between the political activists and the military activists. He asserts that the targeting of Hamas by the PA is an American and Israeli plot, and to defeat it Hamas must retaliate against Israel: "The PA arrested Hamas activists and put them in jail, even though they would not surrender if they were fighting the Israelis, but because the resistance movement considers Palestinian blood as *haram*[30] and a red line this strategy crippled the PA's ability to continue in organizing our people against Hamas. This organization against the resistance was through pressures from Israel and the United States and that is why the Hamas retaliations were always against Israel. In spite of the arrests and the torture, had the Palestinian people fallen into the traps that Israel set up for us, there would have been no intifada. But there is an intifada, a militarized, organized, and popular one."[31] These policies have served Hamas well in building its credibility and popular support within the community. The shocking level of support that Hamas gained in the Palestinian municipal and parliamentary elections of 2006 attests to the credibility and legitimacy that Hamas has achieved. Resisting corruption, deflating internal Palestinian political tensions, remaining focused on the engagement with Israel, not allowing military members to engage in or show off activities that might lead to cult formations are all policies that directly counter the tribalization strategies pursued by the state of Israel. These policies play a major role in building up Hamas's credibility and popularity and help to explain how Hamas is achieving popular and political dominance in Palestine in a relatively short period. Still, the policy of dealing with internal conflicts by retaliating against Israel has not gone unchallenged within Hamas. Anwar explained that the organization is facing growing opposition from the younger generation of what he described as the "Bin Laden School." Its members believe that the PA and its Palestinian police should be declared infidels, which would make their targeting a religious duty. Anwar explained: "Hamas is running into some thoughts that are affected by the 'Bin Laden School.' There are *fiqhi*[32] differences between Hamas and the 'Bin Laden School,' which lead to differences in the manner of work. The point of difference is the *takfir*[33] of the rulers and the leaders in their persons and their programs, *takfir* of the armies and what this leads to in how to deal with them, whether their killing is permissible or not. For example, the operations in Iraq, why doesn't Hamas execute similar operations against the Palestinian police? Hamas did not execute any operation against the Palestinian police even though there are some martyrs who were killed by their hands." Recent events connected to the Hamas takeover in Gaza show that at least there Hamas's policy about not engaging the PA has undergone a shift. At the same time Hamas has remained with no overt military presence in the West Bank. Today two parallel power structures are being constructed, that of Hamas in Gaza and that of the PA and Fatah in the West Bank. Hamas itself is playing two roles in two separate environments: it leads a power structure and engages in governance building in Gaza, and it functions as the opposition and underground resistance in the West Bank.

International Development, Local NGOs, and Factional Politics

Similarly, the traditional left of the PLO factions the PFLP, the DFLP, and the People's Party (formerly the Palestinian Communist Party, which changed its name after the collapse of the Soviet Union) are all associated mainly with the bureaucracy of the Palestinian NGOs. These leftist groups, which spent the 1960s, 1970s, and 1980s talking to Palestinians about imperialism and its strategies to oppress the masses around the world are now the main recipients of imperialist funds. Most local mid-level leaders of the groups that played a role in the first intifada are now running Palestinian NGOs funded by western industrialized nations. There is no doubt that a number of interventions by international development agencies have had a positive impact on the life of Palestinian communities, especially interventions at the macro level in the areas of municipal infrastructure, roads, health care, education, and relief work. However, at the micro level of community development projects, most funds are tied to the agendas of donor agencies and governments, and they seem to do more harm than good.

Many of the community development programs aim at what is often termed democratic education. The leaders of NGOs speak the language of development—"stakeholders," "capacities," "democracy," "gender" —and implement programs that seek to "develop" Palestinian society or more accurately *form* it into what the global donor agencies see as "developed." Leaders of these N G Os make monthly salaries exceeding $5,000 and spend large amounts of money on meetings, conferences, travel abroad to conferences, and flashy reports. Some work as N GO professional consultants and take part in several N G O projects, simultaneously collecting compensation from each. These consultants can make over $10,000 a month in Ramallah by just participating in discussions and generating "working papers" for different donor agencies. Hardly anyone looks at these "working papers" beyond the conference. It is a way to spend the budget and keep the personnel of the donor and recipient organizations working. All of this is happening before the eyes of the Palestinians, who see that these funds are generated under the name of their suffering while the average monthly salary of a working Palestinian is approximately $400–$600. Thus former leftist Palestinian activists have developed into professional fund recipients, spenders, and report generators and maintain strong ties with the representatives of their "international" partners, the global donor agencies. These Palestinian leaders of the main N G Os, some of whom have become N GO celebrities in the West, have emerged as a group formation on their own and call themselves "Palestinian civil society." They are developing into an élite class. The leaders of this class in Ramallah function as a cult, protecting their ties with internationals and coordinating with each other to maintain exclusive access to international donor agencies. Present and former activists of the Communist Party take the lead in this cult formation, followed by former activists of the P F L P and D F L P. Fatah's activists are just catching up in the N GO business, because unlike the leftist opposition they did not have training in telling the "democracy" and development fairytale.

Certainly this picture is not inclusive of all international agencies' interventions in Palestine, nor does it affect all Palestinian N G Os in the same way. There are well-intentioned professionals within the Palestinian grassroots who maintain integrity in their work and implement development programs with a high level of sincerity. There are also international groups that support development schemes informed by local perspectives and local assessments of the need for intervention. A full analysis of development interventions in Palestine is beyond the scope of this research. My interest here is in how these interventions contribute to the construction of violence by local actors, and on the role of NGO élites in Palestinian NGOs.

These local Palestinian NGO élites and their international partners present themselves as the concerned "international community" that responds to socioeconomic and relief challenges created by the isolation schemes imposed by Israel. While the discursive effects of the violence of geographic isolation are social fragmentation, an alteration of social groupings, and cult formations, there is at the same time what Jonathan Friedman calls "vertical polarization" through the connections of a class of "professionals" with the international development agencies (Friedman 2003). These agencies are not so isolated. They are mostly based in Jerusalem and Ramallah, the center of their activities, where the Palestinian Authority is based. Their members pass through Israeli checkpoints and are not required to line up with other Palestinians, instead showing their international NGO ID cards and proceeding unhindered. The Qalandia checkpoint between Ramallah and Jerusalem has a special line for the "internationals." Palestinian assistants or employees who accompany the "international" staff get similar treatment, and if traveling separately their international development agencies' ID cards get them preferential treatment. A vehicle with an international NGO marking that is occupied by local Palestinian staff still jumps ahead of the Palestinian line at the checkpoint and is given priority to pass by the Israeli army. In my observation of the Israeli checkpoint crossings, I witnessed many Palestinians expressing resentment at "these people who bring stickers to stick on their cars and can jump over the line." The preferential treatment that they receive from the Israeli army at the checkpoints helps to define them as a class and separate them from the rest of the community.

This class of local NGO élites, along with representatives of the international NGOs that are active on the ground, collectively see themselves as the "international community" (Friedman 2003) and depend on "development" funds from international donor agencies, which vary in size, depending in part on the degree of political stability. Thus a whole class of people, locals and internationals, have vested material interests in perpetuating the conflict. Judging from my engagement with this class of people during a five-month period in Ramallah, where I was a consultant assigned to the PA Ministry of Planning through the United Nations

Development Program (UNDP), and from the Palestinians' categorization of members of this class as al-muntaf'in ("the ones who benefit" from the conflict), it appears that a system has developed similar to that described by Michael Maren (1997) in his inquiry into the international aid and charity system in Africa. There aid and charity have developed into what Maren calls a "self-serving system" rather than one that has a positive impact on the lives of the communities supposedly being served. International development aid has indeed evolved into the primary industry in the Palestinian towns of Ramallah and Bethlehem. The NGO élites do not necessarily have to do anything to keep the conflict intensified: Israeli practices are a great source of instability and conflict as it is. The problem lies rather in what these agencies do not do with resources supposedly allocated to "help the Palestinians," and in the globalization and hybridization of local identities that end up contributing to the construction of local violence.

The local NGO élite class must model itself in a way that is palatable to the discourse of global development and aid agencies. Entry into the class requires professionalism in talking about concepts such as "denunciation of violence," "non-violence training," "rehabilitation," "capacity building," "youth development," "democracy," "women representation," "medical relief," and "agriculture relief." Self-fashioning becomes a process of identity "hybridization" that also gives more meaning to the performance of political violence as a means to reestablish distinctive local identities (Appadurai 1998). But people's concerns are not so much with the "mixed-up" categories that result from hybridization—in particular the new local élite class—as with how this hybridization will ultimately threaten the distinctiveness of Palestine, the place where Palestinian identity is substantiated, as a representation of authentic Palestinian culture.

In my interview with Marwan, a member of the El-Funoun El-Sha'abiya Dance Troup whose dance plays and folksongs assert a relationship to the place and often engage issues of modernity and tradition through artistic mediums, Marwan stated: "There is a continuous renewal of a state of shock. This stage is still being renewed continuously. It's a process of deconstruction. Every stage repeats the construction of your identity, reforms it. Some tell you not this way, and you are reforming your identity, a process of a new construction. This is the load. Every

Palestinian is carrying this project, the identity project. . . . The project of Palestine is the project to construct the place, as a minimum. I mean, what that place carried or represented. It's a crime to deform the place, not only to change its characteristics. We contributed to the deformation of the place by allowing for our deformation."[34] Marwan's formulation presents the tension that Palestinians find in the constant construction and deconstruction of their identity as they cope with local challenges and global ideas. Yet it is also clear that the concern with identity "deformation" is a concern about how deformation might deform the place—a concern that these new hybridized categories might be *out of place.*

In contrast, Hamas and Islamic Jihad neither take part in the PA institutions nor have an entry into the NGO bureaucracy: donor agencies are obliged to isolate both groups because of their "terrorist" activities. They have not made detrimental political compromises like the PA, and where they were active in public institutions like the *Zakat* Committees,[35] Islamic Endowment committees, and local kindergarten programs, they have proved credible. They are also active in the mosques and provide a medium through the mosques and the statures of the imams[36] to solve communities' local disputes in the absence of government and under conditions of encapsulation, geographic fragmentation, and isolation. In my discussion with Dr. Iyad Barghouthi, he stated: "The Islamic trend is not an outburst or merely passing by. It is a primary part of the nationalist movement. It rises within the conditions of corruption, *mahsoubiyeh.*[37] The mistakes of the PA give them credibility. They are less corrupt than the PA institutions. . . . People want credible persons. They provide that. Their internal struggle will dictate whether they continue on the political path. It is in the [Palestinian] people's interest that they continue in the political line. Their political program is acceptable but people have reservations toward their social program. [Islamic groups] have a conflicted following between the political acceptance and the social rejection." Barghouthi is discussing the tension that Palestinians have between their support for Hamas's political program of resistance to Israel and its policies and their lack of enthusiasm for Hamas's program to transform Palestinian society by organizing it according to strict Shari'a law. The social program referred to here is not the social welfare program that Hamas provides in Palestine through a network of social organization. It is rather the social outlook on life and organization of society under the anticipated Palestinian state. The tension that Barghouthi is describing is a widespread tension among Palestinians in the West Bank: a tension between on the one hand the support that these groups get for a resistance that represents a popular call and a cultural discourse woven into the communities' life, and on the other hand the lack of excitement for the sociopolitical programs of the groups that are the forefront of the resistance. The resistance is the primary subject in people's daily thinking and conversation because the daily encounter with Israel positions it there. Thus the groups in the leadership of the resistance play the leadership role of society at large; the resistance and its forms reconfigure society, groups, and groups' political programs. These dynamics explain the "shocking" victory that Hamas scored in the Palestinian parliamentary elections of January 2006. The results should not have come as such a "shock" once the traditional PLO factions abandoned the practice of resistance before achieving their goals.

CHAPTER FOUR

The Carrier

In this chapter I present descriptions of Palestinians' daily life in Palestine. My aim is to show how the encounter with Israel is an integral component of Palestinian daily life. I narrate specific episodes of the Palestinian encounter with Israel to reveal an intimate view of the social dynamics of these encounters. Then I analyze how the encounters affect Palestinian cultural formations and transformations, and generate a process of oppositions and parallelisms such that the cultural order of the occupied society cannot be adequately studied separately from the effects of those encounters. The encounters lead to the articulation of ideas and generate processes of ideas embodied in material processes that inform actions. The nature of the encounter itself—the nature of the practices of the expanding state, here Israel—has a tremendous impact on the nature of ideas being formulated among Palestinians and the forms of the social processes that these ideas generate. In what follows I present ethnographic descriptions of events in their local settings, the ethnographer's tales, followed by an analysis of the narrated events and of how the events figure in the social processes, sociopolitical transformation, cultural embodiment of ideas, and motivation of action.

The Burden of Palestine

Being Palestinian has become an increasingly complex and cumbersome identity for Palestinians to bear. A long history of enduring, combined with a harsh, inescapable present and an unknown tomorrow, are prominent features of Palestinians' lives in Palestine. These conditions and experiences weigh heavily on Palestinians' identity. The Zionist Jewish

The Carrier Camel, by Suleiman Mansour. Courtesy of Suleiman Mansour.

national project that started in Palestine around the beginning of the twentieth century continues its expansion to this day, affecting Palestinian lives in many ways. Palestinians find themselves subject to perpetual episodes of violence: home demolition and ethnic cleansing, land confiscation and the uprooting of trees, encapsulation and restricted movement, denial of access to natural resources and the surrounding environment, and isolation from the rest of the world by the state of Israel. These practices characterize Palestinian lives today and Palestinians have been subject to these conditions for sixty years now. Above all, Palestinians do not see a way out. The future is dark, unknown, making it something to fear rather than long for.

The painting from 1980 entitled *Jamal al-Mahamel* ("The Carrier Camel") by Suleiman Mansour, the famous Palestinian painter from Jerusalem, came to signify this burden for many Palestinians. The burden of the struggle, the heavy weight of history, and the wondering about tomorrow are depicted in Mansour's painting. Mansour portrays a traditionally dressed Palestinian elderly man wandering in open space, carrying the city of Jerusalem on his back. His age symbolizes that the struggle has gone on for too long with no end in sight. The load appears too much for the old man to carry; he appears weighed down from carrying it for a long time, not knowing where he is going, but he is determined to carry on, showing strength as his fists bear the load of Palestine or Jerusalem. This painting became so popular in Palestine that almost every house had a copy. It was reproduced in all forms: framed as a painting, embroidered on fabric, molded in clay, crafted in wood, printed on stickers and postcards. Palestinians related to it at all levels across generations.

Over time Palestinian identity became loaded with questions: Why must I bear this load? Why can't I just live my life in Palestine? Will life ever be normal again? What is the future of Palestine and of our lives in it? Mansour's painting evokes these worries and the inescapable burden of being Palestinian. It depicts prominent features of Palestinian life: a heavy history that one cannot shed, just like the heavy load of the city of Jerusalem over the back of the old man; a harsh present difficult to navigate; an unknown tomorrow with no clearly defined path. All these features are sensed and experienced by those who live in Palestine. In my interview with Mansour, he stated that when painting *The Carrier Camel* he

was only "trying to express the relationship of the Palestinian to Jerusalem."[1] He mentioned that it was Emile Habibi, a famous Palestinian
poet, who gave the painting its title. The "camel" in classical Arabic
literature signifies patience. Mansour agrees that the title has contributed to the broader meanings sensed by so many Palestinians. Here is an
example of a cultural representation whose creator is not necessarily the
meaning maker. The meanings that the Palestinian general public attaches to The Carrier Camel go far beyond the Palestinian relationship to
Jerusalem that Mansour was trying to depict. Reproducing the painting
in many different forms is a cultural performance that has taken on a life
of its own, attaching new meanings, evoking experiences, and raising
questions not necessarily thought of by the original creator. Understanding the relationship between the creator and the meaning making of
cultural performance is an important methodological step in assessing
cultural performances in relation to their meanings and the impact on
their audiences. This methodological step demands that one consider
the various players making the cultural space of a performance rather
than simply the performers themselves. Doing so will become relevant in
the following chapters, where in considering the performance of violence in martyrdom operations I explore narratives and dimensions beyond the perpetrators or performers themselves to understand the cultural processes that make the performance meaningful. In this chapter I
present ethnographic material through which I hope to reflect the landscape of everyday life in Palestine by presenting experiences and episodes
that I lived as an ethnographer during my fieldwork in Palestine.

Closure

During the course of Al-Aqsa Intifada many areas and cities in the West
Bank were placed under closure by the Israeli army. When a city is placed
under closure, the Israeli army cuts off all access to the city and places the
city residents under curfew. Closures can extend from weeks to months at
a time, based on the Israeli army's plan of operation in a given city.
Closure of cities entails the closure of schools, shops, and access roads.
All forms of social and economic exchanges in the community cease; to
attempt to circumvent the closure is to risk one's life.

For the first twelve days of my arrival in Palestine, the city of Jenin was under closure. During the night of 12 October 2003 I learned that Jenin would be open tomorrow. The next day I heard that Jenin was indeed "open" after twelve days of being closed. I was excited that I was finally going to get to Jenin. On the night when I learned the news, I had been staying in the village of Berqin, south of Jenin, where I was conducting some interviews for my research. I first assumed that since the city was open, I would take the taxi or the bus to Jenin. I soon learned that "open" meant only that the Israeli army was not in town and had lifted the curfew inside the city, but all entrances to the city remained closed. I took the way from Berqin to Jenin through the olive orchards on the mountain, as this was what everyone was doing. The taxi drivers figured out how to get around the tanks scattered on the hills and in the fields around Jenin. A number of teenagers with cell phones monitored the movements of the Israeli army vehicles and informed the drivers, who constantly checked with other drivers over the phone about which avenues had soldiers and which did not. The taxis were chasing each other through the mountains. Drivers were rushing, trying to make it to town before something happened and worried that the roads might be blocked again. I was totally confused. I thought the roads were closed, and that is why we were going through the mountain. The taxi driver explained, "Oh, it's a dream to think of the actual road to be open. We are happy when the army is not in the mountains so we can get through." Our driver was very reckless and hit another car trying to sneak in front of us. We were caught in a traffic jam in the middle of the hill. Cars were scattered throughout the mountain and our driver was driving through the olive orchards, not on any specific track. We reached a dead end at the edge of one orchard. Passengers got out and started removing the *sinsileh* in order to open the way. We did that every time we reached a dead end.

We finally made it to Jenin at 7:50 in the morning. I was first struck by how the vegetable market was very well stocked, how the farmers immediately took the opportunity and managed to deliver fresh produce. The market's produce stands and pushcarts selling novelties were all set up early in the morning. The market seemed fully functioning after weeks of closure. The walls of the city were filled with posters of martyrs. Those killed by the Israeli army and those who went on martyrdom operations were commemorated by hundreds of posters hung around town. Martyrs quickly became icons. Most posters are of local martyrs, but others of national martyrs and historical heroes, such as the Palestinian American scholar Edward Said, who had passed away in the United States a few weeks before. In music shops and near pushcarts with CDs and cassettes one heard revolutionary songs of the intifada, Qur'anic readings, and recordings of Islamic sermons.[2] Revolutionary songs, Qur'anic readings, the sound of sermons, and posters of dead Palestinian fighters all mixed with the hustling and bustling of the market, a speedy market jammed with people who want to get as much as possible done while the city is "open."[3]

I needed to go to the bank to withdraw some funds. I got to the bank at 10:00 a.m. Outside the bank was a long line at the Tyme machine, about fifty people. Inside the bank I took a number for the teller: my number was 415, and the "now serving" number was 66. I sat down only to write the day's notes because there was no point in waiting. The bank closes at noon and there was no way my number would be reached by then. As I came out of the bank I met a man from my village, Ahmed, and he commented: "What you are doing? Are you working on your research? Are you researching terror? This is the terror. The seizure is the terror. The boy barred from his school is the terror. Tell your American friends about the terror."

Around noon I wanted to return to Berqin. I went to the garage and was told that there were no taxis to Berqin. The Jabriyat, the mountain route closest to Berqin, was said to be closed. I was told that after we had passed in the morning, Israeli tanks held whatever cars were still in the mountains. "How do I get back to Berqin?," I asked. They said, "Go through Swaitat, it is 'open.'" Swaitat is a southeastern mountain which goes in the direction of the village of Qabatiya, which is southeast of Berqin. I got to the Swaitat bus. The driver said, "I drop off at the Swaitat and you crossover walking, then you will have to take a taxi from there." I said, "What taxi?" He said, "Whatever you find. If you find a taxi to Qabatiya from there, get a taxi to Shuhada and from there get a taxi to Berqin, or you find a taxi to the Arab-American University [very far east] and after the students are out of class ride in their taxis to Berqin, or you might find a taxi to Al-Shuhada and from there connect to Berqin." I got the picture. You take the taxi that has an empty seat and is moving

A poster for the Palestinian-American scholar Edward Said among the posters of martyrs on the wall of Palestinian towns after his death in September 2003. The poster reads: "Edward Said, we will continue your path and your intellect will remain eternal." Photo by author.

regardless of the direction. You just need to keep inching toward your destination every time you change taxis. Off I went, gradually learning the tricks of navigating around Israeli tanks and hummers roaming the region's countryside and blocking roads.

In the bus the talk of the passengers was about how long Jenin would be "open." Some said that it was open "until further notice," others that according to students at the school it was open for "one day only." The bus was hot, dusty, and filled with the talk of the route; which roads, or rather which rocky mountain trails, were "open" and which were not dominated the talk. The bus driver said, "Thank God for what you got today. Today is better than tomorrow."

We were dropped off at the southeast edge of Jenin. There was a deep ditch and a large mound of mud where we had to cross. The Israeli army dug these ditches all around the city and access roads leading to and from the city in the fields. The ditches were about ten feet wide and six feet deep, with the dugout soil piled up on the sides, making it harder to cross. Busloads of people of all ages—men and women, boys and girls who came to the city to get some shopping done—crossed these ditches on foot, since the bus could not cross, looking around nervously, fearing that they would be caught by the Israeli patrol unit. Those who were caught were normally held in the mountain for hours, well into the night, and subjected to harassment. We walked and crossed over the mound, about two hundred yards. There we waited another forty-five minutes until a bus came. The bus was going to the village of Qabatiya. The bus driver was nice to me and drove me to Al-Shuhada after he dropped the others in Qabatiya, which was closer to my destination. From Al-Shuhada I found a taxi to Berqin.

In Berqin I would hear stories from almost everyone I met regarding their ordeals in the past few years of the intifada. I was stopped by a farmer who told me about his turnip crop, which was ready to harvest. He did not know what to do because of the current closure. He said that three weeks earlier he had been offered 30,000 NIS (approximately $6,500) for it and refused. Now he didn't know if he should pull his crops out of the ground. He had nowhere to sell them. This was the ordeal of many farmers, especially vegetable farmers, whose product spoiled if not consumed. They put all their energy and capital into bringing the crop to harvest. If the harvest coincided with a closure period, it would mostly go to waste. Many instances of extended closure in the cities make the city and the camps starve while the villages throw away the food they have produced. While living in villages through the course of my research, several times I would hear of farmers with nowhere to sell their crops who would open their fields for village residents to pick what they wanted. Other farmers, unable to maneuver their way around the checkpoints and army patrol units, failed to enter the city to make a delivery and would come back to their farm with a truckload of vegetables that they would dump for their animals.

A few points are worth discussing. The first is about the ontology of the cultural order: how social conditions relate to the formation of ideas and influence people's actions (Kapferer 1988). Uncertainty about tomorrow is as much a source of social suffering as the harsh circumstances of the day, as noted by the bus driver who said, "Today is better than tomorrow." Not knowing which road is open, when the city will be open, what one will be able to do tomorrow, is a major cause of distress and anxiety.

People going to the city are unsure of how they will come back, or even whether they will be able to come back at all. Their space has been turned into an unknown world. The unknown is fearful. People lose a sense of control over their own lives once they lose the ability to navigate in space and time. The farmer who plants a crop does not know whether he will be able to take it to the market; the merchant who buys merchandise does not know whether he will be able to transport it. These crippling conditions discourage people from exploring and realizing their potential. Others, however, find meaning in overcoming conditions imposed on them against their will. People make new meanings or reassert traditions, religious beliefs, and values to affirm a sense of certainty and political unity, and to mediate threats of fragmentation and annihilation.

The condition of suspense that people live under—crossing a ditch at the risk of being caught; fearing that they will run into a tank or hummer up the hill, around the next turn, in the valley, or next to the tree on the side of the road; sleeping in the hallway when bullets might be fired through the window at night—are all examples of violence in the imaginary (Whitehead 2004). This imaginary violence affects people more than the experiences of physical violence itself. First of all, imaginary violence has a much larger set of victims. All those who travel and who fear being caught experience violence in the imaginary; only those who actually are caught experience physical abuse at the hands of the Israeli army. The tales of those who fall victims to Israeli abuse become part of the construction of violence in the imaginary. Second, imaginary violence affects victims for an extended period: the entire time one spends away from home, or on the road, or sleeping in a hallway. There have been recent reports that the Israeli Air Force continued to fly fighter jets at low altitude over Gaza after the Israeli withdrawal, projecting sonic terror (El-Haddad 2005) on the whole city, since a missile could hit anywhere. These long periods are punctuated by moments of fear, each of which feels as if it could be one's last.

The constant suspense produced by the imaginary violence affects people in different ways. Some may become psychologically traumatized, and there are many reports of children with mental problems, particularly in the Gaza Strip.[4] Others react by deploying social processes like the one developed in the first intifada and turn enduring the abuse into a meaningful act. Still others, especially in rural areas, go through a process of "indigenization," to borrow a term from Friedman (2003).

There has been a ruralization trend in the West Bank during the Al-Aqsa Intifada, in which people have limited their movement out of the village, adapting their lifestyle to the village's constrained circumstances. Villages that used to only have a couple of basic grocery shops now have shops that sell clothing, kitchenware, farm supplies, pharmaceuticals, and other basic supplies, making it possible to live in the village without leaving often. I learned from some middle-aged residents that they did not leave the village more than a couple of times during the three years of the intifada. This self-imposed isolation becomes a process through which communities are excluded and marginalized.

Still others turn to ideologies that provide answers and certainty to counter the effect of the violence. The sermons, Qur'anic readings, and revolutionary songs that fill the air reflect the mood of the market as well as the choices of audio shopkeepers who live in the same political context and cultural order. Turning to religious and ideological beliefs that provide a sense of certainty relieves the suspense and anxiety created by long intervals of imaginary violence. Thus people become ideological and more religious. For those who believe that they will only die when God has chosen their death, it is much easier to endure the imaginary violence, because the ultimate form of violence, death, is of God's choosing. Several times, while waiting at checkpoints or waiting to be searched by the army, I would hear religious men saying, "This is God's test." Thus the meaningful practice is to pass God's test by enduring the violence and not allowing it to affect you psychologically and socially.[5]

To contemplate death in this way is not particular to religious people: the imaginary violence affects secular and nonbelieving Palestinians in similar ways. The words of the Palestinian poet Mahmoud Dawish are often sung by the Christian Lebanese singer Marcel Khalifeh, who started out his singing career as the singer of the Lebanese Communist Party. His songs are popular and are sung by members of Palestinian left factions like the PFLP and DFLP. One of these songs communicates similar messages:

Muntasiba al-qamati amshi marfou'a al-hamati amshi
Upright I walk. Raising my head, I walk.
Fi kaffi qasfatu zaytounin wa a'la katifi na'ishi, wa ana amshi, wa ana amshi, wa ana, wa ana, wa ana amshi

In my hand an olive branch and on my shoulder is my coffin, and I walk,
   and I walk, and I, and I, and I walk.
Qalbi watanon abyadh, qalbi bustan, fih, fih al-awsaj, fih al-rayhan
My heart is a white homeland. My heart is a field, in it is the awsaj,[6] in it is
   the basil.

In this scene from the poetics of the resistance, the youths who chant
these words effectively premeditate their death and find the meaningful-
ness of their life in the resistance. The emphasis is on walking in the face
of death (coffin on the shoulder) as opposed to kneeling down to it. If
death occurs when walking to it, it is meaningful in that the body will
become part of the land, the homeland, and bring it peace (white homeland), and the heart will bloom flowers in Palestine. The more the condition of violence in the imaginary intensifies through the practices of the
Israeli army, the more accelerated these social processes of martyrdom in
the making become, and the more people get integrated into it. These
confinements, as in the example narrated above, are experiences fundamental to the meaning making of martyrdom operations. They are directly linked to how martyrdom operations are culturally conceived by
Palestinians and become a meaningful practice to the general Palestinian
public. (I explore these meaning makings of martyrdom operations in
detail in chapter 5.)

   As the violence intensifies and is prolonged, more and more of these
processes of meaning making for life under violent conditions are performed and embodied by individuals and communities. These embodi-
ments of new cultural ideas and the bringing back of forgotten traditions
influence community life in other cultural spheres beyond direct encounter with the "enemy" and penetrate into the very fabric of the inner
community's social life. The Gaza Strip, for example, reflects more "radical" political views and attitudes among all factions on the political
spectrum and is far more religious than the West Bank. The reason is
that the Gaza Strip is a lot smaller than the West Bank, and the population there has been confined and isolated much longer than the West
Bank. Yet the processes of religious assertion and political radicalization
are clearly felt today in the West Bank as well. In the village where I grew
up near Jenin in the 1970s, among the nearly forty to fifty high school
girls who used to gather in the village square to wait for the bus, about

five or six wore headscarves. Today one would find only one or two in a larger group of girls who did not wear the headscarf. The religious beliefs that are asserted to empower communities in the face of violence are maintained by asserting traditions and maintaining distinctions of local identity that influence all spheres of life.

As Palestinians share these experiences within the dynamics of meaning making and searching to make sense of their own being and navigate their lives, they acquire "durable and transposable dispositions" through conditioning to the new order, challenges, and social settings (Bourdieu 1977). New meanings that emerge in the dynamics of the encounter become cultural ideas and concepts that are reference points for subsequent cultural processes. These dispositions become methods that order society, which are then incorporated to look like an objective necessity, or conditions that are deployed in daily life through symbolically constructed systems of ideas (Wolf 1999). These symbolically constructed systems of ideas that are informed by local knowledge, traditions, and beliefs, and modeled to react to and interact with the threatening external intrusion, influence individuals' behaviors and motivate their actions. These cultural processes of meaning making are the cultural forces and subjective meanings that inform human practices. They are constantly transforming and are reconfigured by the various political and cultural forces of society along the dynamics of the encounter. Thus the encounter is a cornerstone in the present cultural order, and one cannot make an accurate assessment of cultural practices like the performance of martyrdom operations without anchoring the assessment in an analysis of the encounter.

The second point that emerges from the ethnographic scene presented above is contained in Ahmed's comments to me about my research and the position of the ethnographer in a community. Native scholars like me face extra challenges both in the field and in academia. Native communities question scholars educated in the West (Said 1993; Smith 1999), and conversely, within western academia some question the legitimacy of native knowledge and native intellectual contributions to scholarly work. Other native scholars working in their own communities, such as Julie Kaomea (2003), find themselves subjected to the cross-pressures of competing expectations: the expectations of the academy to speak from theory, and the expectations of one's native community to speak from experience. Although this may seem like an added pressure to the native researcher, I find that being a native researcher enhances research; it does not weaken it or call one's legitimacy into question. Researchers will always be challenged to present local knowledge and local perspectives in a scholarly, theoretical framework, particularly with regard to fieldwork. Moreover, the question "how native is the native" arises when one begins thinking of events and social processes through theoretical templates of thought and expressing one's observations and ideas (Narayan 1993). I find that being native enhances a researcher's access and understanding of local knowledge, that being under cross-pressure from academia and one's native community delivers more rigorous research outcomes. The cross-pressure ensures dual accountability to academia and the research community. Native scholars are subject to scholarly scrutiny as well as the scrutiny of their communities of origin. By contrast, researchers conducting research in communities other than their own, if not connected to the community by some other means, are rarely scrutinized by their subjects' communities. These communities are not included in the scholarly conversations other than through their representation by the researchers they contact as subjects. Moreover, the academic community is more "qualified" to scrutinize any research outcomes than a native community would be, because academic discussion is carried out within a theoretical framework often unfamiliar to the native community. There should therefore be more scrutiny for non-native scholars, or more accurately, scholars whose relation to their researched community is limited to the research they conduct. These scholars do not necessarily carry the pressure of accountability to their researched community.

Base of Operations

During the closure of a Palestinian city, Israeli army tanks conduct patrols during the day and raids at night. In interviews, many residents spoke of shots fired through their windows and showed me where the bullets hit. In one family the sixteen-year-old boy sleeps in the hallway to the bathroom, since once a bullet came through his room's window and hit the inside wall while he was asleep. While occupying a city the army picks a residential home in each neighborhood, occupies it, and turns it into a base of operations while the house's residents are in it. I interviewed a couple of families whose houses had been turned into a base of operation during the recent closure in Jenin.[7]

Salem is a pharmacist who lives with his wife, an eighteen-month-old baby, and his mother, Um Salem:

> Salem: About quarter past eight at night the Israeli soldiers walked in, asked us to sit in one room and put one soldier guarding us. I asked them that since my mom is sick and my wife is pregnant not to bother them. He told me, "Take anything of value and go to one room." I told him, "Fine, anything you want just tell me and I will help you." I was trying to prevent them from destroying the house. As soon as they walked in, some of them lay down on the floor to sleep, some of them stood by the window. There were about thirty soldiers.

> Um Salem: We put our hands up, all of them were aiming at us and they were saying, "Don't be scared." They had been at another house in Jenin the day before. They had been in Jenin for two days. Probably the oldest of them was twenty-one years old. We didn't know how to deal with them. Even they themselves looked stressed and troubled. One was saying, "For over a month I haven't seen my mom and dad because of Jenin." He was somewhat apologetic to us.

> Salem: Another time, two days later, the same group came at eleven at night. Food was at the table ready to eat. The army ate it and they asked for more bread.[8]

Ahlam lives with her mother and father and three other siblings between the ages of fourteen and twenty-five. The Israeli army spent a night at their house in September 2003. Here is her tale:

> Ahlam: We were asleep at four in the morning. Our doorbell rang. My dad went to get his ID and I opened the door. About twenty soldiers dashed into the house. They started searching the rooms. We were six people in the house. They moved us all into my parents' room. They took the mattresses and they said, "There is a curfew tonight in Jenin and we are sleeping here." They left a guard at the door of our room. At eight in the morning I asked to make sandwiches for my young siblings. I asked the guard at the door because the main officer was asleep. The guarding soldier wouldn't let me. The officer woke up at eleven and then he gave me permission to use the kitchen.

> The people in the neighborhood did not know a thing, but some of the

neighbors saw them through the windows. They permitted us after eleven [midday] to use the bathroom and the kitchen, but we couldn't really cook because they were filling the house. In the afternoon they asked me to make coffee for them. One of our neighbors came and rang the bell and they asked us not to answer the door. Around ten the next evening, there were some shootings and already tanks nearby. About one at night they asked us if we wanted to make dinner we could, but we refused. About two at night they brought an Israeli TV crew to take footage and they asked us how the army was to us. In the presence of the TV crew they brought some food and they said we are bringing you food and they left at three in the morning.

Our furniture was filthy after they left. Our computer was taken to pieces and the hard drive was reformatted. They took our mobile phone and cut the wires of our landline. During their stay they had some maps they were studying, some were talking, one guy was reading a book. They messed up a lot of our house trying to cover windows that did not have curtains. They nailed down chairs and other furniture pieces to cover windows.

Our house is situated in Al-Marah above the market, situated in a spot where you can monitor the whole market from it. Before they left the house, two soldiers left first and searched around the house. They spent an entire twenty-four hours in our house. It looked like it was a special operations unit.[9]

The Israeli army, steel-fortified and armed with the latest in state-of-the-art American weapon systems, resorts to using Palestinian human shields to guard against Palestinian resistance attacks when conducting operations in Palestinian towns. As much as this is seen by the Palestinians as inhumane conduct on the part of the Israeli army, it is also seen as an indication that the Israeli army fears a resistance that is poorly armed but vehemently determined. The army's actions are forms of domestic occupation that are intensifying conditions of confinement and domination.

Um Salem's observation of stressed, exhausted young soldiers and of one troubled Israeli soldier who complained about his assignment and missing his family is remarkable. To begin with, Um Salem still feels a human connection to the soldiers who invaded her home and endangered her life and the lives of her family. Although a victim, she ex-

presses sympathy for the conditions of her abusers, young kids subjected to the rigors of war. In describing the soldier who complained to
his Palestinian victims about missing his family and who was "apolo-
getic," Um Salem indicates that even Palestinians who are victims of this
army do not necessarily see Israelis as monolithic: they observe variations in soldiers' behavior and in their attitudes toward Palestinians. In
fact, Palestinians assign grades to soldiers at checkpoints based on their
attitudes and strictness. Some people from the village will find out which
soldiers are on duty before deciding whether to try to cross the checkpoint that day. Some soldiers go out of their way to make people suffer,
having them wait for a long time before calling them, and then harass-
ing them. Others minimize the harassment in carrying out their duties,
even though the state system of which they are a part—not necessarily
by choice—is inherently a system of harassment. These observations
point to the mimesis and the intimacy between enemies that develop
with contact. This process was nicely illustrated by Saverio Costanzo in
the film *Private* (2005), which depicts similar events and encounters in
Palestine.

The camera crew mentioned in Ahlam's testimony is not necessarily
an Israeli TV crew, as Ahlam assumed. I am not aware of reports of these
Israeli army practices in the Israeli media; perhaps they were conducting
Israeli army archiving procedures. The Israeli government archives its
military materials for forty years, and archived records are the primary
sources for historians. For example, materials concerning the ethnic
cleansing campaigns that Jewish militias mounted against the Palestinian populations in 1947–48 did not make it into Israeli historians' narratives until after 1988; until then the narratives of nearly one million
displaced Palestinians, materials documenting the four to five hundred
Palestinian village sites in ruins and the eleven cities emptied of their
Palestinian residents, and other Palestinian historical sources—all were
inaccessible to Israeli historians. When the state finally opened its archives the result was a barrage of "new" histories from a generation of
"revisionist" Israeli historians categorized as "post-Zionists" for acknowledging elements of the ethnic cleansing campaign that were documented in the archived materials. Thus for historians working from
archival materials, Ahlam's narrative has no value now, but it will have
value in 2043.

From Ramallah to Jenin

On 20 February 2004 I was traveling with an American friend from Ramallah to Jenin. I had a meeting scheduled in Nablus on the way. I will explore what would normally be a two-hour trip to illustrate the numerous complexities that the Palestinian daily traveler encounters in the state of Israel.

Settlements

The regular main road, from Ramallah to Nablus, was closed. It had been closed since the beginning of the intifada in September 2000 and was still closed as I wrote this narrative. We took an alternative route that taxi drivers had been using that went through Birzeit south of Ramallah, then down a rocky hill to connect to an Israeli settler road for a short while until it connected to the main road to Nablus, about fifteen kilometers north of Ramallah. One could view major Israeli settlements on the stretch between Ramallah and Nablus. Normally they are situated on mountaintops and overlook surrounding Palestinian villages and towns.

This emplacement of the settlements projects Israeli power over the landscape and surrounding communities. To Palestinians these settlements look foreign to the landscape in terms of structure and placement, in contrast to the Palestinian villages scattered in the landscape. Palestinian villages expand naturally with the community, blending into the landscape as the structures become integral to the landscape. The Israeli settlement activities, however, are planned by the state, placed by the state, and designed by the state. The state has its own political aims in financing and executing settlement plans, namely to reconfigure the country into a Jewish homeland and to emplace Jewish communities there. The state has the resources to plan and construct uniform buildings, cut off the tops of mountains and situate buildings on top of them, and slice through mountains to provide straight access to settlements with roads. The buildings look heavy, even on the mountain; their uniformity gives them an alien, unnatural feel, and the access road looks like a tear through the canvas of what otherwise would have been a breathtaking landscape. Israel designs and situates these settlements in relation to the Palestinians and the territory, not the environment.

In a recent visit to Hebrew University to give a presentation in the winter of 2005, I was surprised to find that the university, a place for intellectual engagement and learning, had been designed in the same way: as a fortress on the Mount of Olives overlooking East Jerusalem, which is mostly inhabited by Palestinians. Inside the campus one can see only heavy stone and concrete walls. The magnificent city is below, but one cannot see it. Yet from the city one views the fortified heavy structure hovering above. Since the beginnings of Jewish immigration the trend in settlement building has been to keep Jews separate from Palestinian Arabs (Abu El Haj 2001). However, the settlement activities in the West Bank have extended what Abu El Haj calls Israeli "territorial self-fashioning" in terms of power and dominance. This structural fashioning of power in the landscape makes Palestinian inhabitant-viewers subject to constant domination and intimidation in their own environment. The visual representations of power are in addition to the state's efforts to isolate the occupied population through land confiscations, territorial confinement, denial of farmers' access to the land, and denial of cross-community exchange through closures, checkpoints, and roadblocks. This territorial fashioning of power on the landscape is a constant reminder to Palestinians of what they see as Israeli abuse of Palestine. The uniform buildings that abruptly cut through the mountain and sit on top of it are an irritating, alien presence in the landscape that the Palestinians regard as hostile to nature itself and to their sense of home at home. Palestinians have a strong attachment to the land and the environment, which anchor many of their symbolic cultural representations (Abufarha 2008). Altering the landscape in ways foreign to the local Palestinians is perceived by the Palestinians as tampering with their souls and bodies. The aesthetically discomforting Israeli settlements and access roads are as much a source of rage for Palestinians as the abuse of Palestinian communities.

The settlement access roads may be used only by Israeli cars. Palestinians who use them risk being shot and killed. Some Palestinians have lost their lives after using them mistakenly.[10] The traffic signs are marked in Hebrew only. But at some intersections of the roads dedicated to Jewish settlers and the regular West Bank roads, one finds traffic signs in Hebrew, English, and Arabic. The same is true for some historic sites. For example, a sign for the Jordan Valley gives the Hebrew name on top (in Hebrew), the name "Jordan Valley" in the middle (in English), and "Wadi Yardin" on the bottom (in Arabic). The Arabic name for the Jordan Valley is *Wadi al-Urdon*, but the sign transliterates the Hebrew name *Yardin* in Arabic letters. This practice is also followed on the signs to Jerusalem, on which the Arabic letters render the Hebrew name "Urshalim" rather than the Arabic name al-Quds. The Israeli state expansion over Palestine and Palestinian communities is engaged in reconstituting the landscape of Palestine into the national homeland of Israel. This process is not limited to territorial and population control but extends to attaching symbolic meanings to the land. Feld and Basso (1996) emphasize the significance of place names and how naming creates senses of place with historical, moral, cosmological, and biographical references. The erasing of names, the attaching of new names, along with the erecting of alien structures, reconfigures a place in foreign ways. The reconfiguration creates a sense of denial: a denial of existence, history, the right to self-representation in space, and territorial entitlement. This denial of the attachments of communities' historical names to their place is a denial of historical events and narratives that are the context of these communities' definition of self in their present. Places' constructions are strongly tied to people's identity constructions. The process of denial is strongly connected to the construction of violence as a means to assert one's existence. Violence becomes a mode of communication to assert existence of denied identities and mediates belonging and exclusion. The performance of violence in contested places is in part about expressing attachments and reasserting the rootedness of identities excluded from these places.

Checkpoint

The taxi from Ramallah dropped us off at the Hewara checkpoint, entering Nablus from the south side. I had a meeting scheduled in Nablus and then planned to continue on our journey back to Jenin, my main field of research. At the entrance to Nablus my American friend was denied entry by the Israeli army officers because she lacked a special permit from Israel, but I was told that I could enter because I had a Palestinian ID. Once the soldier found out that we were from Wisconsin, he told my friend that he had friends at the University of Wisconsin. My friend asked the soldier where he was from and he happily replied, "California." He was a young American Jew serving in the Israeli army. He commented that he hadn't been to college yet. So when he insisted that we could not pass and should just wait for the next shift, I agreed that we would wait right there. In the meantime, people whom the soldier needed to let through were lining up on both sides of the checkpoint, and he saw that I was not willing to turn back. He had already seen my university ID, my letter from the university regarding my research, my American passport, and my American friend. I was a little more daring than usual because I was accompanied by a "real" American, one who was not also an Arab like me. The soldier knew that I was on official business. He asked if my research "was for both people," and I replied, "Of course it is." My friend added, "Of course, it's Anthropology!" (Her remark seemed to stereotype anthropology as a romantic, enchanted field, which is ironic considering the fieldwork I was doing.) Then the soldier said, "Go! Go!" When my friend passed through the metal detector it beeped, and she stopped and turned to look at the soldier, who yelled, "Just go! Go!"

We went into Nablus, I attended my meeting, and the people I met from Nablus drove us to the checkpoint at the other side of town, north toward Jenin, to exit the city. Nablus is the largest city in the West Bank. It is situated in a valley between two high, very rocky mountain ridges. With an army checkpoint at each end of the city, the Israelis keep a tight seal on the city because it is very difficult to go through the mountains north and south of the city. The soldiers at this western checkpoint were intrigued to talk to Americans, especially since my friend was female. One soldier was happy to ask if she had seen a Chicago Bulls game and to volunteer that he liked Michael Jordan. (Many soldiers assume we are from Chicago, because our passports are issued there.) The guy next to him looked at my passport and gave it back without comment or obvious concern.

Past the checkpoint we got on a bus, waited for twenty minutes until more passengers got on the bus, and then drove westward to a point called Innab where the Israelis had blocked the road with a metal gate and heavy blocks of concrete on both sides and no checkpoint. The gate was placed on a narrow mountainside road: on one side was a sharp valley dropoff, on the other side the mountain. The gate was not manned by any soldiers and people were able to go around it and underneath it by foot, but cars could not pass through it nor go around it because the road was narrow. Soldiers periodically appeared to prevent people from going around it. The gate had obviously been there for a long time, because a whole transportation network had evolved to various cities on both sides. On both sides of the gate people sold coffee, sandwiches, and snacks. The road is a major thoroughfare between Jenin, Nablus, Tulkarem, and Ramallah, so the presence of a gate without a checkpoint could only have been intended to cut off these cities from each other and to restrict cultural, social, and economic exchange.

It was late on a Friday afternoon, and when we saw one yellow taxi we ran to it to get a couple of seats and were happy to have done so. It was scary at first when the car didn't start, but it did after a push. As we were pulling out, a driver from an incoming car told our driver where a checkpoint had just been placed and recommended that he avoid that road. Our driver asked which road he should take instead, and the other driver suggested a route that was safe, along hilly gravel roads that connected past the checkpoint to a road leading to Jenin.

Holdup

We drove through villages and beautiful countryside with terraced olive orchards. It had been raining for a while and I had been explaining to my friend what the abundance of hannoun[11] flowers meant to Palestinians. We had been talking the whole time about the beauty of the Palestinian countryside, its diverse scenery, the green mountains in what has been a good winter. We were on the high mountains west of Nablus, on a dirt road, on a clear, sunny late afternoon with a view of the Mediterranean glistening in the afternoon sun. You could view the high-rises in Tel Aviv area and the calm sea from where we were, and at the same time turn back and look north and east and see rolling hills of olive orchards and blooming almond trees with white and pink flowers. We were enjoying the multifaceted scenery and landscapes: the fields, rolling hills, trees, flowers, and terraced orchards.

Then we got on the main road to Jenin. After five minutes we ran into Israeli foot soldiers pointing guns at the taxi. They shouted at our driver to stop and gestured to him to enter a muddy side road in the olive orchard, but he couldn't because there was another taxi similar to ours already stuck in the mud in front of us. While we waited the soldiers asked the Palestinians in the other taxi to get out and push the taxi out of the mud and into the orchard. We watched them struggle for about five minutes, and at one point the wheels were smoking while the soldiers pointed their guns at them. Eventually the passengers pushed the taxi out of the mud and onto the dryer muddy track inside the orchard. As the car moved, some of the passengers fell into the mud. The soldiers ordered our taxi to pull ahead about forty feet and stop.

They then ordered our driver to follow. We were able to avoid getting stuck because our driver accelerated with force. As we were driving into the muddy road in the olive orchard, Israeli soldiers around us assumed a fighting stance, their machine guns pointed straight at us as we were following their orders into a mud puddle. They were shouting and very worked up. My American friend was terrified.

Next the soldiers yelled at us in Hebrew to get out of the car. Once we were out, the soldiers pushed people to get down on their knees, with their hands on their head and their back to the soldiers. I faced the soldiers, walked toward one of them, and asked, "Can I ask what is going on?" He yelled, "No!" and then started speaking in Hebrew. I said, "I don't speak Hebrew. I'm speaking to you in English." Then he told me in Arabic to turn around and go down on the ground. I pretended I did not understand and said again, in English, "I ask you, why did you take us off the road?" He spoke in Hebrew again. I said, "I don't understand Hebrew." Then he said in English, "Sit down like them and turn your face the other way." Then I put my bag down and said, "What do you want?" He turned away and began to harass the people in the next car that had pulled into the muddy road in the orchard.

In the meantime, my friend was telling another soldier that she was an American. She had been taken on the other side of the car and a soldier was checking her passport. After questioning her for a few minutes, he asked her to sit in the car. Then she told him, "He is American too," pointing to me. The soldier asked me to approach him; I showed him my letter from the university and my passport and explained that I was a researcher from an American university, had been conducting research for six months, and had got through every checkpoint. He said in a rude way, "I understand, I understand." And then he told the man who seemed to be the commander—the one who had been ordering me to get on my knees and with whom I had been arguing in English—that we were Americans. The commander, realizing that I was an Arab American, replied that we were *arabim* (Arabs).

The soldiers clearly had not expected to find two Americans among those intercepted, and they began talking about it in Hebrew. I could not fully understand the conversation, but the words "Americans," "university," and "doctor" were repeated in the dialogue. Certainly our presence among the group had spoiled whatever plans they had in store for the Palestinians they pulled into the mud. At this point there were three taxis in the orchard, the passengers on their knees in the mud, with their hands on their head and their backs to the soldiers. We were in the middle car. My friend and I were ordered into the car by the soldier who had our papers. In the meantime, the soldiers had begun pretending that they were checking the cars, so they asked for the driver and started looking at the trunk and engine of our car and the car behind us. The one in front of us was not checked.

The soldiers then ordered people to go back in the cars, except for the two Palestinian men in the car behind us, who were left on their knees. They ordered the car in front of us to leave, and then ordered our driver to leave. Our driver asked whether he could turn around back to the main road, since the road was so muddy and his car was low. He was hoping to be let back to the road so that he could move the car behind us (which would have had to move anyway) and so that the two guys still held on the ground could be let go. But the soldier aimed the gun right at his head and shouted at him to move, so all of us left the two men behind to be subjected to further harassment.

We amazingly made it through the mud for two kilometers until we got to a gravel road in the hills. As we drove, people in the car congratulated each other for having reached safety. Certainly everyone was relieved to be alive. This wasn't something that you necessarily expect to turn out "that easy." Shortly after the hold-up we went through more stunning landscape, including the Sanour Plains, which are situated between mountains and are so flat that in a good year of rain, the area can become a lake. This had been a good year and although there was no lake yet, the plains had started to collect water. The passenger sitting next to me explained how the Romans before "us" (Palestinians) had dug eighteen wells in the plains to collect the water and store it underground; this kept the plains dry, and there must have been a mechanism to use the water in the summertime so that the plains could be farmed year-round. Another person in the car explained how when the plains fill with water a spring west of Jenin bubbles up, and in his village they believe that the spring comes from these plains. Then there was a discussion of the underground water system and the land. The underlying tone of the discussion was the beauty of the land and the inability to live it fully because of the political conditions. We finally got to Jenin and there was no tank at the entrance as there sometimes is, so we went through the main road. Since we had had enough of soldiers for the day, we decided not to continue to my village north of Jenin, which would require getting through another checkpoint, so I arranged to sleep over in Jenin.

The constant fear of violent harassment like what we experienced on the road, coupled with experiencing a landscape that is both familiar and foreign, heightened our awareness of a country, a landscape, that the Palestinians have but in which they cannot live as Palestinians. The landscape is in their view, their roads, their orchards, their hills, but to live in this landscape is a challenge. Although Palestinians physically live there, the restrictions imposed on their movement and the constant fear create a sense of exile from the land. These ontological conditions of confinement and inability to live fully in one's place represent the opposite pole to conceptions of accessibility and rootedness, freedom and independence, continuity and flow. These conditions of displacement create a sense of exile and at the same time become a source of rootedness. In the absence of free physical access to the landscape of Palestine, the intense sense of rootedness is then mediated through the generation of poetics by means of which the meanings of people's relationships to the land are performed. Hence the cultural performances that provide a medium for conceptual rootedness become popular. At this juncture, between on the one hand displacement and confinement and on the other an intensified sense of rootedness, lies the acts of martyrdom that in their performance and cultural representation are a sacrifice for the land, a sacrifice that mediates issues of uprooting and rootedness achieved through the physical and conceptual fusion of Palestinians' lives in the land. This fusion is realized through the poetics of martyrdom in defense of the land, and the new life created for Palestine in the cultural imaginary along the representations of these performances. The

cultural conceptions of the performed violence extend the force of violence to cultural spheres where the performance of violence becomes
meaningful and culturally appropriate to the broader public.

Assassinations

Another feature of life in Palestine in the current ontological conditions
of the West Bank and Gaza is the Israeli policy of targeting Palestinian
leaders, activists, and resistance operatives for assassination. During the
Al-Aqsa Intifada, these assassinations presented a dynamic within the
resistance movement that enabled individual members to accept the
eventuality of their death while they were alive. (I will pursue this point in
the following chapters when I explore the tales of the resistance operatives.) Here I want to explore the broader impact of these assassinations
on the community and how they provide opportunities for the resistance
factions to galvanize youth and become sites where cultural ideas about
sacrifice and martyrdom are embodied in material processes through
which witnesses become ready for martyrdom.

Sheikh Yassin Assassinated

Around 7:30 a.m. I learned that Sheikh Ahmed Yassin had been assassinated in Gaza around 5:30 a.m., after the morning prayer. I was in the
village of Jalama, where I reside, and decided right away to go to Jenin
before the checkpoint closed. I arrived in Jenin at 8:30 and was surprised
to see a mural, about eight by twelve meters, covering three floors of a
building in the center of town. It pictured historic Islamic heroes, including Sheikh Ahmed Yassin and Sheikh Izzidin Al-Qassam.[12] Also in the
mural were Yahia Ayyash,[13] Hassan Al-Banna,[14] and another sacrificer
who had taken part in a previous martyrdom operation. The selection of
martyrs gave a historical dimension to the resistance movement and also
an Islamic one. The mural had a map of Palestine colored with the colors
of the Palestinian flag and supported by a machine gun vertically (along
the vertical eastern border of Palestine); the gun was cracking the Star of
David[15] on the bottom. The pictures of the martyrs were placed in the
windows of the Dome of the Rock. The last two windows of the mosque

Banner for Hamas hanging on the side of a building in the center of Jenin the morning of the assassination of Sheikh Ahmed Yassin. Photo by author.

Members of Al-Aqsa Martyrs Brigades shooting in the air at a rally in Jenin in protest of the assassination of Sheikh Ahmed Yassin. Photo by author.

on the poster had question marks in them, referring to those who would carry on the struggle and perhaps have to sacrifice themselves to achieve their end. As passers-by looked at the mural, members of various factions took over the loudspeakers in the mosque and spoke about the killing of Sheikh Ahmed Yassin. Hamas's speaker was giving instructions about a memorial planned for Jenin later that day. The Fatah speaker stressed their standing with Hamas and the resistance, promised retaliation against Israel, and issued a stern warning to those who might collaborate with the Israelis.

About 9:30 a funeral procession that seemed to be coming from the Jenin Refugee camp reached the center of town. There were two cars with loudspeakers and about twenty men in the center with machine guns shooting in the air. From the second block a group of about four hundred women joined in, chanting their own chants. I got to the center of the procession and took pictures of the kids on the trucks, the armed men, and the crowd in general. As I was taking pictures of the men who had huge machine guns—some of them 500 mm and 700 mm guns taken off Israeli tanks during the Israeli invasion of Jenin—a man five feet away carrying a big machine gun got excited and shot a whole magazine in the air. All the others started shooting as well. The sounds were terrifying, mixed with high emotions and vehement chants.

As the funeral procession advanced through town, people poured in from different streets, the number more than tripling to four or five thousand. There were different chants during the demonstration, some, like Hamas's official chants, organized and memorized, others extemporized expressions of the moment.

The women chanted:

la ilaha ill-allah, ish-shahid habib allah
No God but Allah and the martyr is Allah's beloved
ya Qassam, hat, hat, hat islah lil banaat
Oh Qassam, bring weapons to the girls[16]
ya Yassin, irtah, irtah, ihna nuwasel il-kifah
Yassin, rest, rest, we will carry on the struggle
ya Sharon, ya haqir, dam ish-shuhada ghali ikthir
Hey Sharon, you vile, the blood of the martyrs is very dear

Hamas's script is one that everyone knows. As it is chanted over a loud-speaker, the crowd joins in:

> fi sabeeli illahi qumna nebtaghi raf'a al-liwa'[17]
>
> For God we rose, we must carry the flag
>
> al-jihadu fi sabeeli illahi esma amaneena
>
> Fighting for God is the premier of our wishes
>
> Wal-ya'ud lid-deeni majduh, ya'ud lil-aqsa 'izzuh.
>
> Let the glory return to the religion, and let Al-Aqsa prosper again.
>
> fel-turaq minna ad-dima', wal-turaq minhum dima'
>
> Let some blood bleed from us and let some blood bleed from them.

Here is an example of an improvised chant:

> min Ghazzi hatta Jenin, kulluna Ahmed Yassin
>
> From Gaza to Jenin we are all Ahmed Yassin
>
> ya Qasam, yalla, yalla, khaliha tikhrab bil-marra
>
> Qasam, go, go, let it get totally ruined (turn things to hell for us and them)
>
> ya Sharon, hadder likyas, illayle ir-rad min Hamas
>
> Sharon, get the body bags ready, tonight is the answer from Hamas
>
> 'al-makshouf, ou 'al-makshouf, fakhekhni ti'amal ma'arouf
>
> Out in the open, out in the open, set me up [as a suicide bomber] do me a
> favor.[18]
>
> 'al-afouli raddna, ya waylu illi ey-suddna
>
> Our retaliation is going to be on Afula [an Israeli town], we dare you to
> stand in our way
>
> bab el-aqsa min hadid, ma byiftahu illa ish-shahid
>
> Al-Aqsa door is made of metal, no body but a martyr can open it

There are also slogans calling for unity between Sarya and Qassam, the military arms of al-Jihad and Hamas. Other slogans call for unity between Fatah, Hamas, and the PFLP.

The demonstration rounded back to the center of town and continued with a rally on the city square where speeches were delivered by members of Hamas and various factions of the Palestinian resistance. The speeches, especially of the Islamic factions, made use of Qur'anic verses and Arabic poetry that commented on current events and the confrontation with Israel, using national symbols and stating Islamic principles. During the speech Hamas vowed to retaliate within twenty-four hours. Of the Israeli attack it stated: "the target was not Yassin, the target was Hamas and its choice for armed struggle and the Israelis will definitely fail in reaching their target." People clapped and fired shots in the air when such statements were made. Twice the speeches were interrupted by breaking news reports. The first was about an operation carried out by Al-Aqsa Martyrs Brigades in Tulkarem and the other about an operation under way in Tel Aviv. Every time breaking news was read the crowd burst out whistling, shouting, and shooting. Apparently Zakariya Zbaideh[19] was at the demonstration. When people saw him they began chanting with high emotions:

ya Zakariya, ou ya habib, biddna irrad ib tel abib
Zakariya, our beloved, we want the answer in Tel Aviv

The main Hamas speaker closed by saying: "Everyone who thinks that the assassination of Sheikh Yassin will weaken Hamas, we tell him that you are disillusioned. His martyrdom will only increase the strength among our members. We tell you, our people, to rest assured that Hamas is well, and will remain well, and it will just get stronger."

Certainly every killing and assassination of an activist or leader is another demonstration of commitment to the struggle. Members of the charged crowd called for a response that night in Tel Aviv, in Afula; chanting that they would volunteer to take on a mission that would make a response, they saluted certain political leaders and political tracks and dismissed others. These actions marked a chain of sociopolitical transformations that intensified with every immense episode in the encounter, every assassination or destruction of home or land. Young and old, women and men came together to show their commitment and unity. Every demonstration like this is a renewal of a contract to carry on by individuals and active groups. The demonstrations remind communities of their challenges and priorities. They bring the encounter with Israel to the fore of their daily worries and thinking. The excitement among the crowd every time an operation or attack is reported over the loudspeakers demonstrates the crowd's desire to retaliate against Israeli targets.

For the youth in particular, these episodes are a means of expression and provide sites where they can demonstrate alignment and group-ing. In these moments the youth who are carrying the machine guns and firing into the air are the most prestigious. Hence belonging to these resistance groups becomes appealing to more youth. The Hamas speaker's closing remarks that Hamas "will just get stronger" get trans-lated into material processes through the demonstrations protesting the assassination.

When a martyr dies the funeral home is open for five days as opposed to the usual three, a tradition that arose during the intifada. The funeral normally takes place in the home of the martyr's relatives or, if the martyr is a national leader, in the city hall, town hall, or camp. The funeral homes are open from morning to midnight and are open to the general public. They become sites of active political discussions that situate the loss of the martyr in a broader political context and give it meaning, establishing a narrative of the martyr's life and developing his heroic and iconic image. These discussions are often led by members or associates of the group with which the martyr was allied.

The speakers' use of Arabic poetry as a vehicle for political commen-tary and mobilization builds on the language discourse that character-izes Arab and Islamic life during the golden Islamic periods, when po-etry was the source of proverbs that define the modes of conduct in the good society. Arabic poetry was a medium of nation making in the Abbasid, the Umayyad, and Andalusian eras. The revival of Islamic and Arabic poetic discourses validates the Islamic movement's adoption of the Islamic religion as a strategy to combat Zionism and compete at the global level. By adopting these discourses, Islamic factions com-municate to audiences that holding on to Islamic traditions is key to liberation and to regaining one's position in the global power struc-ture. Tradition here becomes a defining element in the reaction and a medium to express difference and discontent, and to further validate violent practices by association with tradition and historical legacies (Appadurai 1996).

Rantisi Assassinated, 16 April 2004

Dr. Abdel Azziz Rantisi, the new Hamas chief after the assassination of Sheikh Ahmed Yassin a few weeks ago, was assassinated on the evening of 16 April 2004. I was in Ramallah when I learned of the assassination, two hours after it happened. It was evening already. I went to the Ramallah city center, a circle called Al-Manara, the main square in the town where public events normally take place. There were nearly a thousand protesters, highly charged, mostly youngsters, demonstrating and chanting to protest Rantisi's killing:

lil-amam, lil-amam, ya Qassam
Forward, forward, hey Qassam.
Ya mufawedh, barra, barra
Hey you negotiator, Out! Out!

The Hamas spokesperson continued his speech over the megaphone: "We say to the leader who offered all of the compromises, we tell the leaders of disgrace that this insult is for you. Our people are the people of resistance, God is greater and victory is for Palestine." The crowd chanted:

fal-yasqut ghusn iz-zaytoun wal-tahya il-bunduqiyeh
Down with the olive branch, long live the rifle
al-intiqam, al-intiqam
Revenge, Revenge
siri, siri, ya Hamas, anti al-madfa, wa-ihna erssass
Go, Go Hamas, you're the canon, we're the bullets
ya Qassam, hat, hat, sayarrat mfakhakhat
Qassam, bring, bring, booby-trapped cars

The speaker closed with: "We tell you that the resistance here is the only path to our people's dignity." I talked to a couple of people from the crowd, including one youth, about nineteen, wearing a green headband that read, "la ilaha illa allah" (No God but Allah), the headband normally worn by the istishhadiyeen when they appear in their operation videotapes.[20] I talked to him because he was not chanting, only looking silently at the speaker and the crowd, with eyes about to spark fire. His comment was: "We have to have a quick response to this. This should not pass unchallenged. We are all projects of martyrdom for God and the homeland, and on the road of our leaders we will continue marching." I asked about his headband and what it meant to him. He said, *Kulluna shuhada' ma' waqf at-tanfith* ("We are all martyrs with execution on hold"). He continued, "Jihad [struggle for God and the homeland] is the highest of our wishes. It is a jihad, either for victory or martyrdom. There will be no kneeling down other than on our bodies." He seemed ready to go on any mission set up for him. The possibility of dying was already sorted out in his mind and emotive state. His use of the legal term *waqf at-fith* (a hold on execution) to describe his commitment to martyrdom was revealing, because it implied that he was *sentenced* to martyrdom. The conditions to which Palestinian youth are subject and in which they must grow up are in fact perceived by some as a sentence to martyrdom. That is the state the interviewee was expressing: he had already been sentenced to martyrdom and was just waiting for the moment of execution. He proudly accepted his fate as a means to overcome his life conditions. For him life is a life of struggle. The resistance lives as sacrificers offer themselves to martyrdom. Not only are they alive, as promised by Islamic teachings about martyrdom, but they are alive in the life of their struggle and in the ideas of homeland, liberation, and freedom for their people. They see more life in death than in life. Life in death is a life in meanings. These meanings are the main medium through which the decision to partake in the act of martyrdom is produced after one's death has been meditated.

The Official Rally, 17 April 2004

On the next day in the same place, Al-Manara, Hamas prepared for a rally scheduled to start after noon prayers. Its members set up a stage with a sound system and banners. The main banner on the stage bore a picture of Sheikh Yassin and the newly assassinated leader Rantisi. The banner read: *khayaruna al-muqawameh* ("Our Choice is the Resistance"). Many people gathered round the circle, and one person on the sound system and on stage played nationalist and revolutionary songs with traditional, folkloric sounds and music. Then the MC asked people to go to the mosque, where the demonstration was to start: "Hamas invites you to participate in the walk for a blood contract to the martyr, the fighter, Dr. Abdel Azziz Rantisi." He asked the crowd to make a pact for his blood and with their blood, and their voices. Then a song began: "The soul of the martyr is asking, Hey people, where is the sacrifice, where is the dignity, where is the pride, where is the courage, where is the feeling?" Then another song: "Hey my country, be happy, wipe off the sadness with jihad. Don't ever accept humiliation, don't ever accept disgrace. Gaza is fire that's always burning. In Gaza there are youngsters who can protect the house, be joyous my country." This song was followed by zaghareed.[21] Then we heard the voice of a child, aged seven or eight: "Did you see those who stole your land, did you see those who hit your mom?" Then we heard what sounded like a hybrid of song and public address. It started with a very prominent voice addressing the crowd: "I swear by God, the grateful" (repeated three times) "that we will guard Al-Aqsa Mosque." The crowd chanted: "By soul, by blood we sacrifice for you, Aqsa." A new voice on the tape then made a statement in a combative tone: "The oil lamp may turn off. The fuel given to Al-Aqsa may turn off, but our reply that we will light Al-Aqsa with our blood, because what is lit by blood will not be extinguished. Yes, will not be extinguished." The song then began, accompanied by traditional Palestinian sounds:

Dear Aqsa, you are not alone, we fenced you by our hearts.
We will never compromise you as you are the light of our roads.
Your light is oil and blood, don't you worry, your freedom is our quest,
    our quest.

Then the speaker was heard again in the song: "Our houses are stakes tied by the noble Aqsa, our land is an extension to the holiness of the noble Aqsa. It is our history, our present, and our future. We will stand in one row, one body, we will all stand to say we will not allow anyone to think that he can tear down our present and our future." The song picked up again: "Dear Aqsa, we are with you to the roots of history. With our souls we sacrifice to you, who needs the missiles, we smile for death and for you we raise our voices. Our wars are until victory." Then the voice returned, the music in the background: "He who attempts to tear down Al-Aqsa, will be torn down, God willing. And his house will be torn down, God willing. We fear only God and nothing but God."[22] Here the crowd began to chant on the tape: "By soul, by blood, we sacrifice for you, Aqsa." Then the song picked up again:

Dear Aqsa, we are coming as lovers, you are the glory of the free. The blood
  is beating, looking forward to blooming flowers.[23]
From beneath you Aqsa, or from above you, with the ribs our chest, we
  guard you.[24]
The ababil[25] birds are hovering over Gaza, over Hebron, the glory of Al-
  Aqsa will not come down, and we will make the collaborators stand for
  justice.

This song was produced and performed as a ceremonial pledge by the
masses for resistance. Pledge to the martyrs' blood, to the land, to the
religious shrines and sanctuaries, as well as a pledge to fight collaborators and those who might compromise the sanctity of the homeland, the
shrines, and the martyrs' blood.

The MC appeared on stage and read a poem: "We remain offering for
the homeland our blood and we remain offering for Islam, a bridge to
pass through. The people are behind you, Hamas, walking with heads up
high. We are the past, we are the guardians. Oh, by God I am coming
back to you, my country, coming with strength and ability to revive glory.
Your sun is lit, is lit. Your mountains are full of sacrificers and on victory
we have made a pledge, your victory Hamas."

The MC who had been wearing a headband followed: "Our country,
we live on it, we die on it, and for it we struggle." He then asked the
people again to "walk for a contract of blood for the fighter Dr. Abdel
Azziz Rantisi." And then the walk started down the main street in Ramallah. Nearly eight thousand people demonstrated that day. There were
a significant number of women, quite a few of whom did not wear hijab
(head cover). After the noon prayer people started pouring into the center from two main directions. The chants went like this: "Hamas, don't
you worry, every martyr you get an army." Youngsters and youth then
chanted in support of the brigades with stylized clapping:[26]

Revenge, Revenge, hey Saraya, hey Qassam[27]
Hamas [three claps], Hamas [three claps], Hamas [three claps]
We declared it to all, we want your head, Sharon.

Then the crowd returned to the stage area after demonstrating throughout town. There were speeches delivered by Hamas and other leaders,

followed by a poem: "I am not dead, my homeland, speak out. I am a witness that you [the homeland] are experiencing pain." Then a Hamas speaker addressed the crowd: "The land knows and so do the seas that the people of Palestine will not calm down. God is greater, hey, my country, chant, God is greater . . . We assure you that our choice is the resistance, our path is the resistance, and there is no way for our dignity in our land other than through resistance. The pride is in the shade of the swords. All of the peoples that refused but to live lived through resistance. Our people are strong, and they still have the ability for resistance. Martyrdom is a characteristic of our country and our people. Our blood is priceless for our country. Our country is dearer to us than ourselves, and dearer than our blood. Let everybody know that the road to freedom is the road of blood and martyrdom."

The multiple performances in the demonstration—speeches, poems, chants, songs, and leaflets—draw on an enormous and complex store of historical, religious, and local cultural references, connecting them to events and political processes on the ground. The performances fuse human lives in history, land, and religion. The song, for example, extends the religious qualities of the holy shrine (Al-Aqsa) to the rest of the land of Palestine. The speaker's words, "Martyrdom is a characteristic of our country and our people," is a new articulation of identity along this encounter, one that attaches identity to resistance, in particular the act of martyrdom, which is presented here as an organic feature of Palestine and Palestinians. These cultural ideas become embodied in a material process of resistance soldiering and istishhadi making. Cultural ideas of sacrifice and martyrdom, for a country that is "dearer than ourselves," are asserted as objective reality. This process represents a transformation in identity along the dynamics of the encounter with Israel. The new and emerging identities and cultural representations are generated and heavily influenced by this dynamic. In the events responding to the assassinations narrated above, the militarization of the resistance and rebellion intensifies, and a shift in the political grouping takes place based on the level of commitment to resistance. As Ferguson and Whitehead (1992) point out, the encounter with state expansion reconfigures the sociopolitical formations, modifying political groupings and creating new ones. Here grouping is reconfigured as calls intensify for a mimetic response to state violence.

The description of everyday life in Palestine presented here demonstrates how the encounter with Israel is a daily part of Palestinians' lives, constantly present in Palestinians' thinking and daily conversations. The encounter influences their decisions on the practicalities and details of everyday life, as well as their interaction with their environment. The mixture of familiar and foreign scenery in the landscape frame, the complexity of reactions to natural events such as rainfall—an event normally welcomed by farmers—turned into nature's cultural performance, a performance that evokes the feelings of losing land, making the nature's event—like rain—become another encounter with Israel.

The isolation, fragmentation, and constant threat of violence with which Palestinians are forced to live reconfigure Palestinian society in fundamental ways. The loss of command of one's own space and the constant fear produced by physical and imaginary violence projected by the state of Israel lead people toward ideologies and thoughts that provide certainty. The assertion of religion and radical political ideologies becomes a medium seen as necessary for the survival of the community. These ideological transformations, along with the state encounter, reconfigure the inner social fabric of society and set in motion social processes that influence the inner community's social settings and value systems. These social settings generate social processes that transform meanings and cultural representations. Thus the cultural representations of the Palestinian ethnographic present are primarily a product of the cosmology and ontology of Palestinian life.

Under these life conditions, Palestinian cultural identity cannot be seen separately from its setting. It cannot be seen as free from its reactions to the encounter with Israel. Within this setting of Palestinians' encountering a tenaciously expanding state of Israel that is exclusively ethnicized, we cannot perceive "culture" in a simplistic form and say that this act or the other is characteristic of Palestinian culture. It is rather the cultural discourse of the Palestinian-Israeli encounter that must be considered as one whole dynamic, in order to understand acts and practices in relation to ideas and forces that culturally form and transform the encounter. Realizing these ontological and cosmological conditions of Palestinians' lives is not only important for assessing where and how cultural ideas are formulated, but also for appreciating the extent of polarizations that are created through the performance of Palestinians' sacrifice and violence against Israelis. Their cultural representations of these acts of violence and sacrifice often place people's aspirations at opposite poles of their ontological conditions. I will explore examples of polarizations created in the cultural representations of violence in the next chapter.

CHAPTER FIVE

Dying to Live

In this new period of Al-Aqsa Intifada, Palestinian factions that engaged in martyrdom operations gained increased popular support and those that did not carry out similar operations in the resistance discourse compromised their support. Subgroups within the PLO, such as Fatah, formed their own wings and started participating in martyrdom activities in 2002. The Fatah leaders who supported these initiatives, like Marwan Barghouthi, gained wide grassroots support.[1] Other PLO factions like the Popular Front for the Liberation of Palestine (PFLP) and the Democratic Front for the Liberation of Palestine (DFLP), historically secular and Marxist organizations, also joined in conducting martyrdom operations on Israeli targets. By 2002 the Palestinian martyrdom operations were no longer the unique practice of Islamic movements but rather a popular Palestinian form of resistance embraced, executed, and supported by Islamic, secular, and Marxist forces in Palestinian society. It was no longer necessary to recruit people for these operations: there were enough volunteers. In this chapter I uncover the cultural momentum that the martyrdom discourse generated in this period. I seek to understand how martyrdom became a cultural discourse that in effect forced itself on some of the factions rather than being a strategy of choice. I would caution the reader that my intent from these explorations is not to promote this form of martyrdom but rather to explain how it has become popular.

Al-Istishhadiyyat: The Martyrous (Female) Ones

By January 2002 Fatah, the main PLO faction and a secular group, joined in executing martyrdom operations and introducing yet another dimen-

sion to them by sending women to carry them out for the first time
introduction of Fatah into the organizing groups and of women as carriers helped to widen popular support for these operations. Fatah's introduction of women, istishhadiyyat (the feminine of istishhadiyeen), was
related to Fatah's regional political goals and aimed at distinguishing
Fatah's role in the Palestinian resistance as that of an innovator rather
than a follower.

Since the 1960s pressuring Arab regimes to confront Israel has been a
prominent part of Fatah's political tactics (Gowers and Walker 1991).
Between January 2002 and April 2002 Fatah executed four martyrdom
operations—all carried out by women (Wafa Idris, Dareen Abu 'Aisheh,
Ayat al-Akhras, and 'Andaleeb Taqatqeh) and three carried out in the city
of Jerusalem—and all of the carriers' messages referred to the silence of
neighboring Arab states. During this same period there was intensified Arab diplomacy around a Saudi proposal backed by the United
States that was the main subject of the Arab League Summit in Beirut in
March 2002. Unlike the Islamic groups who construct martyrdom acts
with aesthetics that can achieve a maximum impact on Israel and be
more meaningful to Palestinians, the aesthetics of Fatah's operations are
geared to create maximum pressure on Arab regimes. The performance
of sacrifice by Arab and Muslim women in the occupied city of Jerusalem, thus making the sacrifice for Jerusalem, was intended to have
the maximum embarrassing, pressuring, and destabilizing effect on the
Arab and Muslim regimes in the region. This was clearly the political
goal, as stressed by the martyrs' messages, and the timing of the missions to coincide with heightened regional diplomacy. Frances Hasso
(2005) provides an insightful review of the wider impact that these operations had in the Arab countries and discusses in depth the significance
of gender in these operations in particular. Hasso shows how the ways
these women's acts were presented situated them as "gendered-political
subjects." Barbara Victor (2003) also gives us a window into the intimate
details of the female martyrs' lives as well as the lives of some of their
Israeli victims. Victor reports on a rally held by the PA especially for
women at which Yasser Arafat addressed a crowd of women and girls
and praised Palestinian women's role in the struggle. Arafat reportedly
said, "You are my army of roses that will crush the Israeli tanks" (Victor
2003, 19). Later that afternoon the first woman martyrdom operation
was conducted in Jerusalem by Wafa Idris and credit was claimed by

Fatah's Al-Aqsa Martyrs Brigades. The instrumentality of introducing women into the performance of martyrdom acts came to the fore.

In her analysis of the wide impact that these operations had on the Arab political scene, Hasso finds that three in particular resonated in the Arab media and on the Arab streets in the form of demonstrations. Hasso also wonders why the fourth operation did not have such an impact: "Since she was the first woman to undertake such an attack, Wafa Idris received more international and regional media attention than the typical Palestinian man bomber and more than two of the three Palestinian women bombers who followed her in 2002 (the exception is Ayat Al-Akhras). The lack of significant regional attention to Dareen Abu 'Aisheh is a puzzle, since she was the first to leave a videotape explaining her intentions and actions" (81). Hasso's puzzlement can be explained when the violent act is understood as a performance, of which aesthetics are an important component. Dareen Abu 'Aisheh's mission was the only one of the four that was not performed in Jerusalem. The Arab and Muslim connection to Palestine is symbolized in the historical connection to Jerusalem. Executing the operation in an Israeli settlement in the West Bank, as with Dareen Abu 'Aisheh, causes the performance to lose the component of sacrifice embedded in it. Palestinians do not have the connection to this particular Israeli settlement as a historical Palestinian site or city, much as the primary connection of the broader Arab and Muslim world is to the city of Jerusalem. In the other three operations Jerusalem was the object of sacrifice, the party to which the sacrifice was addressed. Similarly, the aesthetics of Ayat al-Akhras's performance were more pronounced because of her age (eighteen), the timing of the performance (on the heels of the Beirut Summit), the decision to stage her performance in Jerusalem, and the clear, overt reference in her operation statement to the Arab silence. All of this gave her mission added potency, which generated the strongest regional impact among the four. Prompted by the women's performances and right after Ayat's mission the Saudi government, to reduce the political pressures weighing on it, opened a public donation drive on public television that lasted a whole day: over $100 million was raised to support the Palestinian intifada.

Locally Fatah regained credibility, as it was still engaged in the armed resistance and did not abandon the path of armed struggle. This involvement further gave the Fatah and the PA leadership political leverage in their continued engagement with Israel on the basis of the Oslo arrangement. The political leadership of Fatah and the PA implicitly use the work of al-Aqsa Martyrs Brigades to give legitimacy to their dialogue with Israel as diplomacy backed by resistance, even though much of their dialogue with Israel focuses on security arrangements in general and the containment of resistance groups in particular. However, the idea of women's participation in martyrdom operations quickly took on its own cultural life. By the time Islamic Jihad and al-Aqsa Martyrs Brigades executed the joint operation of Hiba Daraghmeh in the Israeli city of Afula north of Jenin in May 2002, women's participation had developed cultural meanings beyond the instrumental political goals set in motion by Fatah. Islamic Jihad later used women's martyrdom operations to project a maximum effect locally on Palestinians and Israelis as well as regionally and internationally in an operation in Haifa in October 2003, which I explore in detail later in this chapter.

Hamas and Islamic Jihad were resistant to sending women on martyrdom operations. Their reasoning was that there was no shortage of male volunteers. However, it is clear from the responses to Fatah's launching of a series of operations carried out by women that women wanted to take part in this form of resistance. The best example is Dareen Abu 'Aisheh: although she was a Hamas activist, her mission was organized solely by al-Aqsa Martyrs Brigades, and on a videotape she wore a scarf decorated with the symbols of Hamas's Izzideen al-Qassam Martyrs Brigades. Her willingness to do so demonstrates the eagerness with which some women wanted to take part in martyrdom operations: Hamas would not give Dareen the opportunity, so she carried out her mission under the banner of another group and decorated herself with the symbols of still another, even without shifting her political allegiance. The circumstances were similar with Hiba Daraghmeh's joint operation between Islamic Jihad and Fatah. Later both groups allowed women to carry out martyrdom operations, partly in response to women's desire to be participants and partly because of the significant impact that the performance of sacrifice by women had on the public.

The "Typical Suicide Bomber"

Many Israeli scholars and think tanks try to draw a profile of the "typical suicide bomber" (Mirrari 1990; Farkash 2003). Similarly, western media commentators try to uncover the "mind of the suicide bomber," hoping to identify some shared psychological characteristics. So who are the "suicide bombers," and what do they look like? What is their psyche? What religious ideas drive them to carry out their acts? These and similar questions have been guiding much of the Israeli and western research and journalistic inquiries on the subject of martyrdom in Palestine and elsewhere (Davis 2003; Reich 1990; Robins and Post 1997; Reuter 2004; Victor 2003).

As I discussed above, participants in martyrdom operations willingly offer themselves to the facilitating groups. In an interview, Kamal, one of the local leaders of al-Aqsa Martyrs Brigades in Jenin, asserted that there were not only enough volunteers but too many: "We started to tell people to look after their kids."[2] Why do so many people want to participate in an operation that will cost them their life?

The cultural processes associated with and generated by the performance of martyrdom operations construct a cultural discourse within which a pattern of motivation to carry them through has developed in Palestinian society under occupation. Most of those who volunteer for martyrdom operations are not active members of the armed resistance but rather ordinary members of society who are not necessarily active in politics. In an interview, a Fatah activist, Shalabi, explained that often members of the organized resistance would prefer to go on a shooting operation, in which they would engage with the Israelis until they die, rather than strap themselves with explosives in a martyrdom operation.[3] People are motivated by a variety of reasons, depending on their personal history. But above all it is the discourse of martyrdom in Palestine that blends personal experience with local knowledge and situates cultural ideas in relation to mimetic encounters with Israel and opposition to its policies: this discourse generates a poetics rich in sensory meanings and political goals that provide a system of motivation.

I have reviewed the personal profiles of mission carriers who executed acts of martyrdom between 2001 and 2004 and interviewed some of their parents and family members. I found that many but not all of the mission carriers had firsthand experience with physical violence at the hands of the Israeli state. Furthermore, there are no special indicators that might identify participants based on economic conditions, education level, level of religious belief, or the presence of specific psychological conditions. Participants included members of the poorest communities, the middle class, and, rarely, the affluent communities of Ramallah. Moreover, participants have been school dropouts, university students, and university graduates, people religious and secular, male and female, as young as seventeen and as old as forty-nine. As Reuter (2004) reports, the Israeli army think tanks as well as prominent Israeli psychologists have been trying to develop a profile of the "typical suicide bomber" and find that to do so is a mission impossible. The Israeli psychologist Ariel Merrari of Tel Aviv University, who has been studying suicide bombers for a long time, could not come up with any narrow profile of a Palestinian martyrdom mission carrier.

Mission carriers may be motivated by the history of social suffering, their own experiences with state violence, a fascination with the notion of sacrifice for the land and the symbolic, sensory meanings of sacrifice, a fascination with the concept of martyrdom and ideas about the after-life, a preference for the cultural life of the martyr over their present lives, or a commitment to or fear of the Divine. In addition, they can be motivated by ideas of prestige and social grouping, or the prospect of reclaiming one's honor after being suspected of collaborating with the Israelis. But these experiences can only motivate a person to execute the martyrdom operation within a cultural discourse that melds personal experiences with cultural ideas. In this respect, the individual is not sepa-rate from the social analysis, and the cultural representations are not separate from firsthand experiences (Kleinman, Das, and Lock 1997). Martyrdom operations have a fully developed cultural form beyond the political goals of the organizing groups and the motivations and experi-ences of the individual actor. Alongside their multiple performances, in different multiple settings and with different aesthetics, martyrdom op-erations are given meanings by multiple Palestinian and regional viewers and cultural performers, and they generate social and political processes within which this form of violence takes its own cultural form. The martyrdom operations gained their popularity through the multiple ar-ticulations that accompany their application in the broader Palestinian cultural discourse of resistance, the sensory meanings embedded in the aesthetics of their performance, the nature of the encounter with the state of Israel, and the ways these operations mimic Israeli state violence. This discourse is not a calculated strategic construction by groups and individuals but rather a product of the natural reactions, expressions, and social processes that the performance of martyrdom operations generated in various sectors of Palestinian society when conceived against a backdrop of Israeli practices.

It is precisely within this cultural discourse of martyrdom in Palestine that a system of motivation arises, a product of personal experiences melded with political goals and cultural ideas through symbiotic articulations, manipulations, and transformations over time, along with mimetic encounters with the "enemy" over the landscape of Palestine. Once this motivation system is fully developed, it becomes real for everyone that lives in the habitus. It is within the habitus that this cultural discourse takes place once the individual becomes socially integrated into it and the cultural representations of the experiences of others are no longer separate from the process of experiencing. In my analysis I refer to this system of motivation as the "poetics of the resistance," building on the notion of Whitehead (2004) of a "poetics of violence" to refer to the effects of the semiotic performances over time. Still, the articulation of this discourse does not necessarily illuminate the agency of individuals and groups. All that the analysis tells us is that participants can come from any group integrated into this cultural discourse. But participation is still the result of individual and group choice. People may conceive of the same similar cultural ideas expressed through martyrdom as the martyrs do but choose to express them differently. Participation in martyrdom is still a choice, even though the choice may have been made within a cultural discourse that paved the way for making it. This chapter explores the articulation of this martyrdom discourse and uncovers its magnitude.

The Life of the Martyr

I begin by looking into the life histories of three participants: Ragheb, a seventeen-year-old istishhadi (masculine) mission carrier, Hanadi, a twenty-nine-year-old istishhadiyya (feminine) mission carrier, and Eyad, an organizer of martyrdom operations with Islamic Jihad who was eventually assassinated. Since the identities of the martyrs and by association their families, whom I interviewed, can easily be found in numerous articles and other publications about the acts of martyrdom, I asked for and obtained permission from the three families to use the real names of the participants.

I chose my interview subjects to obtain a representative sample of participants in martyrdom operations. Eyad was an activist from the first intifada who during the Oslo peace process changed his allegiance from Fatah to Islamic groups; many of the leaders who organize martyrdom operations have similar histories. Ragheb is representative of many ist-ishhadiyeen who are young and not active in politics, and whose participation in carrying out an operation came as a surprise to family and friends. Hanadi took part in an atypical mission as a result of undergoing unusual life experiences. Exploring the life histories of these three participants will enable us to see what they had in common as well as how they differed.

The families of all three participants subsequently had their homes destroyed by the Israeli army. Some family members have been arrested and released. During the interviews, I refer to the parents of each martyr based on the Palestinian tradition of calling the father *Abu* (father of) and the mother *Um* (mother of), followed by the first name of the martyred son or daughter.[4] For example, I call Eyad's father Abu Eyad, and Eyad's mother Um Eyad. All three subjects are from the Jenin area, and all carried out operations for which credit was claimed by Islamic Jihad. In the following pages I examine their personal profiles, activist profiles, personal experiences with violence, conceptions of martyrdom and sacrifice, and ideas about land, whether in their thoughts or in the cultural contextualization of their operations.

Most of the information that I present about the participants' lives is from my interviews with their families and friends. I explore two martyrdom operations by examining their preparation and execution, as well as the cultural discourse created by their performance. I chose not to interview people who were preparing to go on a mission for ethical reasons and because of security concerns. The ethical dilemma would arise if I knew of a specific mission that would cause physical harm to others and were in a position to prevent it. And there were security concerns because even if an organization planning a mission were able to conceal its details and the identity of the mission carrier, if the mission failed (and many missions do), I would become suspected of being responsible for its failure and might be viewed as a threat to the organizers.

Eyad Sawalha

The information presented here on Eyad's life history is based on interviews with his family members (father, mother, and younger brother)
and leaflets and publications issued by Islamic Jihad.

Personal Profile

Eyad was born on 2 February 1972 in the village of Kufor Rai'i. He was a
member of a family of fifteen, with five boys and eight girls. He was the
sixth child in the family. His father started working in the Gulf in 1953.[5]
After his parents got married in 1960 the father continued working in the
Gulf but left his wife behind in Palestine. The father started as a plumber
but later opened his own electric supply shop in Abu Dhabi, which he
called Sharikat al-Fida' (Sacrifice Corporation). The mother, Um Eyad,
brought up the family alone, the father visiting only in the summer for a
month or two. His mother described what it was like to be the head of
the family, manage the orchard, and build the house on her own: "There
was no electricity, no water, and no gas. I used to collect twigs and use it
to heat water to wash cloths, cook, and everything." She added, "I built
the house. I used to sift the nai'meh,[6] get it ready, get the water, and
get everything ready for the jableh."[7] Abu Eyad said, "She also planted
the olive trees." In addition to raising her children, Um Eyad took care
of eight dunums[8] of plum and cherry orchards and planted forty-five
dunums of olive trees, maintaining them and harvesting them.

Eyad finished the eleventh grade, then transferred to Qalandia Technical Institute in the fall of 1988 and spent one year learning welding and
mechanics. His family and friends describe him as having a very cool
temper and an exceptionally generous soul. His mother said, "I would be
screaming at him and he would keep his smile and cool." Eyad stayed in
touch with his family throughout his time on the run. His mother said,
"Under the worst circumstances he made sure he stays in contact with
us, especially his mother, and in contact with the needy in the village."

The Activist Profile

When the first intifada started in 1987 Eyad was fifteen years old. He
became active in the intifada, making Molotov cocktails. He once got

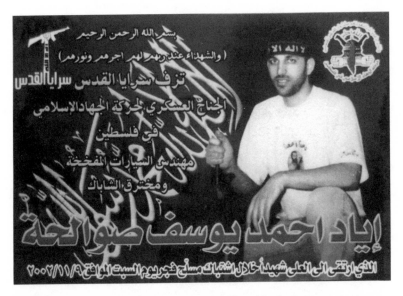

One of several posters for Eyad Sawalha distributed in the Jenin area.

arrested and spent eighteen days in administrative detention. After he moved to Qalandia he became more closely connected with larger groups of activists and activists from different regions. His mother reports that many of his friends were killed during the intifada, especially in the Nablus area. Later during the intifada Eyad joined al-Fahad al-Aswad (Black Panthers).[9] During his time with al-Fahad al-Aswad, Eyad became active in interrogating alleged collaborators and setting up ambushes for the Israeli army in the Jenin area, especially the army base near 'Arraba known as Tudan. Eyad was carrying a piece of a weapon called a *gallila*. Eyad was accused of killing the *mukhtar*[10] of Jabaa', a village across the valley from Kufor Ra'i (Eyad's village). Eyad's mother says that he "did not kill him, but the man had a heart attack during the interrogation." Eyad was arrested on 9 June 1992. After confessing to carrying weapons, shooting at the Israeli army, and interrogating collaborators, he was sentenced to two life sentences by the Israeli army court.

Um Eyad says that Eyad was in solitary confinement and subjected to torture for six months during his sentence: "There was a constant red light shining on his face, after a while his ears were dripping liquid, he almost lost his sight, and the handcuffs remained on his arms. He stayed in this condition for a long time and was not released out of this torture

until after a long campaign that involved the Red Cross and Arab members of the Israeli Knesset, like . . . who got involved through the Red
Cross. I was always running around and writing to people and getting
people and institutions involved until I got him out of solitary confinement." In jail Eyad shifted his affiliation from Fatah to Islamic Jihad.
Jihad reports in a booklet released after Eyad's assassination that the
shift started through a friendship that Eyad developed with one of Jihad's
members in Jnaid jail, and that he then learned more about Jihad and
Islamic thought and ideology during his time in Asqalan jail, where he
read *kayfa nata'amel ma'a al-Qur'an* (How Do We Treat the Qur'an), a
dialogue between Muhammed Ghazali and Omer Obeid Hasaneh, and
al-mustakhlas fi tazkiyat al-anfus: nazariya mutakamila fi tazkiyat an-nufous
(The Extracts of the Purification of Selves: A Comprehensive Theory in
the Purification of Selves) by Said Hawwa.

Eyad did not declare his change of allegiance to Islamic Jihad and kept
his official membership in good standing with Fatah so that he could be
included in prisoner releases as part of the Oslo process. His mother
noticed a change in his behavior; he started praying and fasting but
would not tell her about his organizational shift while he was in prison.
The release of prisoners during Oslo mainly included Fatah members, a
few from other PLO factions (the left), and rarely any representation
from Islamic groups like Hamas or Jihad. These selective releases, coordinated between Israel and the PA, were driven by the PA's needs for
soldiering to build security apparatuses. The activists of the intifada, and
mainly those of Fatah, were the primary pool from which the PA built its
security structures. Eyad was released from prison on 9 September 1999.

The Violent Profile

When Eyad was released from jail he was planning a mission along with
a friend he had met in jail, Mu'tasem, from the village of 'Anabta west of
Nablus. Their mission was to kidnap Israeli soldiers and use them as a
bargaining chip to secure the release of Palestinian prisoners, especially
those with Islamic group affiliation, who were not included in releases
connected to the Oslo process. A few months after his release Eyad
traveled to Mecca in December 1999 for Omra,[11] and a few weeks after
his return he enrolled in Shahid Abu Jihad College in Nablus. According
to his family the PA paid his enrollment fees. He had told his family that

he was training as a jeweler (his mother made a gesture that suggests that he was fooling them). He spent a year at the college. "Who knows where else he was enrolled at the time," his mother wondered.

Eyad spent time looking for a cave where he could hide the Israeli soldiers he was planning to kidnap. The start of the second intifada in September 2000 led to direct, daily confrontations with the Israeli army, and Eyad began to set up ambushes of Israeli army vehicles, mainly on the road from Jenin to Nablus. His family reports that after a while the Israelis cleared the sides of the roads of trees and shrubs, making it difficult to get close enough to the road to harm the army, so Eyad decided to move to the Tulkarem area to join Mu'tasem in his activities there. Mu'tasem at the time was already "wanted" by the Israeli army.

The Israeli Secret Service, Shabak, went after both Eyad and Mu'tasem and recruited one of their friends, Murad Abu el-'Asal, to spy on them. According to Eyad's family, the Shabak recruited Murad by offering him a permit to work in Israel. Murad apparently was very close to Eyad and told him about the recruiting process. Eyad instructed him to play along and so he did. (Um Eyad made some gestures to indicate that Murad had some mental problems.) Murad was used by Eyad to give confusing information about himself and his friend, Mu'tasem, to the Shabak. The Shabak would search Murad every time he met with them and checked under his shirt. After repeatedly asking Murad to give details of how he was searched when he met with the Israeli officers, Eyad set a small bomb made of three hundred grams of TNT in Murad's underwear. In the next meeting with Murad the bomb was not detected by the Israeli officers. Murad set off the bomb while in a car with the two Israeli officers in the village of Taybeh west of Tulkarem, across the 1967 border. Eyad's family and Islamic Jihad report that the Shabak officers in the car were killed along with Murad.

In retaliation for this episode Israel launched an air attack on Tulkarem that targeted Mu'tasem's house with missiles, killing him and destroying the house. Eyad's mother reports that the loss of Mu'tasem "burned" Eyad. After the killing of Mu'tasem, Eyad printed T-shirts with Mu'tasem's picture and the words *wa'adan wa ahdan* (a promise and a pledge) on the top and *lan nansaka abadan* (we will never forget you) on the bottom. From that time Eyad shifted his attention away from conventional ambushes targeting Israeli army convoys to martyrdom operations. By then Eyad was already on the run and was no longer able to be active while blending into the community for cover. Resorting to martyr-dom operations became the "appropriate" method of engagement from Eyad's perspective, his father explained.

Two months after the invasion of Jenin and a sustained Israeli as-sassination campaign that claimed the lives of many of Eyad's friends—especially since the assassinations concentrated on his organization, Islamic Jihad, and Hamas—Eyad set up some of the most lethal car bombs that exploded in Israel. This was a new strategy: using a car allowed for bigger bombs than could be detonated by a bomber wearing an explosive belt. Eyad organized two major bus bombings that inflicted enormous damage. The first targeted an Israeli bus at Megiddo Junction on 5 June 2002 using a car loaded with a hundred kilograms of explo-sives. The car was driven to the bus and set off by Hamzi al-Sammoudi. The explosion destroyed the bus and killed seventeen Israelis, mostly soldiers, and injured forty-two others. The second bombing occurred at Kirkuk Junction on 12 October 2002, where two Palestinians drove a car set up with explosives into an Israeli bus and exploded it. Fourteen Israelis were killed along with the two Palestinians who carried out the mission, Ashraf al-Asmar and Muhammad Hasanain, and fifty-six others were injured.

After the Israeli assassination of Salah Shehadeh, Hamas's leader in Gaza, by an air strike with missiles at an apartment building that killed fifteen Palestinian residents in addition to Shehadeh, Eyad rigged a car with five hundred kilograms of explosives to blow up one of Tel Aviv's high-rise buildings, to match the Israeli strike on Gaza in both form and magnitude—a goal that is consistent with the mimetic nature of the violence performed by Palestinians. The Israeli police caught the car in the Khedara area on its way to Tel Aviv after chasing it because of suspi-cions that it might be stolen, thus preventing an explosion with cata-strophic capabilities.[12]

The Position of the Family

While Eyad was on the run the Israeli army searched his family's house nearly twenty times, according to Eyad's family. One time they exploded the doors of the house (Eyad told his family not to fix them because the army would ultimately demolish the house). Um Eyad would verbally stand up to the Israelis when they came to search the house. Abu Eyad said that one time an Israeli officer told him, "Aren't you a man? She should shut up. You talk." The Israelis held up and arrested his mother and sister several times. Um Eyad reports that one time family members were held at the 'Arraba junction near Jenin and the Israeli army officer told her, "We will keep you here. Eyad will come to look for you and we will kill him." She said that she told them, "In your wildest dreams. My son knows his mother and knows your tactics." She said she challenged the soldier to face him instead of taking her and her daughter: "If he is arrested he is in God's guard, and if he gets martyrdom the pride is mine." Eyad's younger brother, who was present at the interview, had been arrested and released four times. Two days after my interview I learned that he was arrested yet again.

On the night of 21 April 2001 over twenty-five Israel soldiers came to Eyad's family home to demolish it. The family claims that everything in the house that was Eyad's survived the demolition of the house, his framed picture lying in the rubble unbroken, his clothes and his engagement ring found intact (Um Eyad now wears his engagement ring). "Everything that is his came out intact, our belongings were burnt," Um Eyad asserted. This account circulates within the community and creates a social understanding that a higher power is working on the side of the fighters.

During the interview Um Eyad kept saying niyyaluh[13] while talking about Eyad's tales or describing him. She seemed proud of Eyad and his accomplishments, even though he was her only son who did not complete high school and did not enroll in the university. His older brothers are all university graduates or students, and his sisters are either married or at school. Most attended the university. Um Eyad feels that "Eyad brought the best certificate." He is being glorified in an Islamic Jihad booklet that honors him as the engineer, the leader. His mother said, "He earned his engineering degree." Two weeks after the demolition of his family's house Eyad was caught and killed by the Israeli army in the old part of Jenin.

Ragheb Jaradat

I spoke with Ragheb's father, mother, and sister at their home in Jenin in March 2004. Their house is decorated with pictures of Ragheb, who had gone to a local photographer and made several nice pictures of himself a week before his mission.

Personal Profile

Ragheb was born in 1985 to a middle-class family. His father owns a pharmacy in Jenin. Ragheb lived very comfortably. His father asserted, "He did not need a thing. Our financial situation is good." Ragheb had two brothers in universities abroad. His family reports that Ragheb was a good student throughout his school years. From first grade until the first term of twelfth grade Ragheb was the first in his class. In the second term of twelfth grade he was doing poorly, and his teachers were baffled about the sudden change in his performance. His family described him as very personable and helpful to others. He used to open their pharmacy by himself and operate it, which he was fully trained to do. His father stated that Ragheb would not let him go to work during the times of unrest and would insist on running the business by himself. While the father was describing Ragheb's personality, his mother started crying.

Activist Profile

Ragheb was not politically active in any group. The only sign of political activity that his family noticed was that a few months before his mission he started hanging the posters of martyrs in the house. Yet Um Ragheb recalled that during Ragheb's early childhood, in the intifada years, an Israeli soldier harassed Ragheb: "He was in the entryway of the house. He was only four years old. One soldier held his head and twisted his whole head and told him, 'Don't you become a terrorist.' " When Ragheb was six, a play about the intifada was staged at his kindergarten's summer camp. According to his teacher, Ragheb would not accept any role other than that of the martyr.

Once there was a funeral in the village for someone whose body had been held by the Israelis for some time. Upon the return of the body Ragheb composed a speech that he read at the funeral. His family stated that this was the only time they saw Ragheb involved in a political activity, and it seemed to have affected him. Like other episodes—an assassination, the destruction of a home, a large-scale attack on a city that

Ragheb Jaradat playing the role of martyr in a kindergarten play at the age of six. Courtesy of Ragheb's family.

forces people to smuggle food supplies from the villages—the funeral of a martyr is a site where new commitments are forged. It is a site where the impact of the martyr's life is most pronounced and where participants are best able to imagine and connect with the life of the martyr.

Martyrdom and Sacrifice

Judging from accounts of discussions that he had with his family the day before the operation and comments that he made regarding his surprisingly bad performance in the twelfth grade, Ragheb seems to have placed a high value on martyrdom. His mother told him once, "With these grades you will live between the feet of your brothers who are all doctors." He replied to her, "By God, my certificate will be better than their certificates." The principal of his school had also talked with him about his grades and he told the principal, "I promise you, Uncle Abu Yusef, that I will get a certificate that you will take pride in." The "certificate" is highly valued in Palestinian culture, and a university diploma is a well-regarded credential to which Palestinian youth and their families aspire. All parents want to see their kids succeed and have a certificate.

From the 1960s to the 1980s the Palestinians were known for having a high percentage of university graduates.[14] A high social value is still placed on gaining a certificate, even though many Palestinian graduates no longer find employment opportunities that enable them to put their certificates to good use.

The Arabic word for "certificate" is *shahadah*, derived from the noun *shahid* ("witness") and the verb *shahada* ("to witness"). The shahadah certificate is a form of witnessing or certifying an accomplishment. Related words include *musha'hada* ("seeing," past tense *sha'hada*) and *istishhad* (martyrdom). Shahadah (martyrdom) is dying for the *shahadatayn* (dual of *shahadah*) and is the first pillar of Islam. *Shahada* (they bear witness) that there is no God but Allah and that Muhammad is his messenger. In early Islamic wars the goals were to get the other side to recognize and state the shahadatayn, after which they become Muslims. When a Muslim recognizes that death is imminent he or she recites the shahadatayn. Saying *istashhada* (he was martyred) means he stated the shahadatayn, that is, he said *ashhadu an la ilaha illa allah wa anna muhamadan rasulu allah* (I witness that there is no God but Allah and that Muhammad is Allah's messenger). The word *shahid* (martyr) was originally applied to a person who died witnessing the shahadatayn and in pursuit of the shahadatayn from others. Today anyone who dies fighting the "enemy" is considered shahid. So the two meanings of *shahadah*—"certificate" and "martyrdom"—are both indications of socially appreciated accomplishments. When Ragheb assured the principal of his school "I will get a certificate that you will take pride in," he sized up the two certificates in his mind and assigned a much higher value to the certificate of martyrdom. This is a common belief in Palestine today, since diminished job opportunities have made the university certificate more valuable in social terms than economic terms.

Ragheb left two notes before his death, one addressed to the Palestinian public through Islamic Jihad and the other to his family, his father in particular. In the note to his family Ragheb wrote:

Father hear me . . . Hear the echo of my voice . . .

I am alive between the people . . . Fighting . . . In spite of my death . . .

No, I did not die . . . I now started living . . . Along with the beloved in heaven . . .

Here we clearly see the life of the martyr through the impact of the sacrificial performance. Being "alive . . . in spite of . . . death" brings the martyr a form of living in death, a preferred form of living over the crippled present life. Ragheb sees himself fighting in spite of his death, and further sees that his strength in death is more than what he can project in his living life. Conceptualized as such, death becomes something not feared but a form of living that is more meaningful than life of the physical sort. In this context, death is about living, and to die is to live. The sacrifice of the body and its *concentration* through the performance of this form of violence against the backdrop of the encounter with Israel and its histories is a concentration of the *sacrificer*, here the social person performing the sacrifice. Thus the social person is made an icon through the sacrifice of his body. Hubert and Mauss (1964) note that the sacrificer is the moral person whose conditions are modified by the sacrifice for bearing the cost of sacrifice. The istishhadi, the performer, is idealized. This concentration is further extended to the community at large through its representation in posters produced for the istishhadi, the distribution of the istishhadi's picture, the documentation and narration in booklets of his or her life, the poetry and obituaries that idealize them, and so on. All of these representations produce an iconic image of the istishhadi that concentrate the social person in a way parallel and complementary to the concentration of the body through the ritual of sacrifice as performed through the application of the martyrdom operation.

Not only does this form of living make the social person alive in the immediate community, but as we see in Ragheb's message, there is a consciousness of the broader ability of the life of the martyr to shape the cultural order at national, regional, and potentially global levels, an ability that "begins" with the dying of the body. Thus the conceptual space that the martyr's life occupies is much wider than the physical and social space that the person occupies in life. It is primarily this social life of the martyr that is constructed in the cultural discourse of martyrdom, in the poetics of the resistance that makes death through sacrifice sought after. As martyrs become immortalized in the representations and the poetics that these representations produce, the Palestinian *people*, whom these icons signify, become immortalized. Hence the immortalization of martyrs' physical fusion in the land of Palestine through the "blood

covenant" of sacrifice becomes an immortalization of Palestinian peoplehood and the rootedness of the Palestinian nation in the land of
Palestine.

Most martyrdom mission carriers are described, like Ragheb, with a
heightened sense of awareness, as thoughtful rather than impulsive actors. Thus it is not surprising that martyrdom operations carriers should
often be characterized as above the norm in personal qualities and intelligence, though this pattern has puzzled some observers of the Palestinian resistance (Reuter 2004). A public opinion survey by Khalil Sheqaqi
points out that approval of violence rises with the level of education
among Palestinians.[15]

The cultural life of the martyr in the social world is distinct from the
other life promised by the Divine in heaven. It is precisely this cultural
life that explains why both Islamic and secular groups organize martyrdom operations and both religious and nonreligious individuals carry
then out. Most participants, including Ragheb, believe in an afterlife in
heaven, but I find that the cultural life of the martyr is most prominent in
the motivation process. It is about the life in the living world and not
about the lives of the dead. People can "go to heaven" many different
ways, and they can do so without giving up their present life. In contrast,
the cultural life of the martyr with the capacity to extend well beyond the
biological life of the body and the present social life of the person can
only be achieved through the sacrifice of the body. This makes the act of
martyrdom connected more to the cultural discourse of its poetics rather
than to the belief in life in heaven. This cultural discourse is materialized
through the various cultural productions for every martyrdom operation:
news of the performance, a political statement from a group claiming
responsibility, and the process of placing the act in a political context
through posters, postcards, five-day funerals, booklets about the martyr,
stories about the martyr told at his or her funeral, obituaries, poetry, and
political commentaries in the media, all of which create the new life of
the martyr.

The Night of the Mission

During the battle in the Jenin Refugee Camp in the first week of April
2002, Ragheb was fasting. His father recalled, "One evening he brought

a Pomila[16] and he said, 'I want to peel this for my father.' He sat next to me and wanted to get close to me." Abu Ragheb continued:

On Tuesday, April 9, he came in the late afternoon and had a new Marines haircut. He told his mom, "I need to take a shower." So I decided I am going to get on his case about this Marines haircut. He came out of the shower and I forgot. He was wearing jeans and a long white undershirt. He is tall and wide so one of my cousins was around and said, "By the grace of God, what a body!" Ragheb said, "This body impresses you; this body will impress you tomorrow." He called his brothers in the Ukraine and Jordan and he told them: "Do not forget the Jenin Camp." In the evening he broke his fast, which was strange for us that he had fasted on a Tuesday. About the 'asha[17] time before he left he asked me if I wanted cigarettes or anything and he asked his mother whether she wanted anything and she said, "No." I told him just come back by 9:00 or 9:30; he said, "insh'allah (God willing)." Apparently he had stopped by his cousins and had tea with them. He also stopped by his aunts. About 11:00 p.m. I got worried about him as he did not return yet. I got all the kids of the neighborhood looking for him and asking about him and no one knew where he was.

The dynamics described above of Ragheb's preparedness to carry out the operation reveal a sense of excitement for the moment. His remark that "this body . . . will impress you tomorrow," alluding to his plans to offer his body in sacrifice, reveals his excitement at being a moral person who would gain new social status for bearing the cost of the sacrifice.

The Operation

Ragheb was dropped off by a fairly new car next to a bus stop near Haifa where many army personnel take the bus. He was dressed in an Israeli army uniform. Ragheb cocked the gun as he got on the bus to Jerusalem.[18] He carried on him an Israeli army card and an Israeli army bus pass. Ragheb knew little Hebrew. His family said that according to the Israeli media a female soldier was exchanging looks with him on the bus. Abu Ragheb says, "The girl told the press that she was planning to get off the bus wherever Ragheb gets off in order to meet him and hook up with him. She reports that he was chewing gum and flirting with her through blowing bubbles and exchanging looks with her." Ragheb stayed on the bus for about twenty-five kilometers before he detonated himself. The explosion killed twenty-two Israelis and Ragheb.

The Aftermath of the Operation

Normally, shortly after the organizing faction reveals the identity of the mission carrier, hundreds of people from the town gather at the mission carrier's home and begin the process of making the carrier an icon. Abu Ragheb described how the family learned about the operation and then found out that the mission carrier was their son:

> On Wednesday morning, the next morning we heard on radio Monte Carlo that there was a suicide bombing in Haifa. Even though I am convinced that my son wouldn't do such an operation, but when I heard the news, it was as if you have dumped cold water on my back. A doctor who is a friend of mine called in a joking manner and said, "Do you believe that your son Ragheb carried out this operation?" He asked where Ragheb was, and I said Ragheb had slept outside the house. My friend said I was joking and that he did not believe the people. He told people, "I know this boy and he cannot kill a chicken." I felt that my head was split. The phone dropped from my hand. Within minutes there were over two hundred people in the house. For us our God has dignified us, he gave us this goodness, I had worked hard in raising him. I spoiled him. I did everything for him.

Um Ragheb's first reaction: "For me it didn't occur to me at first. I was very pleased when I heard about the operation. But later me and this daughter [pointing to her daughter present at the interview], we started exchanging looks of suspicion. Once I realized it is Ragheb, I made coffee and made tea, and kissed the hand and the head of Abu Ragheb . . . I swear I did not weep over him; I did not pull my hair, nothing." Um Ragheb sought to demonstrate control over her emotions toward the death of her son because the death of a martyr is not supposed to be a sad thing. However, she did cry during my interview with her. Her repeated insistence that she demonstrated control, even as she was in tears while narrating her experiences, points to the polarization that is created in the performance. Ragheb's funeral was to be celebrated like a wedding. These polarizations generate the poetics, a cultural force, by means of which new meanings are sought and formulated. They are lived not only by Ragheb's family but also by the community at large that mourns him and celebrates him at the same time. The struggle to balance the cultural expectation of restraint, pride in the son's or daughter's act, and the emotions brought on by loss is strongly felt among most of the families I interviewed, especially mothers. Um Ragheb stated: "If he had told me that he wanted to go, I wouldn't have let him. Our religion says that if martyrdom is accepted then he will go to heaven. At his funeral I carried his picture and walked out in the street. There were some men who were crying. But for me, God gave me patience. My sister was crying. I told her: 'Stop it, he is a martyr.'" Today she wears a gold pendant with Ragheb's picture inscribed on it. She says that Ragheb stays with her all the time: "His voice stays in my ears while I am awake and through my sleep. I see him a lot in my sleep."

After the operation much of the discussion at the funeral and at gatherings at the homes of the mission carrier's relatives focuses on where the operation took place, how many were killed, and who got killed. The people in the village describe the fluctuation in numbers and who were among the dead. Ragheb's family reports that according to Israeli papers the total number of people killed was eighteen. Then the number is changed to twenty-one. It is later reported that four of the wounded died later, bringing the total to twenty-five. According to an Israeli press report one of the soldiers killed in the operation was just leaving Jenin after the invasion and being sent home, having been relieved of duty. Another report states that among the dead was the daughter of the Israeli ambassador to the UN, and that the Palestinian ambassador to the UN had offered her father his condolences. These narrations and descriptions make the event more meaningful: it reached one of the soldiers in Jenin and the daughter of one of Israel's top diplomats, and it killed twenty-five Israelis the week after the invasion of Jenin, where the operation was planned and from which it was sent out. The more the act reaches the Israeli political system and its army personnel, the more legitimate it becomes in the perpetrator's locale. However, the meaning is not limited to the application of mimetic violence. Other operations performed in a civilian setting become more meaningful and carry a wider impact, as I will explore in looking into the dynamics of the operations.

The Israeli army arrested Abu Ragheb on 17 April 2002 and held him for three days. Abu Ragheb describes the arrest:

When they came to the house they took Ragheb's poster down from the wall and the officer told me, "I am captain Jamal. I destroyed Jenin." He said to me, "Your son is a terrorist." He said, "Your Qur'an is fake." He said, "This Qur'an that says Moses rather than Israel is the book that taught you terrorism." I said to the soldier, "He is not a terrorist. He is not a terrorist." He asked me, "Why didn't I look after my son?" I said that he was a good boy and nobody ever complained about him. There was no reason for me to keep an eye on him. Then the soldier opened Ragheb's room, searched it, and didn't find anything. They took whatever documents they found in the house, our land titles, our marriage certificate, and so on.

When he took the poster down he said: "Get up," I said "Where to?" He said, "I want to take you and teach you a lesson the hard way." I said, "I need to go to the bathroom." The solider said, "If there is another operation, from al-Sileh I will tear down your house, I will burn your pharmacy, and explode your car."

Um Ragheb added: "The soldier said to me, 'You are his mother, you brought a terrorist.' "

The narration of these encounters is in itself a source of social prestige. People hear their stories about facing the Israelis and enduring harassment, which are seen as signs of courage and heroism that add to the family's heightened social status. The narrations also add to the life of the martyr that *begins* in the community after his death. This life, which starts with the martyrdom operation and continues with the funeral procession, is represented in posters, poetry, booklets, and statements issued by the sponsoring organization, in graveside memorials, and in the cultural poetics that create a new life for the martyr. This new life takes its own course, partly material and partly imagined, within which new meanings emerge.

The Meaning Making

After his operation, the posters of Ragheb pointing a gun filled the walls of his village. One of these posters still hangs on the front window of his father's pharmacy in Jenin. His friend, his teachers, and local poets wrote poems of his martyrdom. The posters, the funeral procession, the bulk of literature produced about the mission after his death—whether by the organizing groups or by local poets, friends, and teachers—all build the iconic status of the martyr and give his act meaning beyond the goals of the organizing group. The organizing group often refers to the operation as retaliatory violence in response to Israeli state violence. In this case the operation immediately followed the invasion of Jenin, and the enormous destruction and killing of over sixty Palestinians that the city suffered during the invasion.

Islamic Jihad titled this operation 'amaliyyat kasr al-sour al-waqi (the Breaking of the Protective Wall Operation). The message is being conveyed to the state of Israel, to Israelis, and to the Palestinians that the wall erected by Israel will not be its savior and, more importantly, that Palestinians can break out of confinement and siege. In the words of the Jihad statement:

> We emphasize the ability of our heroic warriors to penetrate and break all the security barriers of the criminal enemy, and no wall or fence will bar us from reaching the enemy's security depth.
>
> Saraya al-Quds[19] emphasize that this heroic qualitative operation is part of our painful retaliation to the massacres in Jenin, Nablus, Bethlehem, and Hebron.

The statement by the organizing group sets out the meaning-making process. Every operation has a title. The reference to the ability to "penetrate and break" barriers is a formulation that connects the bodily practice of sacrifice and violence to conceptions of unconfined life, unsegmented peoplehood, and unfragmented Palestine. These aesthetics create a polarization between on the one hand the ontological conditions of encapsulation and fragmentation and on the other hand the unity and freedom of Palestinians and Palestine. Statements like this one normally contain other information regarding political goals as well as sensory meanings. But statements are only the beginning of the meaning-making process. The broader cultural productions in the poetics of resistance and the commentaries broaden these meanings, reflecting a wide range of perspectives. In the statement quotes above Islamic Jihad gives the operation several meanings: political goals as a challenge to the geographic isolation and encapsulation that Israel is imposing on the Palestinians by building a wall; retaliatory violence in response to Israeli attacks on Palestinians in Jenin, Nablus, and Hebron; and the challenge to Israeli identity itself. The term "hitting in Israel's security depth" came up again and again in my interviews with Brigades members. The strikes on

Israel's secure spots—the inner city, the transit systems—are seen as a challenge to the whole presence of Israel and its normalcy in Palestine. Since the territorial violence is a battle over which people occupy the territory, disturbing the normal life of the Israelis who occupy these places poses a challenge to Israel's identity itself. The challenge to Israeli identity in these contested places is an assertion of Palestinian identity. Thus the operation takes on a sociopolitical space and a cultural meaning beyond the instrumentality of the act and the organizing group.

Poems evoked by the events, each from the point of view of a different writer, put the act in a context and attach other meanings to it. A local resident from the nearby village of Berqin wrote in a poem that was published in a booklet about Ragheb:

> The lion of Jaradat[20] as a volcano rocked them
> and returned the Rabbi of Zion to his past.
> Reminded by the fear shocked in his Khayber,[21]
> There in no longer a bunker in the volcano to save him.
> The Rabbi of Zion is fearful, hysterical,
> no longer knows the sleep in his night.
> Oh, Ragheb of the glory, my poem when I write it for you,
> I feel my heart beat in it.
> Welcome to your courage, welcome to your stand,
> About your glory the lips of the flowers will tell.
>
> You exploded yourself, belief and sacrifice,
> the vengeance awakens in the highest of its meanings.
> And the bird chirped his peek in happiness,
> Oh the Sila[22] of glory in the arms hug him.
> The olive trees of Berqin in the valleys were whispered
> by the winds, and they were told to kiss him.
> The sanabel[23] of wheat sang wheat tones,
> and the flowers rejoiced dancing to the rhythm.
> Here Palestine returns, in spite of the chains,
> to hug him and to form a ring of flowers to gift him.

In most of the poetry about martyrdom operations two themes are prominent: the heroism of mimetic, retaliatory violence; and the landscape. The retaliation is an opportunity to apply the same violence that is presented by continued Israeli practices. The violence of martyrdom operations projects terror on broader Israeli society that mirrors the fear that Palestinians experience because of Israeli state violence. The landscape dimension is related to the historical Palestinian positioning of the act of sacrifice for the land of Palestine.

The poem carries the consistent theme of *penetrating barriers*, as exemplified in the volcano. The wheat singing, the flowers dancing, the wind telling the olive trees to kiss Ragheb—all are images depicting the happiness of Palestine (in the cultural imaginary) for the sacrifice. This happy life comes to Palestine through the exchange of the martyr's blood to nourish the plants and make the birds happy. Ragheb is placed in a homological relationship with the land of Palestine as his body parts transform into corresponding parts of Palestine. The last two lines of the poem—"Here Palestine returns, in spite of the chains, to hug him and to form a ring of flowers to gift him"—mean that the captivity of Palestine did not prevent her from taking the Palestinian sacrificer into her soil, and that she will reciprocate by blooming a ring of flowers, continuing the poetic relationship between the Palestinians and the land of Palestine in spite of captivity and isolation. The notion of unity with the land is illustrated in the image of Palestine hugging the martyr. The scene of joyous Palestine renaturalizes Palestine, reunites it, and presents it as being full of mercy and love to its people, the Palestinians. Palestine is also appreciative of the heroes who sacrificed for her. These meanings assert a sense of conceptual rootedness in a Palestine from which Palestinians have been uprooted and excluded, and the unity of Palestinians and Palestine in the face of fragmentation and segmentation. Thus the polarization of sensory meanings and political goals pronounced through the application of violence generates a poetics through which a fusion occurs. This fusion in the Palestinian context is a fusion of Palestinian lives in land (of Palestine) and history (of Palestine), achieved through the violent sacrifice of a Palestinian body and violence against Israelis that disturbs their sense of normalcy.

Hanadi Jaradat

The first operation three days after my arrival in Palestine was carried out by Hanadi, from Jenin, in the coastal city of Haifa on 4 October 2003.

She exploded herself in Maxim restaurant overlooking the Mediterranean Sea. The explosion killed twenty-one Israeli restaurant patrons and injured fifty more. The information I present here about Hanadi's history and mission is based on an interview with Hanadi's family in Jenin in addition to a review of responses and commentaries in the Palestinian and Arab media, most of which was also recirculated in Palestine as handouts by activist groups.

Personal Profile

Hanadi was born on 22 September 1975 in the city of Jenin and grew up in Jenin city. She attended school in Jenin and she graduated from the law school at Jarash University in Jordan in 1999. Hanadi worked for two law offices in Jenin over the span of three years as a trainee lawyer. Her family described her as kind, loving, concerned about others, outgoing, and articulate. She was an opinionated person who defended her views. Her family describes her as resolute; when she set her mind on something she followed through. She did not engage in any formal political activities before taking on the mission. She held a "typical" Palestinian political position that "this land is ours and our rights to it will be restored at some point."[24]

Her father, Abu Hanadi, was born in the Palestinian city of Bissan[25] in the northern Jordan Valley before it was depopulated of its Palestinian residents in 1948. Her mother, Um Hanadi, comes from the Palestinian town of Zir'in, in the central plains north of Jenin. The village also was depopulated of its Palestinian residents by Jewish militias in 1948 and subsequently destroyed by the Israeli army (Khalidi 1992). Abu Hanadi explained that he was too young when the family was forced out of Bissan to remember life there, but his father constantly talked about it, so a picture of life in Bissan has always been a vivid image in his life. He in turn always talked about Bissan to his children. Abu Hanadi became active in the Popular Front for the Liberation of Palestine in the early 1970s. During six years of activism he was arrested by the Israelis several times, and Hanadi as well as two of her sisters were born while their father was in Israeli jails.

After the activism period Abu Hanadi focused on working to provide for his growing family. He described working hard to improve their economic situation, but they were constantly under the pressure of making ends meet and coming up with rent for their apartment. The family had seven girls and two boys. The eldest boy, Fadi, quit school early to help the family, especially after the father became ill and unable to work. Fadi provided enough money for Hanadi to go to college in Jordan. She was the smartest of the children, with consistently good grades. The family was excited for Hanadi's university education. She graduated in the summer of 1999. Hanadi got engaged to one of her cousins in 2000. Her fiancé was killed by the Israeli army in the beginning of the second intifada.

Her father became severely ill with a liver ailment and needed medical treatment that was not available at the local hospital. Hanadi tried to get him a permit for treatment at the Israeli Rumbum hospital in Haifa and was repeatedly turned down by the Israeli military coordination office in nearby Salem. The father, accompanied by his wife, left for medical treatment in Jordan. The family had a cousin, Saleh, who had been on the run from the Israeli army for several years, charged with being a local leader of Islamic Jihad. Saleh had a wife and a toddler whom he had seen only a few times, both of whom lived in the village of Al-Sila al-Harthiya. While Hanadi's parents were in Jordan for medical treatment, Saleh's wife and her child came to Hanadi's home in Jenin to meet her husband. While they were sitting at the front doorsteps of Hanadi's home, an Israeli special force unit surprised them with gunfire that killed Saleh and Hanadi's brother, Fadi.

The details of this incident were narrated by Hanadi herself in an interview with a local website (AbrarY) after the assassination on 13 June 2003 that was recirculated after Hanadi's martyrdom:

Saleh came to our house to visit his wife and child. We sat in front of the house as normal. We were drinking coffee and he, Saleh, was playing with his son, hugging him and kissing him when a white car with an Arab license plate was passing by. The car suddenly stopped. I thought it must be some of Saleh's friends. Two men came out of the car and directly started shooting at Saleh. Another car came in a flash and started shooting. We all went down on the ground. Saleh's wife grabbed her son and ran into the house. My brother was wounded and bleeding. I held his arm and started pulling him to cover behind the seat we were sitting at to shield him from the bullets. I started screaming Fadi, Saleh. Fadi was asking with difficulty help me, help me . . .

[After fifteen minutes of tearful crying, she continued:]

One of the armed men came over me and threw me down on the ground, he took Fadi from me and told me, "Go inside to the house or I'll kill you" . . . I screamed, "Leave me, this is my brother, he needs help, he is bleeding" . . . They attacked and asked, "Where is his weapon?" I said he has no weapon, by God he is going to die!!! . . . They forced me down on the ground with the gun on my head and face on the ground. One of them said, "You bitch, you terrorist, we'll kill you with them." . . . Then I heard one saying, "Pull them and pile them to the side here." . . . I could not bear, I started resisting and screaming, "You terrorists, you dogs, leave them! Leave them!" . . . They hit me and threw me down to the ground again, dragged both of them a few meters, shot several shots again to insure their death.

The Israeli army simultaneously launched an attack on the city of Jenin as a whole, concentrating on the Dabbus neighborhood where the assassinations were carried out to provide cover for the safe exit of the army's special unit. In the attack the Israeli army stormed the neighborhood with gunfire and three other Palestinians were wounded, among them a young girl. Hanadi asserted to her interviewers that the units that held her surrounded the house and went through it; they could have simply arrested her brother but were determined to kill him. She described the bodies of Saleh and Fadi filled with gunshots from all sides. According to another report from the same site Hanadi is reported to have called a zaghruda[26] during her brother's funeral and declared, "His blood will not be shed in vain. The killers will pay the price. We will not keep crying alone. Damn the whole world if our people will continue to be denied freedom and dignity." These words were echoed four months later in Hanadi's martyrdom note.

Martyrdom and Sacrifice

Um Hanadi told me about a dialogue between Hanadi and her brother Fadi, who was killed by the Israeli army four months before Hanadi's mission. The dialogue concerned news of a martyrdom operation carried out by a girl. Hanadi asked her brother, to whom she was very close, "If this operation was by Hanadi Jaradat, what would you do?" Her brother replied, "I will fill the magazine and empty it for you,"[27] referring to the act of shooting the magazine of his M-16 gun in the air as a celebratory expression. But Hanadi's brother was killed before the mission, which she carried out in part to avenge his killing.

In the note that Hanadi left behind for her family, she explains her choice to carry out the mission:

> I have chosen this path for myself by my own determination. I have worked for this until God rewarded me with martyrdom, God willing. Martyrdom is not for every human on earth, only for those who are dignified from God. Are you sad because God has dignified me in martyrdom!? Do you repay God by what he does not like and I don't like either!? Give me to God. . . . We are all dying. No one is eternal on this earth, but the rational who gives himself to God's call. This is a *jihad* country only. We live in it for *jihad*. It is incumbent upon us to lift the oppression we live in over the past years. I know I will not bring back Palestine. I know this fully. But I also know that this is my duty and I have done my duty in front of God. I have answered the call after my belief in my religion . . .
>
> My main concern has become to see the light of God. This is his country and this is his religion and they want to extinguish his light and we know that. My duty towards God's religion and his obligation on me is to defend him. Nothing is in my possession other than this body, which I will turn into shrapnel, that will uproot the heart of everyone that tries to uproot us from our country. Everyone who plants death for us will get it even if it was a small fraction . . .

Here Hanadi expresses several aspects of her conception of martyrdom. First, martyrdom is a reward from God, which he grants to good people who gain it through their good deeds. Second, martyrdom is performed through a sense of responsibility toward ongoing events. Here the responsibility that lies with Hanadi is toward the Divine for all that she has witnessed and for her beliefs. Her assertion that it is her duty to defend God, "My duty towards God's religion and his obligation on me is to defend him," indicates her fear of the Divine's greater violence if she were to remain silent. She offers all that is in her possession—her body— to defend and express her commitment to the Divine: "Nothing is in my possession other than this body, which I will turn into shrapnel, that will uproot the heart of everyone that tries to uproot us from our country."

From another angle, the reference to the body as the only possession with which Hanadi can express herself shows how grief is expressed

through the body. As Veena Das (1997) points out, "Transactions between body and language lead to an articulation of the world in which the
strangeness of the world revealed by death, by its non-inhabitability, can
be transformed into a world in which one can dwell again, in full awareness of life that has to be lived in loss" (68–69). Hanadi expresses
through her body what she could not communicate in language. The
overwhelming suffering, accompanied by a discourse of ignorance, silence, and complicity with the conditions of suffering, makes the world
uninhabitable. The cultural meanings associated with martyrdom and
sacrifice for the land, the people, and the Divine make more life in the
loss of life. Hence the loss of life through a martyrdom operation is *dying
to live*. Dying to live describes two sensory meanings. The first is that
death is a form of living preferable to the lived life of suffering. The
preferred living is in the iconic life of the martyr in the community. This
form of living also generates new lives. This iconic image of the martyr
brings life to the community as well as the promised better life if the
sacrifice is accepted by the Divine. The second meaning is that *dying to live*
expresses love for life. Here the deep love of life in conditions that deny
life drives people to the extent of death to seek a good life worthy of
living, such as that of the idealized martyr. Through the cultural conceptions associated with the performance of sacrifice physical boundaries are broken, political boundaries are broken, psychological boundaries of fear are broken, and cultural boundaries are broken. The sacrifice
creates the naturalized Palestine pre-boundaries and pre-occupation as a
united landscape; *dying to live* this life in freedom, mercy, and unity is
achieved in the cultural imaginary. Along these cultural conceptions a
motivation for sacrifice emerges.

The Night before the Mission

In the evening Hanadi spent time with her sisters laughing, chatting, and
talking about the plans for the wedding of one of her sisters, which was
scheduled in ten days. The sisters described Hanadi as very happy for her
sister, helping her to think through her wedding plans and decide whom
to invite. Hanadi stayed up after her sisters went to bed, and read the
Qur'an for the rest of the night. When her father asked her to go to bed
she said that before doing so she wished to read the last section of the

Qur'an. At 7:30 a.m. on Saturday Hanadi left home for work. She told her mother that she would be handling a land sale in the village of Qabatiya and expected to be late, but that her mother should not worry about her.

The Operation

The operation was orchestrated by the Islamic Jihad group, the same faction with which Saleh and Hanadi's brother Fadi were associated. The operation was timed for the Jewish holiday Yom Kippur. Hanadi was set up by a Jihad member from the nearby village of Zbuba. Hanadi apparently had requested the mission, according to a leader of al-Aqsa Martyrs Brigades. He reported that Hanadi insisted on going on a mission and threatened the local Jihad leader at the time that if he did not set up an operation for her she would go with a knife to the nearest checkpoint.[28] The Israeli military was already on a state of alert—a normal procedure on Jewish holidays—but there were reports that the state of alert was heightened because the Israeli secret service had received tips that an operation in Haifa was under way.

On the afternoon of Saturday 4 October 2003, Hanadi was dropped off by a car with an Israeli license plate in front of a beachfront restaurant called Maxim in the coastal city of Haifa. There are reports that she ordered food and dined at the restaurant and paid for her dinner before detonating herself. The explosion killed twenty-one Israelis and injured fifty others. A number of children were among the Israeli victims, as was the former head of the Israeli navy, General Zai'v Almong.

The Meaning Making

As with every other mission, the meaning making begins with a statement claiming responsibility for the act. The Islamic Jihad issued a statement calling the operation "The Bride of Haifa Teaches the Zionists a Lesson They Will Not Forget." Hanadi's new title, the "Bride of Haifa," gave sensory meaning to the act and became inspirational in the meaning making for many sets of viewers. Much of the literature produced about her mission referred to her as the "Bride of Haifa," "Bride of Palestine," or "Bride of the Sea." This title has a Palestinian historical reference. The city of Haifa was known as the "Bride of Palestine" before 1948 for its vibrant cultural and economic life. This description of Hanadi as a bride offered in sacrifice to the captive Haifa, Palestine's bride, likens Hanadi's sacrifice to the ancient Egyptian ritual of sacrificing a bride to the Nile River so that the Nile would reciprocate with flood water for the Nile Valley's fields. Here the Bride of Haifa, Hanadi is sacrificed so that the city of Haifa can live as a Palestinian city.

The "Bride of Haifa" operation evoked emotions and inspired an enormous number of literary productions in Palestine and the Arab countries. I collected twenty-eight poems, obituaries, and essays published in newspapers and journals by authors from Palestine, Egypt, Syria, Lebanon, Jordan, Arabia, the United Arab Emirates, Oman, and Libya. The aesthetics of the operation contributed to the ability of the performance to permeate many spaces, where it left audiences with a curiosity that generated multiple articulations of the act. That the operation was carried out by a woman—and a mature woman, twenty-nine years old and a lawyer—made it unlikely that she had been manipulated by organizing groups. The site of the performance, on the seashore, provided a poetic, theatrical setting. The photo of the martyr released by Islamic Jihad showed her with a glowing smile, made up with deep red lipstick and facial powder, and bore a caption describing her as a bride. Hanadi's operation produced more literature because it was more influential, and it provides an example of the performative properties of violence. From their different perspectives, literary contributors contextualized the mission and attached sets of meanings to it. These meaning makings and articulations extend the force of the violence to multiple regional and global cultural spheres (Appadurai 1997; Tambiah 1996). However, it is important to point out that these contributors are not pursuing a strategy of meaning making: they are commentators in their own right, and their reactions and perspectives contribute to the articulation of a cultural discourse of martyrdom.

In what follows I present some of this literature and analyze the meaning making that is generated by it. All this literature was written and published in the Arabic language and translated into English by me.

In a piece entitled "The Seagull Returns to Haifa" by Haytham Abu el Ghozlan, the author attaches meanings related to the notions of sacrifice, renewal, and rootedness in the landscape. Here is an excerpt:

The soul earthquakes with worries and sorrow, so strong that it rips the pupils of the eyes apart, and it explodes, tearing down the walls of silence that besieged us. And the bridging waist rises and shakes to revive dead people where death has long passed, where they lived dead/alive walking in humility, shriveling leaves in a fall that awaits falling . . .

We share the wounds and the pain squeezes us. The distancing kills us longing and missing, but it does not defeat us. The knife does not slaughter us even though it is placed on our necks. The seagull is returning to Haifa, carrying the indicators of a new period. He sees Haifa by his eyes, and sees Jaffa, al-Majdal, Deir Yassin, and all of Palestine, without thorns, or fire, and without permanent sadness. In his eyes you find the shine of martyrs slaughtered from the wrist to the wrist and their tears fill out oceans and valleys but don't find who will write an obituary on their death or pity them.

The seagull returns again, shining, destroying the boundaries of misery; challenges the impossible; looks closely at the homeland, kisses its soul, does not fear it; and calls it, with calmness and revelation; bated in anomie of missing; hyper, shivering from the excitement of the meeting and the passing of the days of the open doors; the time for the harvest has come; the beating of the hope has increased; the funeral is like the wedding; ruins, shadows, and sorrow; and a wound whose red drops water our crops poems and homeland love . . .

The seagulls have returned to answer the Jerusalemite call, hugging the horizon, spreading the perfume of the poppies and sprouting the moaning of the wounds into diamond rhythm, into a morning breeze, into daisies covered behind it a journey of silence and a violent tornado, and a coffin that blooms into beautiful flowers and blood.[29]

The first paragraph presents the mission as an "earthquake" challenging the silence that "besieged" the Arab nation. It picks up on the theme of "tearing down the walls," penetrating the confinements of the ontological conditions. It presents the death of the sacrificer as a means to "revive" people who are dead in silence. The dismemberment of her body at the "waist" is to "bridge" disunited peoples. In the second paragraph the author brings out the social suffering of Palestinians subjected to Israel's violence, and takes up the issues of uprooting and displacement by talking about the pain of distancing from the Palestinian cities "Haifa," "Jaffa," and "Al-Majdal" that are now inhabited by Israelis. He makes further reference to "Deir Yassin," a Palestinian village that was the site of a massacre of its Palestinian residents in 1948, bringing out the length of the history of suffering.

Then the "seagull returns." The "seagull" represents Palestinians' lives before the establishment of Israel and the consequent displacement of the Palestinians, which deprived them of access to most of the Palestinian seashore except Gaza. Before the loss of the seashore the seagull was part of the Palestinian landscape, its image included in many Palestinian depictions of pre-Israel Palestine. Thus the seagull returning represents the Palestinians' return to Palestine, as well as the freedom of flowing, of crossing borders and barriers. The seagull "hugging the horizon" brings out senses of unity, harmony, and mercy. That Palestinians sacrifice themselves in Palestinian cities evokes a sense of belonging and rootedness in these places. The illustration of a "coffin that blooms into beautiful flowers and blood" uses cultural ideas of the martyr's blood blooming into flowers in the land, keeping alive the relationship of distanced Palestinians to the land of Palestine.

This representation is an example of a cross-cultural conception of sacrifice as a ritual sequence connected to patterns of creation. Lincoln (1991) explored similar conceptions among ancient peoples such as the Persians, Indo-Europeans, Scythians, and Celts and demonstrated how sacrifices are acts that effect transformations from the microcosm to the macrocosm. Lincoln uses the term "alloforms" to refer to dismembered parts of the sacrificed victims that create parts of the universe. There is thus a "homologic relation" between the human body and the universe. This relationship is conceived of through the breakdown of the human body and the universe into "parallel sets of their constituents parts" (Lincoln 1991, 186). Similar ideas are found in the Palestinian conceptions of martyrdom. In the excerpt above about Hanadi's mission of "tears" and "oceans," "red drops" and "water," flesh and earth in a "coffin that blooms into beautiful flowers and blood," the dismembered body parts of the martyr create a new universe in which Palestine is alive. Through the poetics in imagining the performance, sensory meanings are polarized between realities and aspirations. The polarizations are further emphasized in poetic turns of phrase: "bridging" through dismemberment; the "shine" of a "slaughtered" martyr; a "funeral" likened to a "wedding"; the "moaning of the wounds" that gives rise to "diamond rhythm," "morning breeze," and "daisies"; and the journey

of "silence" and of a "violent tornado." All these polarizations generate
poetics within which a fusion in the new generated life in the cultural
imaginary is achieved. The performance of every ritual of sacrifice by a
Palestinian martyr in the land of Palestine repeats this process of transforming "microcosm to macrocosm," shifting substance from the sacrificed body of the martyr to the "alloformic" parts of Palestine, sustaining
a Palestinian life with Palestinian characteristics against the decay of captivity and attempts at reconfiguration.

Another Palestinian writer, Rashad Abu Shawer, comments on the
mission with a political analysis that presents the mission in the context
of three primary dimensions in the production of violence: the violence
of the state of Israel, global complicity, and cultural ideas such as rootedness mediated by the performance of the mission. The piece is entitled
"Hanadi's Litigation":[30]

If Felicia Langer[31] gave up on the Zionist system, distanced herself from it,
and withered away with its citizenship so she can keep her honor as an
attorney and her concessions as human, what can the Palestinian attorney
Hanadi Jaradat do? Does she litigate in the courts of the thieves that occupy
her homeland? Should she ask for justice from her people's oppressors?
According to the articles of what law would Hanadi litigate before Sharon's,
Mofaz's, and Yalon's courts? How would she persuade the bulldozer drivers
to stop tearing down homes over the heads of their Palestinian residents?
How would she go by invoking mercy and humanistic feeling in the hearts of
the Apache leaders, and the leaders of the Markava tanks that harvest Palestinians daily and terrify their children and daughters, and humiliate them at
the roadblocks!?

Should Hanadi litigate before the Security Council? Before the representatives of the five Great Powers? By what language would Hanadi convince the
American representative of the extent of suffering and injustice that Palestinians are subjected to? The injustice that is supported by the American bless-
ing, is executed by American aircrafts, and is protected by the readiness of
the American Veto all the time?

Why are Hanadi's people denied a free homeland with a simple life where
the human has the right to drink tea with his relative, or his wife, or fiancée
under the olive tree, or a fruiting fig tree, and instead is being taken over by
death decided and executed by the occupiers? Why do Hanadi's people have
to pay daily in death, destroyed homes, uprooted trees while the Zionist

assembly continues to live near the seas of Haifa, Jaffa, and Acre, clear of
worries and relaxed in their security, feeling secure as long as their war
machine grinds the Palestinians and as long as their defense army harasses
Palestinians!?

What a litigation Hanadi exploded in Haifa. Destroying the sense of calm
from the life of a reckless human assembly that shows off carelessness,
relaxed for the wisdom of its generals, police, and security apparatuses that
sentence Palestinians based on the security needs of the settlers . . .

Hanadi's litigation is one of the Palestinian litigations that say in the
articulation of blood that the roots in this land are Arab Palestinian roots that
will be impossible to uproot. These roots are protected by sacrifice and not
by the litigation of writers, journalists, and corrupt leaders. It is time for this
litigation, Hanadi's, to be the pointer and the statement of truth in a court
hall that extends through the continents, so it is heard in the ears of the
oppressed whose moaning or complaints are not rescuing them. Hanadi is
executing Hammurabi's law and what was revealed in religious and the
humanistic laws that are absent in this Sharonite and Bushian era.

In the first paragraph the author presents the situation in which the
Palestinians find themselves locked, in their local setting, where the only
recourse is the very system that is violating their lives—the very same
system of regulations and military orders that strip Palestinians of access
to their places, restrict their life, harass them, and project enormous fear
in them. The passage brings out the daily violence that Palestinians
suffer at the hands of the Israeli army from house demolitions, tanks
that invade towns, uproot trees, and destroy fields, roadblocks, and
constant harassment and humiliation. In the second paragraph the author brings out the global system's complicity with these forms of Israeli
state violence against the Palestinians. The author implicates the UN
Security Council, which pays lip service to Palestinian complaints with a
six-decade history of not doing anything practical to stop Israel's viola-
tion of the Palestinians. He also notes the American role, in particular its
history of protecting Israel against international pressure by using its
power at the Security Council.

Abu Shawer highlights the contrast between Palestinian lives in Palestine, lives with no sense of calm, normalcy, or space to enjoy the
simplest of daily activities, and Israeli lives in *Palestine* (Haifa, Jaffa, Acre),
where Palestinian life no longer exists. He continues with Hanadi's "liti-

gation," an explosion targeting Israeli civilians whose effect is that of mimetic terror and fear projected on the Israeli public. This positioning of the martyrdom operations sets it apart from other forms of conventional violence aimed at Israeli army personnel. The targeting of civilians in public spaces threatens the entire Israeli civil order and Israel's sense of normalcy. The force of the violence permeates Israeli society and lasts well beyond the moment of impact.

Abu Shawer makes two other points: the power of cultural assertion through sacrifice and violence in a morally failing global system, and the resurgence of tradition as a form of resistance to a global order that asks a people to live with injustice. Abu Shawer regards Hanadi's mission as applying humanistic law and religious law at a time when just laws are absent. Sacrifice, traditions, and religious laws are contrasted with the uniform legal embodiment and the "new world order": "Hanadi is executing Hammurabi's law and what was revealed in religious and humanistic laws that are absent in this Sharonite and Bushian era." This positioning of the act makes clear the failure of the global system and local discontent with it, which leads to a resurgence of tradition and shapes the form of violence applied. "Hammurabi's law," the first known code of law to be inscribed in Babylon, called for al-*aynu bil ayn wa essinu bi essin wa badiu' azlam* (an eye for an eye, a tooth for a tooth, and the one who starts is the harsher), an explicit justification of violence that mimics the form of violence suffered. In Palestine the Palestinian civil order is ruined by Israeli state violence, and therefore the violence applied through martyrdom operations in Israeli public places attacks the Israeli civil order. In the absence of a system to seek justice, such old ideas can be revived and asserted, not only to deal with the "enemy" but to affect the cultural order of the society of the actors as well.

Another article from the al-*Hayat* newspaper in London by an Egyptian writer, Amin Huwaidi, comments in a piece entitled "The Bomb Hanadi":

Her grandfathers' land is occupied, its groves are being destroyed, their homes are being destroyed, her people are being killed. Cities are besieged, people are on sidewalks with no cover or food. As we know the environment forms the thoughts of people who live it . . . Hanadi found that everything is permissible. Everything is legitimate and the international legitimacy is silent and further partners with the criminals and supports them, or at least does not stop them! So what is Hanadi to do in her logic of the destroying belt as it is clear that she would be a killer and killed?! Hanadi is no longer a human like the rest of the humans. She no longer feels that she walks like a human, thinks like a human, or feels like a human. Hanadi transformed into a human bomb. Humans do transform into wolves sometimes, or into vampires, or killers sometimes. But she refused to become like Sharon and Mofaz and chose to become the bomb . . .

And you, General Sharon, when isolating the Arabs you isolate yourself. Did you gather from every place on earth to live in a walled place so you live in the walls of steel and hatred?! Where is the Maginot Line? Where is the Siegforb Line? Where is the Berlin Wall? Where is the Bar Lev Line? You jail yourself, General. You are the jailer and the prisoner exactly like the human bomb, the killer and the killed at the same time. You are building the Ghetto where your fathers and grandfathers lived. Hanadi passed all the barriers, lines, and checkpoints to hit in the depth because she knows if you have the advantage in the power scale she has the advantage in the scale of fear. If you have the exclusive rights to the aircraft and the tank she has the exclusive ownership of the human bomb. No one but her owns this weapon and it is homemade, it walks in every landscape, space, and all directions.[32]

Huwaidi anchors the mimetic act to state violence and points to the conditions to which Hanadi is subjected, in which all sorts of violence and violations against her and her people are permissible. The habitus in which people grow up can condition all kinds of violators, but Hanadi's habitus gives her act the moral high ground: she was not a killer who killed and continued to kill but one who kept her humanity by ending her life at the same time as she took the lives of others. Margalite (2002) also makes this point when he argues that Palestinian martyrdom operations are motivated by vengeance, and that by blowing themselves up Palestinian bombers assume the moral high ground. Positioned as such, the act of sacrifice gets further cultural meaning in the dynamic of the encounter with Israel and the process of differentiation from the "enemy." Huwaidi also notes the cultural power of sacrifice and how it affects the dynamic of the encounter.

In the second paragraph Huwaidi presents an argument that Islamic groups in Palestine often use to explain the political strategy of martyrdom operations. That strategy is based on achieving a balance of fear and terror with the Israelis, since the Israeli monopoly on technology prevents the Palestinians from achieving a balance of power. How this fear is to lead to a political outcome is not fully explained, but the groups argue that fear deters further violence. (I present excerpts from my discussions with these activists in chapter 6.) The theme of penetrating and breaking down confinements recurs in Huwaidi's representation of Hanadi's mission. He states that "Hanadi passed all the barriers, lines, and the checkpoints to hit in the depth." This language will resonate with Palestinians who are unable to get things done because of the state of siege, or forced to undergo the risk and hardships of checkpoints and barriers. To them, breaking barriers is a worthy and meaningful performance.

Another Palestinian woman writer, Jihad al-Rajabi, writes in "They Are the Dead, Not the Sea!!":

The Bride of Jenin lights up the sea! She perfumes the clouds that extend to our wounds, and she rains on us from the clearness of tartil.[33] Hey, Bride of Jenin, the pain is tugged by pain! Cold in the links and the warmth is moaning . . . and longing to you, you the mirror of resistance from a dawn that we do not see! We feel its calmness as you depart us quietly in the whispering of your soul.

The sons of your patient nation have no horses to carry them to you as you hover from above, a woman of jasmine! They chew the silence and silence swallows them! They concentrate in the darkness of their souls and the darkness lives in them! Ashes topped by ashes and under it ashes and the coals in them is frost that burns them!

The odor of blood intensifies in the streets of Gaza, in Jenin and Hebron! The screams intensify! And the same careless face searching for leftovers at the dining tables of the powers. Confused walking, closed eyes touching the thorns with bare hands and bent down! Not as a heavy stalk of wheat but like those who hide their head in the sand. Goes by and the years have pecked his flesh and the nights chewed his bones and made his dreams carry black rain that drowned those who are waiting![34]

In al-Rajabi's depiction we see again the imagery of freedom and breaking out of confinement as the "Bride of Jenin lights up the sea" and "perfumes the clouds" that "extend to our wounds." We also see the worship qualities of the act, which is likened to reading Qur'an in the calmness of dawn, undisturbed by the activities of the day, a ritual of the most dedicated Muslims. The dawn prayer, the dawn tartil, and the dawn tasbih have sufi qualities that permit a more intimate engagement with the Devine. The author describes the Bride of Jenin ascending to heaven, which all the grooms who hoped to seek her in marriage have no means to reach.

Al Rajabi characterizes the act as bringing "dawn that we do not see." All the attributes of this new period are not necessarily clear, but the dawn is inarguably the end of night. This image is a prominent one in contemporary Palestinian resistance, which rests on the principle that *even if the future is unknown, we have to break out of this present.* (I return to this point in chapter 6.) Al-Rajabi presents the act against the backdrop of Israeli violence. "The odor of blood intensifies in the streets of Gaza, in Jenin and Hebron!" She contrasts Hanadi's act with the silence of the Arab leaders and their "beggar" relationship to the "great" powers. These contrasts are typical of literary works inspired by martyrdom operations, as new articulations of Arab identity are distanced from "corrupt," "silent" power structures whose leaders can only close their eyes and bury their heads in the face of "heroism." The act of martyrdom is a rain that will drown them. Especially for Islamic groups, the act is thus seen as a form of liberation from corrupt political regimes and an assertion of Arab and Muslim identity.

Another commentator on Hanadi's mission sees the operation as a source of empowerment to other Palestinian communities that face challenges and threats of destruction. Imad Awada wrote a piece entitled "I Am Hanadi, Hey Rafah" in the Lebanese newspaper, *al-Safir*:

> Hanadi left with her blood. The birds chirped for her. The mothers cried and the moon sprouted grass. The jasmine massed at the windows of her wedding, the horses neighed and the procession started. The rain came, and the hearts of the flowers shivered . . .
>
> I have decided to carry the death that they surround us with to surround them with death, so I make their mothers weep tears and blood . . .
>
> Rise up, Rafah, and listen to Hanadi calling . . . Palestine is my country . . . I sacrifice for my Jerusalem with my body . . . My country is my wounds . . . Rise up Rafah . . . Rise up, Rafah, of the children I am Hanadi . . .
>
> I am who I am . . . I am Hanadi . . . I am Hanadi coming from the eyes of the rain.[35]

Here Awada presents Hanadi's mission as an example of sacrifice and resistance and calls for the residents of the city of Rafah and the Rafah refugee camp to take part in Hanadi's form of resistance. At the time, the Rafah refugee camp and the city of Rafah were experiencing a sustained campaign of home demolitions against Palestinian residents by Israel, which sought to evacuate Palestinians from near the Gaza Strip's border with Egypt. Falah (2005) presents an excellent analysis of these home demolitions and the extent of the geographic "enclavisation" that Israel hoped to obtain from these demolitions. Rafah city and camp suffered the most severe destruction of Palestinian homes and neighborhoods during the second intifada. This observation is yet another reference to mimetic violence. The mission projects onto Israelis the same fear that Palestinians experience from the state of Israel: "I have decided to carry the death that they surround us with to surround them with death."

Awada also articulates the sacrificial nature of the act, presenting images of the life that flourishes after the mission, or after Hanadi's death in sacrifice. Sacrifice entails renewal and the birth of new life. The coming of the rain, the happiness of the flower for the rain, and the chirping of the birds are not only imaginaries of life from sacrifice but also images of Palestine before Israel. These images bring to life the history of restricted access to water that led to the uprooting of hundreds of thousands of citrus trees and limited the farming and green life around it. The lack of water changed life as Palestinians knew it. The transformed landscape, the departure of birds that used to mass in the orange groves that no longer exist—these images are vivid in memories and narrations in which Israel stands as the obstacle to recovering life as it was lived.

Hanadi's mission became the medium for artistic expression beyond the Middle East. It was the subject of a multimedia work of art featured at the exhibit "Making Differences" at the Stockholm Museum of Antiquities in January 2004, which accompanied an international antigenocide conference sponsored by the Swedish government. The art, by the Israeli expatriate Dror Feiler and his Swedish wife, Ganilla Skold Feiler, was entitled "Snow White and the Madness of the Truth" and consisted of a sailboat floating in a basin of red liquid, its sail made up of an icon-shaped photo of Hanadi smiling (the same photo released by Islamic Jihad after her mission), while a recording played Johann Sebastian Bach's "My Heart Is Swimming in Blood."[37] The metaphorical use of "Snow White" recalls references to Hanadi as the Bride of Palestine. The artwork was attacked and vandalized on a visit to the museum by the Israeli ambassador to Stockholm, who denounced the artwork as "obscene" and a "monstrosity." In defense of his artwork Feiler stated that it had a message of "openness and conciliation" and that the text accompanying the artwork acknowledged that innocent people had been victims of the operation.[37] This incident prompted a series of commentaries in the Israeli and Swedish press. While one writer in the Israeli newspaper *Ha'aretz* argued that "violence" should prompt Israel to "take a closer look at its concept of tolerance," the Swedish tabloid *Expressen* wrote that the ambassador's action reflected "not only a strange view of the limits of freedom of expression, but also growing Israeli arrogance in relations with the rest of the world."[38] Hanadi's mission generated discussions worldwide on a range of issues, from Israel's treatment of the Palestinians to its relations with the rest of the world and its claims on history.

Hanadi's mission became a medium for artistic creativity in part because of the contrasts embodied in the performance of the mission itself. The violence was performed by a woman in a beachfront restaurant bordering a beautiful sea, and twenty-one people died. Violence of that scale, especially against a backdrop of such beauty, is a source of human fascination and a staple of Hollywood. The operation permeated several cultural spheres and prompted a dialogue between an Israeli expatriate and an Israeli government representative, and then between Israeli commentators and Europeans about fundamental issues of Palestinian-Israeli relations.

The aesthetics of Hanadi's performance enabled it to enter all these spaces simultaneously. As a cultural performance, violence can permeate many cultural spheres and generate sets of social processes well beyond the physical space of impact or the immediately affected victims. These processes have an effect on the society of the actors, the society of the "enemy," as well as regional and global allies. Different performances will have different results. And sometimes the performance of violence will affect social processes, but without guiding one way or the other: the processes have a life of their own, and the course that they take will be greatly affected by the existing power structures in the spaces reached by the performance of violence. Yet it is also true that the mere generation of these processes can disturb the status quo sufficiently to alter the power structures themselves. In other words, the performance of violence raises questions, but it does not necessarily present answers.

The Poetics of Martyrdom

The cultural ideas expressed through the performance of martyrdom and its cultural representations in Palestine are also expressed through performative expressions in media such as music, dance, and theater. I attended a dance performance of the Palestinian Popular Dance Troupe (El-Funoun El-Sha'abiya) on 13 May 2004 to commemorate Al-Nakba (the catastrophe)[39] at Ramallah City Hall. The piece was entitled "Haifa, Beirut and Beyond," the three places standing respectively for pre-Israel Palestine, the Palestinian exodus and exile, and the continuing resistance and unknown tomorrow. El-Funoun is twenty-eight years old and was formed amid expressions of Palestinian identity through the revitalization of Palestinian folklore. The group made its greatest success in the early 1980s by performing folkloric dance and songs that narrate life in Palestine before the establishment of Israel. It depicted scenes of the Palestinian grain harvest with references to the Marj Ibin 'Amer Plains.[40] The group also reproduced Palestinian traditional village weddings in songs and dance and used history, folklore, symbols, and aspirations to articulate Palestinian identity. It represented the Palestinians as the Canaanites entrenched in the land of Palestine, as the olive tree, and narrated the life of a lively community with intense interaction with its landscape, telling stories of boys and girls meeting at the spring, dancing for the harvest, and making wedding plans, and stories of heroic Palestinians challenging invaders through different periods of Palestinian history. The group then moved more toward resistance songs during the first intifada.

It took El-Funoun eight years to prepare "Haifa, Beirut, and Beyond." El-Funoun's artistic production came to a standstill during the Oslo period of the 1990s, as did most Palestinian artistic forms of expression during this period. Several artists communicated to me that the Oslo period hampered their creativity and their ability to express ideas through their artistic medium. The famous Palestinian painter Suleiman Mansour pointed out in an interview in Jerusalem that many artists did not survive Oslo, that there was emptiness, a loss of direction, and hence a lack of expression. It was a time when some artists moved to abstract art, others expressing what Mansour described as "empty non-sense ideas" like painting "someone fucking a shoe." Mansour explained that there seemed to be a calculated attempt to gut Palestinian art of its local content and that he himself could not paint during that period but reverted to sculpting with mud instead; this decision was probably what enabled him to survive the Oslo period as an artist.[41] This pattern—the huge impact of the Oslo process on society, and the new surge of expression by artists like Mansour—will become more clear as I further explore the dance performance of El-Funoun.

"Haifa, Beirut, and Beyond" was presented in 2001, during the Al-Aqsa Intifada. El-Funoun's presentation was a complex Palestinian experience of love and life; dispossession, exile, and ruined nationhood; and a resistance filled with defiance, death, and dreams. The dance begins with a scene of pre-Nakba, or pre-Israel Palestine, in which the dancers, men and women, were mixing mud. (It is traditional to cover the roofs of mud homes in Palestinian villages every fall with fresh mud in preparation for the winter season, to cover any cracks that appeared over the summer.) This opening scene is followed by dances of dispossession, in which people are forced to flee into exodus, and then by scenes with themes of exile and the reformulation of Palestinian identity into a refugee identity. The fourth and last theme further articulates the refugee identity, as the key[42] becomes the symbol of the Palestinian struggle for the right of return during the Oslo period, which threatened to compromise this right. The group performed several dances with large keys on their shoulders, representing a heavy weight, in spite of which the Palestinians mounted a determined struggle. The performance concludes with dances that fuse themes of death and dream. In this last dance the dancers mix the mud again, although not joyously as at the beginning of the dance. Here the mud mixing is tense and the dancers display fear and love, worry and resistance, strength and determination.

These themes of cultural expression reveal a strong link to the land at a time when the Palestinians felt that it was in serious danger of being severed. This threat came from Oslo and its attempts to resolve the conflict without acknowledging, let alone preserving, the Palestinians' right of return, their entitlements in historic Palestine. The players in the Oslo process assumed that by brushing this hard issue aside they could keep the peace. In my view this brushing aside of a complex relationship to the land and history is a primary reason why there was such an outpouring of expressions of the Palestinian relationship to the land of

Palestine that is now Israel. The artistic expressions were paralleled in Palestinian performances of sacrifice that saw Palestinian bodies mixed in the mud of Palestine through missions of martyrdom. Both artistic works and performances of violence expressed the relationship to the land and sought to assert cultural fusion with it. The sacrifice represents the ultimate expression of that relationship by achieving a physical fusion with the land.

El-Funoun's performance made rich use of symbols, historical references, and folktales from Palestinian memory, performed in a mixture of traditional and modern styles to traditional and modern music. The performance contained a range of expressions: festive and happy, sorrowful and sad, rebellious and aggressive, powerful and strong, weak and fearful, yearning and loving. In its final form the performance is a rich mosaic of cultural symbols, history, and question marks that reflect the complexity of everyday life in Palestine. The performance itself becomes a form of identity embodiment rather than a collection of symbols manipulated by the art form. El-Funoun creatively projected time to give historical depth to the symbols, so that the performance came closer to representing the Palestinian presence than any of the symbols themselves could do. The art reflects Palestinian lives, their suffering, violence, resistance, defiance, worries, hopes, and love for a life missed. The poetics generated by the performance become cultural representations and cultural expressions that on the one hand reflect the Palestinian state of being and on the other generate an emotive force among audiences and inform future actions. This form of artistic expression also reflects the tension between the reality of the cultural order and the artists' aspirations. This tension parallels the polarizations generated by the acts of martyrdom and their cultural representations, as explored earlier in this chapter. The acts are a product of the historic moment at which Palestinians live, and the state of being within which they live.

The more successful the performance is in pronouncing this historic moment, the more people will connect with it. Here lies the power of the poetics of the performance: it moves the audience by interweaving history with the challenges, worries, fears, and aspirations of the present and questions about the future. The viewer who knows the past and understands the present will be affected more deeply. In interviews after the performance, members of the audience revealed the intense emotions that the performance evoked in them. One woman described it as "too much to handle." The performance also provoked the curiosity of the audience, generating a new, shared meaning. This same dynamic applies to the cultural conception of performances of martyrdom. The more the martyrdom operation pronounces the historic moment and Palestinians' state of being, the more people will connect with it.

The program for El-Funoun's performance was decorated with an old door key, the symbol of dispossession and the quest for the right to return. Also decorating the program was a wheat stem signifying the land, against a mud-brown background, the color of the Palestinian soil. The MC for the show introduced the dance performance in Arabic:

> From Acre, Haifa, Jerusalem, and Jericho to where the winds have spread our souls. To exiles where we hide memories, dreams, and our little things. An old key, but not an incapable one. Old, but shines as a glass of heart. We carry it on our shoulders that are heavily weighted down with worries, so it may carry us to our home which we have not forgotten. And we dance with it, with wishes and excitement, holding onto language, history and stories. We open a door of a memory that will never burn out, and with [the key] we look for walls of mosaic of forgiveness.
>
> In this work there will be a number of fields and spaces open. Imaginations that have been confined in the cocoon of shock will be born. The music that is pregnant with the pressures of the open tomorrow, and lived with longing of the prolonged moment, calms down and charges, domesticates and differs, gets ordered and gets loose on its own, as it wishes, and according to the echo of the collective tone that is forcefully charging in the unknown, through the painful wires of the sea and the charging land waves.
>
> The held body spills out in the questions of existence and the limbs and eyes dislocate from the Iqal[43] of assertion and withdrawal. So it is frank and clear. So it swims through the horizon, declaring an opinion, a point of view, a hint, or a Mawwal.[44] Inventing the forms of living, with happiness and sadness, with love and life, with worries and calmness, and with all the machineries of survival and the preferred presence in spite of the laws of civilized death and the molds of the technology of modern behavior.
>
> Samples of blood and flesh, the love for the place has mixed them, and the intrinsic chains of details have formed them. They came out of the land's mud so that they draw the characteristics of the place but no longer are its face . . . will they finish??

> In this work the questions of Palestinian fate come out and remain, setting the sail before the sun's eyes and in the face of the wind so that the picture does not stay blurred and to balance the scale.

These same words could have introduced the performance of martyrdom in its Palestinian formulation and cultural conceptions. The memories of the Nakba and its tales represent a field that defines the making of the contemporary Palestinian identity. It is a history that the Palestinians inescapably carry on their shoulders, in good times and bad. They sing and dance these tragedies so they may heal their suppressed collective trauma, so they may come to terms with their past and move beyond it. But with a history that never stops, an encounter with an expanding state that continues to ruin their peoplehood and places, dreams that continue to shatter, the dances and songs become a means of transforming history into defiance and resistance.

At the same time the introduction refers to Palestinians "inventing the forms of living," implying that acts of resistance have a sacrificial nature, that life is lived culturally though the life of the identity. Such assertion of identity and forms of living challenge the modern order, the modern "civility" that requires negating identity and conforming to modernity and its order. Here the Palestinian narrator makes clear his awareness of the "moulds" of "modern behavior" and the "preferred presence," but death of the body is his preferred form of living, a choice that may seem incomprehensible to the "civilized" order. These constructions, which are also conceived of in the performance of martyrdom, are formulated in a polarized global order that demands "civility" from the occupied, oppressed, dispossessed, squeezed Palestinians—in response to the modern technology of war and numerous cultural invasions, they are to make their diverse cultural representations conform to fixed molds. Challenging this global order and the forms of modernity itself becomes a meaningful act. Martyrdom operations, which do not conform to the rules of "modern behavior," become a means of asserting difference from the molds into which everyone is expected to fit.

The ideas expressed in this dance are similar to the ideas expressed in the commentaries, obituaries, and poetic representations of martyrdom explored earlier: fusion with the land, breaking free while under siege, and resistance to conformity, among others. These ideas are generated by people's realities. The idea of birth from "the confinement in the cocoon of shock" parallels the penetration of barriers and the process of breaking free from confinement. In an interview, Marwan, the person who introduced El-Funoun's dance performance, stressed the importance of place in their work:

> The odor of the place is fragrant in our work. It is clear in the picture, in the music, and in the song. This mosaic in Palestine is rich and complex in this country. We try to embody the place in particular characteristics through the dance. The place means a lot to us. It is a form of our embodiment, a form of our identity. The most important element in the elements of our existence and our identity is the place, through our presence in it or love for it and bond to it. The Palestinian is not living a state of no place. The Palestinian is outside of the place, working for the opportunity to live inside of the place. The Zionist project is realized through the isolation of the Palestinian human from his place and then the isolation of the Palestinian from himself, from the family. If you are happy for a happy occasion, you find a barrier, a checkpoint. If you are sad, you will find a barrier, a checkpoint. If you love, you find a barrier, a checkpoint. In order to work, you find a barrier, a checkpoint. Barriers and checkpoints that split us into shrapnel. This tearing apart even when you are inside the place, you are torn apart, until your relation to the place ends. We embody the importance of the connection to the place and we remind people of our isolation from the place. We have a strong tie to it, but forcefully are forced out of it. This place, we made it, we formed it. We love it and any fusion with it means an end to the [Zionist] project.[45]

The relation of Palestinians to their place lies at the heart of the Palestinian struggle to realize Palestine. As they are squeezed more and more from their place, performances that exemplify this strong bond to place become popular. Marwan's comments emphasize the Zionist attempt to disrupt Palestinians' cultural relations to their place, and Palestinians' struggle to maintain fusion with the land as a counter to the Zionist project. But more importantly, his conception of the relationship to place points out the dialogic relationship between Palestinian identity, place characteristics, and constructions and the ontological conditions of confinement and isolation. The attempts to isolate the Palestinians' from their identity, community, peoplehood, and culture are also attempts to isolate Palestinians from their physical place with roadblocks, barriers, and checkpoints.

The poster produced by the Palestinian Independent Commission for the Protection of Citizens Rights in response to the massacre in the Jenin refugee camp in April 2002—showing a poppy blooming amid the debris of destruction—draws a relationship between the victims who died in the attack and the land. The poster bears the statement muhawelet qatl al-makan (The attempt to kill the place) placed over the scene of destruction. The words muhawelet (the attempt) and al-makan (the place) are in red, while the word qatl (to kill) is printed in black and seems to have fallen from its place, now occupied by the poppy flower, shown in red bloom. Next to the roots of the flower two young girls play in the ruins. The illustration interprets the violent Israeli attack on the camp as an attempt to "kill" people's relationship to their place and environment, to their acculturated space and homeland. At the same time the flower raises the hope of renewal and a stronger relationship with place. The symbol keeps alive those who die, embodied in the place, and later generations are strengthened through representations of the martyrs' experiences.

These cultural actors, whether they are painters, poets, writers, dancers, or fighters, express similar ideas and engage in similar social processes. Each chooses his of her own medium to make that expression. Martyrdom will not be the medium of choice for everyone. But what gives martyrdom its potency is its capacity to make these expressions and to be noticed by a wider set of viewers. The conditions of containment and confinement that I explored in chapter 4 and mentioned here by Marwan are the main conditions against which the conceptions of place and space are generated. Through the performance of martyrdom, physical barriers are broken, penetration is achieved against the "enemy," and cultural conceptions of freedom and rootedness are generated. So my mother's comment to me on the first day of my arrival in the field—"See how they took the road from us?"—turned out to be at the heart of my inquiry into violence and martyrdom in Palestine.

A number of common themes and processes of polarization recur in the performances of martyrdom and their cultural representations explored in this chapter, as may be seen in the commentaries, istishhadiyeen notes, and poetics that I have cited. These cultural themes and meanings associated with martyrdom operations in Palestine and the polarizations generated by these performances can be summarized as follows:

1. *Transcendence of Boundaries.* These performances transcend all bound-aries, physical and conceptual. The istishhadiyeen "penetrate" the Israeli segregation wall, "break" all the barriers, and "pass" all checkpoints. By simply reaching an Israeli town, the istishhadi achieves the breaking of boundary conceptions in polarization with the ontological conditions of encapsulation and confinement. Furthermore, he or she conceptually transcends the oppressive political order, the negligent international order, the moral order, and even the imagination.

2. *The Revival of Palestine.* The sacrifice of Palestinian bodies in Palestinian places from which Palestinians have been expelled recreates life for Palestine. The sacrificed Palestinians' body parts create corresponding parts of Palestine—streams, nurturing fields, blooming flowers, moving and shaking olive trees and wheat stalks—and bring back birds, singing, perfumes, and weddings. In these cultural conceptions of sacrifice Palestine is revived in Palestinian memory and the cultural imaginary to regain its Palestinian characteristics and retain its Palestinian identity. Palestine is recreated in its natural setting: pre-Israel, pre-colonization, open, free of boundaries and walls, filled with water, birds, and abundant life. This revival of pre-1948 Palestine is a polar opposite to the Israeli erasing of Palestinian signs from the landscape and the process of reconfiguring Palestinian territories into Israel through the Israeli settlement program and of intensifying Palestinians' isolation and alienation in their own homeland.

3. *The Unity of Palestine.* The combination of the above two conceptions —the transcendence of boundaries and the revival of Palestine—is a template for the conception of the unity of Palestine. This unity is expressed through physical reach and physical sacrifice, as well as through the cultural representations of birds flying through the sky of Palestine, trees whispering to plants, and sea waves dancing. These cultural conceptions of the unity of Palestine are in opposition to intensified Palestinian geographic fragmentation and isolation, and persistent conditions of exile and denial to exiled Palestinians of the right of return.

4. *Assertion of Palestinian Rootedness.* The physical spread of Palestinians' flesh and blood in the land of Palestine in sacrifice for it and for the Palestinian people fuses Palestinian peoplehood with the land of Palestine. This process asserts a rootedness of the Palestinians in Palestine against the denial of rootedness, accessibility, and physical attachments

and experiencing of the land. The sacrifice further configures the land of Palestine by attaching new historical events to places, as the sites of explosions become sites of martyrdom and sacrifice by Palestinian icons, thus building stronger bonds between Palestinians and the place of sacrifice. This process stands in opposition to political processes that seek to finalize the exclusion of Palestinians from historic Palestine in the calls for recognizing Israel as a "Jewish state."

5. *Assertion of Palestinian Peoplehood.* The concentration of the sacrificed victim concentrates the sacrificed identity, creating the immortalized iconic image of the istishhadi. The istishhadi is a Palestinian sacrificed for Palestine and its people—thus, by extension, the act asserts Palestinian identity and immortalizes Palestinian peoplehood. This immortalization of Palestinian peoplehood is generated in opposition to political processes that deny Palestinian identity, as the Israeli and international orders turn their back on Palestinian entitlements to identity. These assertions of a distinct Palestinian identity are a challenge to globalization and the processes of identity "hybridization."

6. *Assertion of Palestinian Independence.* The Palestinian sacrificers who take their lives into their own hands assert agency, control, and independence. Their performance communicates control over self-destiny in the face of political domination, curfews, imprisonment, terrorizing, and constant harassment and abuse that Palestinians are subjected to through their encounter with Israel.

7. *Securing Inner Peace.* The performance of sacrifice or istishhad is a religious ritual performance that fuses Palestinians' Muslim lives with the divine life. The martyrs live in the divine world and also in the cultural world of the Palestinians, leading two lives and fusing Palestinians' lives with the life of the Divine. This conception creates a sense of calmness, harmony, mercy, purity, and certainty, in contrast to the conditions of occupation, which are characterized by brutality, the ravages of war, the harshness and boldness of daily encounters with soldiers, and the resulting "contamination" of self, mixing-up of categories, and fear of an uncertain tomorrow. The fusion with divine life that is achieved through the sacrifice is a repurification of the self. As the system fails to work, a move toward tradition reasserts a sense of control and direction.

8. *Application of Mimetic Violence.* The application of violence at Israeli targets and publics in the "Israeli depth" spreads terror and fear through-

out Israel, just as the Israelis reach the Palestinian depths and spread terror throughout Palestine. In this mimetic process Palestinians spread and expand throughout Israel as Israel expands and spreads through-out Palestine. This mimesis of enemies asserts the power and capaci-ties of Palestinians and further consolidates their legitimate political aspirations.

In combination, these processes represent the poetics of martyrdom that are created between the poles of ontological and cosmological con-ditions and political aspirations. The cultural discourse within which acts of martyrdom are constructed melds personal experiences with cul-tural ideas, whereby the individual is not separate from his or her social setting and cultural representations and performances are not separate from experiences. In the Palestinian context there is a prominent land-scape dimension in the construction of the act of sacrifice. This land-scape dimension makes the site of martyrdom an important component of its performance; together with the timing and cultural references of the mission, it represents a semiotic grounding for the poetics of the performance as a whole. The system of motivation for martyrdom opera-tions is generated through symbiotic articulation, manipulations, and transformations over time, along with mimetic encounter and opposi-tion to the "enemy" over the landscape of Palestine. Thus the mission asserts the unity of Palestine, Palestinian conceptual rootedness in Pal-estine, and Palestinian identity. It does so by destabilizing the identity of the "enemy" whose presence threatens the very identity of the actor and the community of Palestinians in their place: Palestine.

CHAPTER SIX

The Strategies and Politics of
Martyrdom in Palestine

Much of the literature on suicide bombings offered thus far has either revealed the increased intensity of this form of violence or focused on the political strategies of participant groups. None of the political analyses offered to date factor in the cultural aspects of this form of violence. How does the cultural significance of the performance of self-sacrifice and martyrdom politically shape the application of violence? How are cultural conceptions of sacrifice and martyrdom deployed in political and military strategies? In this chapter I demonstrate how the cultural dynamic of this form of violence is not separate from its military strategies and political capacities. I explore how the cultural conceptions of the violence in multiple cultural spheres are integrated into political strategies and further motivate its performance.

Many of the histories and analyses of suicide bombing have proven shortsighted by lumping what I see as three varying forms of violence into one category (Andriolo 2002; Atran 2004; Bloom 2005; Khosrokhavar 2005; Pape 2005; Reuter 2004; Shay 2004). The first type of violence is what I call the "no-escape operation," a military operation from which the participants have virtually no chance of returning alive. Operations of this sort are practiced by most nationalist liberation movements around the world and in certain battle situations even by organized militaries. The Palestinian liberation movement in particular has regularly engaged in cross-border no-escape operations launched from Jordan and Lebanon. Khosrokhavar (2005), Reuter (2004), and Shay (2003) trace the origins of "suicide terrorism" to the Assassins of the twelfth century, who carried out no-escape assassinations in Persia and Syria.

Bloom and Pape go back to the Jewish Zealots of the first century, who carried out no-escape operations against the Romans in Jerusalem. Both historical examples involved the targeting of leaders, officials, and armies and did not include a performance of self-sacrifice.

The second kind of operation does include a performance of self-sacrifice and is applied against state armies, officials, or institutions. Examples include operations of the Lebanese resistance against the American, French, and Israeli military in Lebanon, of the Liberation Tigers of Tamil Eelam (LTTE) in Sri Lanka, and of the Partia Karkaren Kurdistan (PKK) of the Kurdish Workers' Party in Turkey. The Japanese Kamikaze attacks also fall into this category since they included a self-sacrifice component and were applied against military targets, with the notable difference that they were organized as part of a state military campaign against an opposing state army.

The third kind of operation involves a performance of self-sacrifice and is applied against civilian targets. Examples include Palestinian suicide operations in Israeli public spaces and Chechen rebel suicide operations in Russia. Others, at a different level, are suicide bombing operations carried out by groups like Al-Qaeda against civilian targets in the United States, Britain, and their allies.

Although all three types of operation are conducted by a mission carrier on a mission of certain death, they are different in their aesthetics, formulations, and strategies. Treating them all the same complicates the task of understanding their motivations and of formulating effective responses to them. For example, the strategies of coercion discussed by Pape (2005) may explain in part the political objectives of suicide bombings of the second type, which are applied against state targets, but they do not explain this type fully, and they fail altogether to explain similar acts against civilian targets. The martyrdom operations against civilian targets of the sort engaged in by Palestinians, which are the focus of my research, not only mediate social processes among Palestinians, as I demonstrate in chapter 5, but also ignite semiotic cultural warfare that sets the operations apart from similar acts against state military targets. These operations are loaded with cultural ideas and meanings, integrated into political strategies, that move the battleground from the physical fields into the conceptual fields. It is true that the two other kinds of operations also mediate social processes and are intertwined with cultural ideas. But I wish to draw attention to the different impact that the performance achieves in relation to the variations in aesthetics. This form of violence in particular—violent sacrifice in civil public spaces—breaks out of the established rules of engagement, challenging the established perceptions of state and global agencies that combatants and noncombatants are distinct, and brings the confrontation to a different level, forcing the engagement of various nonstate forces.

Both Bloom (2005) and Pape (2005) separate political analysis from social analysis. Yet any political analysis that does not rest on a clear understanding of the social space occupied by the martyrdom operation in the wider community, by the "enemy" and its supporters, and by international observers would be missing vital aspects of the political strategy and how they work or fail to work. Furthermore, the purely political view leads the authors to make assumptions and assertions that contradict the political and social realities underlying these forms of violence. Bloom, for example, asserts: "My focus on the organizations fits the available empirical evidence from Japanese Kamikazes of World War II to most of the Palestinian and other suicide bombers of today. All of the bombers are first and foremost members of organizations that train them, select their targets, buy their explosives, issue orders for when to launch an attack and try to convince the larger population that their cause is just" (85). There is plenty of "empirical evidence" in the field where I conducted my research in Palestine that is contrary to several of Bloom's assertions. My interviews with several organizing factions and families of mission carriers indicate that most "bombers" offer themselves voluntarily. There is even evidence that some mission carriers choose the place and target of their mission.[1]

Murad Tawalbeh, a nineteen-year-old from Jenin Camp who worked for the Palestinian police and is currently in Israeli jail after a failed attempt to execute an operation, threatened his brother, Mahmoud Tawalbeh, the leader of local Islamic Jihad at the time, that if he did not send him on a mission he would go through a different organization. The older brother responded to his brother's wish by setting him up with an explosive belt and sending him on a mission.[2] Mahmoud Tawalbeh, who was killed in the Jenin Camp battle and is the recognized Palestinian leader of that battle, was an officer in Al-Amn Al-Waqa'i (Palestinian

Preventive Security) and defected to Islamic Jihad because Fatah would not provide finances for martyrdom operations.

These personal initiatives demonstrate the extent of individual agency and the primary role that the meaning attached to these operations plays in their construction and application, as well as in the configuration of groups and their strategies. Palestinians have shifted alliances based on which organization is opening the door and facilitating their means of expression, not which organization is giving them more powerful positions or hand-outs. To the contrary, Tawalbeh abandoned positions of institutional power to join a group and engage in a form of activism that most certainly would end his life. The entanglement of the cultural meanings in the act explains why mission carriers and field operatives, even at the leadership level, are committed to carrying through their missions. No political analysis could explain this persistence when doing so means the death of not only the mission carrier but also most organizers, who become targets of assassination. Even some top-level political leaders of organizing groups have suffered the same fate. In the organizational calculus, the loss of leadership's political and military cadres is not something that can be taken lightly, and yet in spite of the loss they persist in pursuing their strategy. So what is it that outweighs the severe losses these organizations incur by pursuing martyrdom strategies?

Pape (2005) views "suicide" terrorism as a strategy of political coercion by weak opposition groups against more powerful and democratic states. In Pape's view, strategies of coercion seek to force democratic states to relinquish control over territories that "terrorists see as their homeland" (21). Pape sees these forms of violence as being carried out in the context of territorial conflicts and focuses his analysis on the reaction to state expansion by the groups engaged in "suicide terrorism," rather than by analyzing the state expansion itself. Furthermore, Pape reduces to territorial terms his analysis of groups that embrace global ideologies and apply this form of violence against global powers like Al-Qaeda, arguing that the ultimate goal of Al-Qaeda is to coerce the United States to leave Saudi Arabia. This reductive approach to pragmatic, visible, and legible political goals across the board fails to see not only the cultural assertions associated with the application of violence but also the complexities brought on by rapid increases in policies of globalization—especially after the collapse of the Soviet Union, the consequent strengthening of globalized ideologies such as political Islam, and the local histories and cultural ideas that create local meanings and through which local communities and groups relate to global ideologies.

Pape's well-regarded *Dying to Win* (2005), with so many tables and graphs of data on 460 "suicide attackers" in Palestine, Sri Lanka, Lebanon, Turkey, Chechnya, Japan, and the Bin Laden campaign, still lacks substance. Despite the claim that the book provides "analysis grounded in fact, not politics,"[3] Pape lacks basic knowledge about the multiple contexts in which his data originate.[4] Gathering a large amount of data from different contexts can only be fruitful if there is an analysis of how the data are situated in the local context. Understanding the data against the backdrop of specific histories and local cultures is a necessary step before attempting to draw an overarching cross-cultural analysis.

Bloom's *Dying to Kill* (2005) arguably complements the work of Pape. While Pape sees suicide bombings as coercing external forces or "democratic states," Bloom focuses on "domestic political dynamics and organizational outbidding." Both Bloom's and Pape's analyses are relevant, and they present some factors in their political analysis of martyrdom operations, but neither the factors individually nor the sum of these factors collectively provides us with a full understanding of how this form of violence is constructed. This form of violence cannot be entirely understood without expanding the analysis to social and cultural realms at the level of individuals, groups, local communities, society at large, regional communities, the "enemy" state, the society of the enemy state and its support, global powers, and international observers. This "holism" approach, after Ferguson (2003), requires a lot of work but is necessary if we are to do justice to the subject and provide a comprehensive analysis that can afford us the tools with which to develop effective responses.

Bloom's analysis of strategies of organizational outbidding still does not explain why groups become popular by applying violence in certain contexts. Also, both Bloom and Pape keep their analyses separate from state expansion schemes. Pape calls the expansions "Democratic Occupations" (99) and repeatedly refers to territories that the "terrorists *see* as their homeland" (21, 30) and that "terrorists *view* as their homeland" (23, 79).[5] Had Pape considered the cultural dimensions of the production of violence, he might have seen that his terminology is part of what

contributes to violence as a medium for cultural assertion and for asserting territorial entitlement and belonging. It is precisely in reaction to
state expansions and globalization that seek to impose uniformity and
stifle expression that violence arises as a means to assert identity and
rootedness.

Bloom (2005) demonstrates the negative impact of counterinsurgency
efforts and their lack of effectiveness in derailing organizing groups by
showing how Israeli assassination policies have increased support for
suicide bombings and their sponsors in Palestine. However, her inves-
tigation of state terror does not go far enough in questioning why these
policies go beyond the state's declared objectives of "eliminating the
threat." Even though it is clear in almost every instance that there is both
state violence and nonstate oppositional violence, most recent political
analyses of suicide bombings by political scientists and journalists, like
Bloom and Pape, scrutinize the oppositional violence separately from the
parallel state violence. Moreover, at a time when their analyses conclude
that state policies are helping to intensify the violence of nonstate actors,
it is assumed that the state is missing the point, or that state strategists,
lacking the scholars' vision and political lenses, fail to see that their
policies are aggravating these violent situations. The idea that the state
may have an interest in continued violence and in maintaining a threat
that must be eliminated is not entertained. This analytical imbalance—
paying greater attention to nonstate actors than state actors—is a fundamental methodological defect. In my view it leads to a shallow understanding of the political dynamics that produce the violence, and to the
formulation of resolution strategies that wholly miss the point.

In his "*New* Strategy for Victory" (2005),[6] Pape calls on the United
States to remove its army bases in Saudi Arabia and go back to the old
policy of "offshore balancing" so that it can "find a lasting solution to
suicide terrorism that does not compromise our core interest in maintaining access to one of the world's key oil-producing regions" (238).[7]
Pape fails to see that the history of "offshore balancing" in the region
played a major role in the emergence of "suicide terrorism" as a form of
resistance applied against United States targets. Pape also does not tell
us how withdrawing United States forces from the Middle East will fail
to be interpreted by organizing groups and their publics as "concessions" to their "strategies of coercion," a particularly curious omission
given that Pape spends considerable efforts in the book warning against

the dangers of such concessions. Moreover, if that is Pape's advice to the United States, we cannot but wonder what would be his advice to Israel. He offers none. Israel occupies Palestine for reasons having nothing to do with its natural resources. Israel occupies Palestine to emplace itself there. Yes, the situation is a little more complex with Israel, so how might the "offshore balancing" policy work for Israel? Should Israel place itself out of Israel and maintain control of the Palestinians?

Bloom's advice to Israel is "to create economic incentives and opportunities for greater collaboration" (41) and to refrain from policies of "mass arrests, deportations, house demolitions, and targeted assassinations" (42). These suggestions are good and may relieve the pace of martyrdom operations, but they will not necessarily provide a solution. Viewing the solution in purely economic terms assumes that these communities have no political and national aspirations. It does not take much analysis to see that those who sacrifice their lives are not necessarily going to be satisfied with greater economic security. That is aside from the fact that Israel is building a wall so that there can be no collaboration, economic or social, between Israelis and Palestinians. In addition, most analyses of colonial rule from similar perspectives argue that communities are better off "economically" if they are colonized. Pape (2005) argues that "for many years most of the Palestinian population preferred to accept the benefits of the economic modernization that occurred under Israeli rule rather than support violent rebellion." He continues: "We do not know exactly why the Palestinian rebellion against Israeli occupation began when it did" (47). These colonialist analyses will remain off target if they continue to assume that natives will be happy as long as they have a job in factories, farms, and construction sites run by the colonialists. But beyond economic aspirations, these communities, like communities around the world, have political aspirations. They seek recognition of their identity and entitlement to land, cultural expression and preservation of their cultural distinctiveness, and an expression of rootedness in specific places, all cultural ideas that are the heart of the meanings associated with violence and generate support for its application (as demonstrated in chapter 5). Reconciling these aspirations with the expanding state and its multiple interests is a complex subject that cannot be fully satisfied here, but I begin a discussion in chapter 7.

In this chapter I provide some analysis of the factional dynamics of the resistance, the formation of subgroups, and the shifts in strategies and tactical procedures that groups experience in the face of encapsulation and tribalization processes associated with state expansion. My analysis is based on ethnographic observations and interviews with field operatives in the resistance factions. I also discuss the strategy of martyrdom in a form of dialogue with members and associates of Palestinian factions, mainly in the the Jenin area. I explore with them the martyrdom strategy from military and political perspectives and demonstrate how these strategies are woven into the cultural perspective that I presented in chapter 5. Here I explore how different factions employ martyrdom strategies toward their political goals or Palestinian national goals by looking at how the various groups view the successes and negative impacts of martyrdom strategies as well as their potentials and limits.

The Martyrdom Discourse

For over a decade the PFLP and DFLP had been militarily inactive, except when the PFLP assassinated a member of the Israeli Knesset in retaliation against Israel's assassination of the general secretary of the PFLP. However, in this intifada both engaged in organizing martyrdom missions. The formation of Abu Ali Mustafa Brigades, the new military wing of the PFLP, was in response to the pressure that the organization felt to participate in the resistance in its new forms. Sami, a leader in the group in Jenin area, explained: "Hamas was not able to prove its presence without the martyrdom operations, and the same case with Jihad. The Front [PFLP] has to accompany the political movement. The leftist, though, should take the lead [in the resistance], not the right and the Islamic thought. The Front does not have [popular] institutions that support it like Hamas and the others. Their resources are limited. When the resources are available there is no problem . . . The street is very pleased with the martyrdom work. The [first martyrdom operation carried out by the PFLP] was in a settlement in Gaza in 2002."[8] The PFLP realized that it would become progressively less relevant if it did not engage in the resistance, and in particular the martyrdom operations. The main idea behind the PFLP participation was a concern with local Palestinian politics. This is not purely a case of "groups outbidding" each other, as posited by Bloom (2005). The PFLP recognized that if Hamas and Jihad were the only groups carrying out martyrdom operations and generating tremendous support by doing so, then leadership of Palestinian society would fall exclusively to the Islamic groups and the PFLP, along with its programs for social change, would die. Martyrdom is the form of contemporary Palestinian resistance that has proved meaningful and captured the imagination of Palestinian publics. To be recognized as a resistance faction, Palestinian groups are compelled to participate in the performance of martyrdom. The cultural discourse of martyrdom has achieved such power that the cultural dynamic is defining the form of engagement and resistance, forcing it on some groups and reorganizing society.

The Islamic brand of martyrdom has become the new form of resistance to various factions, be they religious, secular, or Marxist. Salim states:

> Here there is new development in the thought of the resistance and the concept of the resistance among the Palestinian people and its organizations. Al Aqsa Martyrs Brigades began working only within the West Bank and Hamas inside Palestine (within Israel). This was a monumental development that Fatah, which was in the midst of a peace process and arresting and jailing Hamas activists, is also engaging in militarized activities with even a religious undertone in its public addresses. This was the case for all of the other organizations as well. [Fatah and others] started writing on the hatta[9] 'La illaha illa Allah' (There is no God but Allah). And again we had collective demonstrations, collective and organized strikes, and collective work on all levels with few internal fights. A new coordination committee to work between the factions was developed in almost every Palestinian town. Then, later, Fatah enters for the martyrdom operations as well. It was clear that there was and is military coordination between Hamas and Fatah. All of the tapes released by Fatah of istishhadiyeen cannot be distinguished from Hamas's tapes. The tone, the language, and the dress.[10]

Salim is describing Hamas's leadership in resistance discourse while others are following. Marxist and secular organizations like PFLP and Fatah started referring to what they used to call al-kifah al-musallah (the armed struggle) as jihad. Salim accurately observes that their presentation of martyrdom operations in language, video images, and posters is very similar to those produced by Islamic groups. When the second intifada started and people gave up on the political process and turned back to resistance, Hamas was the primary force conducting resistance, and consequently its forms of resistance became the model for other groups. All other factions organized "brigades" like Hamas's Izzideen Al-Qassam Brigades: Fatah's Al-Aqsa Martyrs Brigades, the PFLP's Abu Ali Mustafa Brigades, and the DFLP's National Resistance Brigades. Salim notes that the brigades became "a source of fear for Israel and were the title of an Arab summit in Sharm el Sheikh." The spread of the brigades and the concept of martyrdom operations that defined the brigades and distinguished them from military wings that these groups had maintained in the past, was in line with the transformation of the resistance and its role in establishing the cultural discourse of martyrdom. Hamas now takes the lead in formulating and applying the discourse of martyrdom. The leadership of Hamas in the resistance at a time when Palestinians increasingly believe that resistance is the proper response to Israel, coupled with Hamas's widespread presence in civil institutions and the growing importance of sermons in mosques, is contributing to the emergence of the group as a well-organized political force with strong popular support.

Navigating Meanings in Armed Factional Structures

In my endeavor to understand cultural meanings associated with the application of violence, I have paid close attention to where these meanings are made and by whom. In chapter 5 I explored the meaning making of martyrdom in broader society; in this chapter I focus on inner group dynamics and their processes of meaning making, as well as their conceptions of these acts of violence and how they fit into political and military strategies. I interviewed three kinds of activists. The first are the organizers, or local field leaders of the brigades. These are the people who are directly engaged in the resistance and could be involved in some capacity in setting up martyrdom operations. The second group consists of musayyiseen (plural of musayyis), meaning the "political intellect," or what I call the meaning makers. These meaning makers are activists, or political cadres, who are intermediaries between the organized resistance and the general public. They are the ones active in giving political and cultural meaning to the act of resistance within the community. The third group consists of the members of the brigades, the soldiers, cell members, or commanders. I also spoke with one of the top political leaders of Hamas in the West Bank to whom I give the pseudonym of Sheik Omar. The following is a list of the people whom I interviewed (sometimes identified by a pseudonym) and their roles:

Political leaders
  Sheikh Omar, Hamas
Military wing leaders
  Kamal, Al Aqsa Martyrs Brigades, Jenin
  Hamzi, Al Aqsa Martyrs Brigades, Jenin
  Anwar, Izzideen Al-Qassam Brigades, Jenin
  Sami, Abu Ali Mustafa Brigades, Jenin
Meaning makers
  Hasan, Hamas
  Salim, Hamas
  Shalabi, Fatah
  Sami, PFLP
Brigade members
  Reda, Al Aqsa Martyrs Brigades

Interviewing these subjects, especially the brigade leaders and members, was not an easy undertaking. Gaining access to some of the groups was long, patient, and delicate work. Aside from the groups' own precautions, my own ethnographic approach was not to rush into nervous interviews. I sought interviews during which I could connect with my interviewees at the gut level. I demonstrated my interest in the subject matter and not the identity of the individuals or tactical information regarding their organizations. The groups made all arrangements for the interviews, including the choice of when and where the meetings were held: I merely followed their instructions. My job was primarily to demonstrate that I was conducting legitimate academic research and nothing more. I made my contact information available to brigade leaders through activists and had no prior conversations or engagement with them outside my interviews. Their identities remained unknown to me throughout the process of arranging the interviews.

Another concern about the interviews was that some of the interview subjects, being wanted by Israel, are in constant hiding and on the run, fearing assassination. While conducting the interviews my life too was in danger. At any point during the interview I could have been hit by an Israeli missile. But can we really research violence without getting into dangerous places and situations? This is just the nature of doing "field-work under fire" (Nordstrom and Robben 1995). Being in dangerous positions gives the researcher a close look at the elements that produce the violence and also enables him or her to better assess the effects of violence, and how these effects figure into the construction of violence. While I was in the middle of an interview with a leader of Izzidin Martyrs Brigades we heard a bombing sound close by that shook the room we were in. I panicked but he remained calm and went on talking. Fortunately the noise was not a missile but possibly a sonic boom. The calmness of my interviewee revealed how common conditions like these had become, making people fearless of fear and fearless of the threat of violence. Breaking the barrier of fear is at the core of the military strategy of martyrdom, as I will explore below.

Interview Procedure

Each interview was unique in its procedure. I will narrate my meeting with Hamzi in February 2004 as an example.

Jenin had been calm for well over a week because of the Eid holiday.[11] This period of calm was not normal, especially since there had been a martyrdom operation the week before, on 29 January. Although the mission carrier was not from Jenin, normally the Israelis would close down the city and further restrict movement between villages. Yet access to the city was still allowed, and the main checkpoints remained "open" as during "normal" times. I received a call on my cell phone from an unknown caller asking me to be in Jenin the next day around noon for an interview. The next day I set out in the morning. The line at the checkpoint was long, and while waiting I received a call from someone who asked where I was. I told the caller that I was still held up at the checkpoint and might be delayed. The checkpoint had a few cars on my side and about a dozen people on foot, but from the other direction it had over twenty cars and a lot of people waiting to pass.

The checkpoint is a large, flattened area that has become completely muddy from the winter season. There are maybe a dozen parked tanks, ready at any moment to enter Jenin. The tank tracks in the mud made the terrain even more sludgy and difficult to negotiate. A soldier perched on top of the watchtower was surveying the scene. On the opposite side stood a concrete watchtower with small eye slots for surveillance. There were about eight or ten soldiers standing around, two on the ground handling those passing through the checkpoint, one up on the tank, at least one in the watchtower, another two in a smaller watch stand on the right side, and two others apparently on some sort of cleanup duty.

As we waited people formed a line, but over time those waiting in the line became less orderly. The longer they were subjected to harsh treatment, the less they were aware of others around them, and their desire to pass through and get on with their day surpassed most rules of order. The soldiers worked one side of the checkpoint at a time, sometimes called people in cars, sometimes people on foot; it was random and totally at the soldiers' discretion. People often shuffled from the car line to the walking line depending on which appeared to be moving more quickly. There were times when the soldiers called no one at all, just chatting in the middle and taking their time. Everyone stood around waiting to receive a small but very important hand gesture from the soldiers, similar to the gesture that one might use to beckon a young child. Each side was at least fifty meters from the soldiers, too far to communicate with them easily. After the soldiers gestured to you, you would walk to them, being sure not to make what might be considered a suspicious gesture or motion. Once you reached the soldiers, you were required to present your I D, and the soldiers would ask you questions: where you were from, where you were going, and why. It is completely within the soldiers' discretion to let you pass or not. They may refuse, and you could try again later with different soldiers and be allowed to pass. There is no regularity or system that can help people predict if they will be successful in passing.

When the soldiers began to call from the opposite side of the checkpoint before I got a turn, I decided to use my American passport and walk out of the line toward the soldiers with confidence. Halfway between the soldiers and me, the soldier on top of the tank screamed at me, initially in Hebrew, to stop because no one had called me. I answered in

English (acting as the international NGO's foreign officials do when they pass) that I had to go to Jenin. He told me to wait. Once the car they were checking was let through, the soldiers called me up. I informed them that I was doing research for an American university and had a meeting in Jenin. They let me pass.

Here was yet another delicate situation for me in my fieldwork: so that I could be mobile, I availed myself of my American citizenship in my hometown, in the presence of people who were still not mobile in their own home. It is rather a peculiar position to be in, especially because of the looks I got (or perceived) from people around me. As I passed them I had to look into the eyes of all the people waiting on the other side, who knew that I was able to jump the queue because of my American passport. The process forces the community to place people in a hierarchy. People in the line are always joking about who passes and who does not, who got held up for a long time, who got shouted at. Even though the soldiers have no set procedures, the dynamic at the checkpoint does affect people's perceptions of each other.

After I passed I had to call a taxi, as none were waiting on the other side. I walked about half a mile before the taxi arrived. While in the taxi I got a call from the caller in Jenin, telling me that he was ready to meet if I was in town. I told him that I would soon be dropped at the Jalama taxi stand in Jenin. He asked me to describe what I was wearing and to wait for him there. I stood by a lamppost near the taxi stand for about twenty minutes. One man came up to me, introduced himself as Ali, and asked if I was the researcher. I replied, "Yes." He said, "Let's go," and we continued walking together. Minutes later another man joined us while walking. He had on a coat, seemed to be armed, and was introduced by Ali as a member of Al-Aqsa Martyrs Brigades. We hadn't walked far when we reached the market. A man in his late sixties sat on a stool in front of a store, and there were four free stools. We greeted the man and sat down. The others began talking to the old man and ordered coffee from the next coffee shop. The area was in the center of the Jenin market. During the interview the member of Al-Aqsa Brigades made phone calls to his friends and changed SIM cards between calls. Abu Kamal, the old man, took part in no political discussions whatsoever. He just chatted about the market, the coffee, and daily life. The member of Al-Aqsa Brigades seemed to be known in the market, and many passers-by greeted him. Fifteen minutes later a man with an M-16 came by, greeted us, and sat down. He was introduced as the man that I needed to talk to. As he sat, Abu Kamal, the old man, excused himself, saying that he needed to go pray.

The market setting was a source of security for the brigade members, and for me too. We felt safe, even though we were in the open, in full view of the public. Many people who passed by would greet the men with whom I was sitting, particularly the one who was holding his weapon on his lap. He seemed interested in talking to me, but he went through some questions about my research first. What is it that I was going to do? Why and for whom? Toward the end of the interview one other person came by; he was also armed with a short gun but did not talk. After his arrival a few other guys gathered around us to hear what was going on with the interview, which by then had devolved into a discussion that the spectators took an interest in and listened to closely.

I conducted interviews in different formats. For example, I interviewed one of the leaders of Izzideen Al-Qassam Brigades at a location within the city to which I was taken. I received a call on my cell phone the day before. The caller asked me, "You have been seeking to speak to someone?" I replied, "Yes." He said, "Come to Jenin first thing in the morning." I was in Ramallah that day so I made the necessary schedule changes and made my way back to Jenin that afternoon. The next morning I sat at a coffee house and received a call at 8 a.m. sharp. The caller asked for my location and then someone came and picked me up. The interviewee introduced himself as a leader with Izzideen Al-Qassam Martyrs Brigades. He did not reveal his identity.

These kinds of interviews require a level of confidence from both sides. I was making myself available for a blind interview, and at the same time the group was arranging interviews of wanted persons by someone they did not know. What served me well is that I am from the Jenin area. I have an address and a village, and I attended school in the city where people know me. When I sought interviews I would give my name and cell phone number, and explain that I was conducting doctoral research through an American university on the Palestinian resistance and al-'amal al-istishhadi (martyrdom work), that I was from the village of Al-Jalama, and that I welcomed questions about me.

My experience is that rushed interviews do not produce ethnographic information but mostly journalistic and "generic" information. At one point I interviewed families of martyrs from the Jenin refugee camp after making arrangements through quick phone calls to a local informant. In those interviews people mostly talked with me as if I were a journalist, giving me political arguments and established points of view on various topics. But in most of my interviews I sought to establish a level of confidence by approaching interviewees through channels they trusted, being patient, and not rushing to an interview before the subject was ready. Such a relaxed environment was important if I was to conduct interviews that went beyond the groups' talking points, especially given the sensitivity of the topic at hand.

The Martyrdom Strategies

In this new period of the second intifada, the Palestinian factions that are engaged in the performance of martyrdom as a form of resistance are Hamas, through its military wing Izzideen Al-Qassam Brigades; Islamic Jihad, through its military wing the Jerusalem Battalions; Fatah, through its military wing Al-Aqsa Martyrs Brigades; and the Popular Front for the Liberation of Palestine, through its military wing Abu Ali Mustafa Brigades, named for a former general secretary of the group who was assassinated by Israel in 2001. I have talked with operatives and activists associated with all these groups except Islamic Jihad. In Jenin Islamic Jihad operatives have been very active, and consequently their leaders have had short tenures. Often a leader would get arrested or assassinated before I could arrange an interview. My aim in interviewing members of Hamas, Fatah, and the PFLP was to understand, from their perspective, the political and military logic of martyrdom operations.

Martyrdom as a Military Strategy

The strategy of martyrdom in resistance varies from one group to another and from one time to another within the same group. The concept of martyrdom from a military standpoint is viewed by different groups from two perspectives. The first is organizational and relates to individual readiness to operate in the resistance and the organization's capacity to recruit individuals to its ranks. The second is tactical and relates to the resistance battle with the state of Israel. At the organizational level, the concept of martyrdom has enabled Palestinian resistance factions to organize, operate, and survive under extremely dangerous conditions. Members of the operating resistance factions are constantly being hunted by Israeli snipers and targeted missiles. The concept of martyrdom deflates the fear of death. Breaking the barrier of fear is a requirement for Palestinian activists if they are to participate in the resistance under these conditions. Below is an excerpt from a taped interview with Sheikh Salah Shehadeh, one of Hamas's founders and the founder of its military wing (Izzideen Martyrs Brigades). He was the target of a controversial Israeli air strike on an apartment building in Gaza in 2002 that killed him and fifteen other residents of the building. The interview is part of a musical tape from a pro-Hamas band in Gaza. Sheikh Salah Shehadeh was talking of an "open grave policy," stating: "It is known that every fighter has an open grave. So every one of us takes a look at his grave in order to work. Without this open grave policy we cannot work. The closed grave or with no graves or that we don't have a view of the open grave, then it would be impossible for us to operate. This stupid Sharon and those around him from the Zionists think that killing puts the fear in our fighters. We take security measures only because it's our duty to do so in order for us to fight. Our desire to stay alive is not for the sake of staying alive but so God can cure the hearts of a believer nation and free this Arab people."

Salah Shehadeh is describing how open discussion of a willingness to die enables an organization to function and enables its members to take on challenges. He is referring specifically to martyrdom operations— fighting until death or offering oneself for death. Being committed to Hamas's military wing or other faction means that you are committed to die, that you have an open grave waiting for you. Joining the resistance becomes the same as offering oneself to die. Through this death and this commitment to die the resistance lives, and so does the idea of Palestine. Some members of the brigades whom I interviewed showed me photos they had made for their martyr posters. Imagining oneself as a martyr is part and parcel of belonging to these operating factions, especially since not many of them survive in the operating field for a long time. At an operational level, martyrdom maintains the morale of the group in the face of the continued loss of leaders and members. Martyrdom figures positively into the calculus of the resistance, making it difficult to lose at the individual and organizational level. If one succeeds in executing an operation, that is a win, and if one dies, that is also a win, because one dies as a martyr and that is a good thing. Hence martyrdom provides immunity against demoralization and defeat.

The organization sees the need to score against the Israelis if it is to survive as a group and recruit new members. As Shalabi states: "You have to bring in Israeli losses for the resistance to continue. The Israeli soldier is very protected in his tank, they hardly get their heads out of their tanks. The lack of weapons that can damage these tanks allows these tanks to come in and tear down half of the Camp and we can't do any damage to it, so we want to retaliate, one way or another. At the organizational level the members of the organization are always pleased, even though its outcome has grave consequences for the members of the organization. Because once an organization is successful in executing an operation, the Israelis go after those activists in the organization, but still they do it. There is a lot of heightening of morale from these operations [among the members]." Similarly, Hasan argues for the need to be able to retaliate: "As Palestinians we demonstrated and protested with the stone and chants and they retaliated by killing sixty-seven Palestinians.[12] Sharon's visit to Al-Aqsa was protested with a demonstration, yes, there were some Palestinians carrying weapons among the demonstrators, but the Israeli reaction was with machine guns and many victims fell. Here I want to make killing on the other side and I cannot reach this soldier fortified in the plane or in the tank or in the hummer, so how am I going to kill from them, how am I going to make them lose so I can limit their hostile attacks? This kind of operation has important effects on Israel and the evidence to that is the failing of several Israeli governments because they are incapable of protecting Israeli security." The military dynamics of the calculus of martyrdom have led several scholars (Bloom 2005; Ruter 2002; Pape 2005) to characterize strategies of martyrdom as "weapons of the weak" employed in a desperate attempt to make a kill. However, this depiction is an inaccurate use of the term as it was first introduced by James Scott (1985) in his ethnography of peasant resistance in Malay society. Scott argued that "weapons of the weak," by combining ideological and physical struggles in attacks and resistance,

constituted an effective means of resistance in the long run. This understanding of the "weapons of the weak" could be appropriate to describe
the dynamics of Palestinian resistance, but it is simplistic to characterize
mission carriers as desperate to kill. To do so is to overlook the multiple
sources of power beyond military strength, which is measured in how it
affects the political and cultural fields and not in the number of casualties inflicted on the adversary. Martyrdom has a high impact, a point to
which I will return when discussing the political strategies of martyrdom. But from a purely military standpoint, Reda explains that being
unable to conduct military training impedes the ability of a group to
carry out effective military warfare. Since most members are organized
within communities and no military training camps or facilities exist,
they are led toward martyrdom to ensure a kill. Reda states:

> It does not matter to the *istishhadi* whether he is going through Hamas, Jihad,
> or Fatah. His aim is to get there and do the operation. The *istishhadi* is not a
> military person. Fatah does more of the armed [no-escape][13] operations due
> to the lack of experts that can set up the belts in Fatah. Seldom did any of
> these people who go on engagement [no-escape] operations finish his mag-
> azine. All of them get killed. The training is very limited. The *istishhadi*
> operation has more chance to kill. These [martyrdom] operations are more
> terrifying than shooting. The saying says *lei'yar elli bisibish bidwish* ("the bullet
> that does not hit the target drives you crazy"). These operations have an
> effect on their [Israelis'] morale. Merely getting to Tel Aviv or Haifa is an
> accomplishment that has an effect. The Israelis are afraid of going out, afraid
> of going to work. For them to know of the operations terrifies them and
> pressures them psychologically. The effect of these operations is far beyond
> the killing. This situation puts the Israelis under pressure to pressure their
> government to move toward a solution.

In other words, a lack of attention to training by Palestinian factions
has led activists to favor martyrdom over conventional operations to
ensure effective performance. Fatah activists across the board have mentioned in interviews that fighters with some level of training prefer conventional attack operations to the self-explosive belt. Similarly, Hamas
activists note that mission carriers are chosen from members with the
least military experience. Reda's remark that the martyrdom operation
"puts Israelis under pressure to pressure their government to move to-

wards a solution" could be read as well suited to the characterization of martyrdom strategy by Pape (2005) as a "strategy of coercion." However, this formulation only surfaced in interviews with Fatah activists whose leadership is engaged in a political process with Israel. Hamas, the organization that first devised the strategy in Palestine and still takes the lead in applying it, does not frame it as such, nor is it engaged in a direct dialogue with Israel. None of the Hamas activists I spoke with framed martyrdom in terms of achieving concessions from Israel. Pape's suggestion that operations timed to coincide with critical points in the Oslo process are evidence of a "strategy of coercion" is a misreading. Hamas's political goal with respect to timing and coordinating the attacks was to derail the Oslo process and prevent Palestinian leadership from granting concessions: it was not a strategy to secure political concessions from Israel but rather a strategy of combating Israeli state expansion. All the statements that Hamas made in conjunction with these attacks during the Oslo process acknowledged as much, as I explained in chapter 3. If we were to accept Pape's argument of political coercion, we would have to assume that Hamas was involved in the Oslo process and coordinating with the official Palestinian leadership that was engaged in dialogue with Israel. However, there is no evidence that any such coordination took place. To the contrary, there is plenty of evidence that Hamas was vehemently opposed to the process as a whole and boldly resisted it.

The second military dimension of martyrdom is at the level of the broader battlefield with Israel—that is, the struggle through martyrdom works toward what organizations refer to as *tawazun al-ru'ub* (the balance of fear). Martyrdom is the form of violence that projects terror on the Israeli public as a whole. As Reda stated, an operation does not have to be "successful" to project fear. As long as some operations are "successful," any attempt has an impact as a form of violence in the imaginary that projects fear among Israelis. Strategies oriented to the "balance of fear" aim to bring a level of fear among the Israeli public similar to that prevailing among the Palestinian public under Israel's occupation. Anwar explained that there was a conscious decision in Hamas to achieve a balance of fear: "There are missiles, tanks, weaponry that terrify the public. The behaviors of the [Israeli] soldiers, the roadblocks, the militarized scene in general scares the public. . . . Hamas's role in martyrdom operations, exploding buses and public places, is asserting to them as we are not safe in our homes you are not safe in your homes. Before

you launch a shell on our people, you must calculate a thousand calcula-
tions for the *istishhadiyeen* and the explosive work. These operations
played a role in bringing such a balance of fear. When they assassinate a
Palestinian leader, their newspapers report that there is what looks like a
curfew in Israel. Their buses would be empty. The last statistics say that
there were twenty-five families that left Ashdod and many others may
leave."[14] Hasan also stated:

> [The *istishhadiyeen*] have a particular message: it is to target the personal
> security of the Israeli. I want to kill from them as they kill from me. The
> Israeli civilian doesn't do a thing to stop these abuses or to limit their size.
> The message to the Israelis is that "you are paying the price." The Israelis are
> fearful from what's coming. The bars are empty, the streets are empty, and
> the restaurants are empty. As they target all aspects of our life, we target their
> life in all of its aspects. The operations now are no longer limited to retalia-
> tion on certain Israeli aggressions; these operations have become a program.
> At any time that these organizations have an opportunity to execute an opera-
> tion they will. [The Israelis] make calculations, they worry that there are
> people who are willing to sacrifice self. You cannot hold them and they know
> that they have no ability to control these people. They hit in every place and
> every time they are able to hit. This is the program today.

Hasan clearly articulates the mimetic property of this form of violence
when he states: "As they target all aspects of our life, we target their life
in all of its aspects." The urge to "target their life in all of its aspects" is
essential to understanding the strategy of martyrdom against civilian
populations. In these spaces martyrdom's main target is the Israeli civil
order: that is what distinguishes it from other, conventional operations.
Herein lies its power, but also the basis for questioning its legitimacy. (I
will return to this point when discussing political strategy.) At certain
periods of increased intensity, these operations did severely harm Israeli
public life. These curfew-like conditions that these operations create in
Israeli public life mimic the impact of Israeli violence on Palestinians.
I was in Tabaria (Tibarias) on the Sea of Galilee in November 2003.
I walked the lakefront street, which is filled with cafés and is normally a
busy area, and saw that all but two cafés were closed. I sat in one for a
late lunch and was the only diner in the café. The city's pedestrian district
looked as if it was under curfew.
    Some media commentators and contributions on martyrdom argue

that groups choose martyrdom operations as a cheap form of military operation (Bloom 2005; Reuter 2002). But almost everyone I talked to asserted that martyrdom operations are the most costly in human and financial terms. Anwar explained the experience of Hamas: "Militarily the martyrdom operation is costly. The military operations against checkpoints are easier, easy to get to, and cost less. The operations inside [Israel] cost more, require more planning, and they cause more harm to [Hamas's] human resources. The operation costs at least two cars, one *istishhadi* martyr, and at least five to six persons between martyrs or life sentences. It is a much higher cost and more difficult. The person who goes on a mission is the one with the least experience. The one with experience provides the maximum of what he's got before martyrdom." This description not only shows that martyrdom operations are costly but also refutes the notion that the groups conducting them are driven to consolidate internal power structures, as Bloom (2005) suggests in her analysis of strategies of "groups outbidding." As Anwar explained, the group loses not only the mission carrier but normally also the organizers and facilitators. The belt maker, the transporters in the West Bank and Israel, along with their cars—all become targets that Israel goes after and often succeeds in uncovering with the cooperation of the PA's secret service. That Hamas's top political leadership has been and continues to be targeted as well as the military leaders demonstrates that if there is a "group outbidding" element in the application of the martyrdom strategy, it is an outbidding of the political programs sponsored by the groups, not necessarily the personalities and power structures. If these leaders were driven to consolidate their internal power, they would at least follow strategies that allow them to stay alive. Furthermore, the "outbidding" strategy fails to answer one important question: Why do sponsors of martyrdom become popular?

The popularity of martyrdom and martyrdom strategies lies in the meanings associated with their performance, which makes the performance an intelligible act. The more meaningful a mission is, the more it becomes effective and relevant in strategies of "outbidding." Without an accurate understanding of the cultural dimension of martyrdom operations, we would not know why or how they alter groups' positions in the community or how strategies of outbidding play a part in the decision to undertake them. Anwar states: "The level of success of the operation . . .

organizationally, it's measured in the target itself. If the target was military or at [the Israeli state] official level. For example, the Café Moment operation in Jerusalem was only a few meters from Sharon's house. Operations in Bir As-Sabea' and Safad are operations that target the Israeli depth. Operations close to the offices of the Israeli Ministry of Defense, these are considered quality operations within the organization."[15] Hamas measures the success of its martyrdom campaigns in relation to their capacity to mimic Israeli violence or to be meaningful to Palestinian publics. Hamas carried out operations close to Prime Minister Sharon's house and to the Israeli Ministry of Defense just as Israel targets Palestinian leaders. Similarly, the operations in Safad (far north) and Bir As-Sabea' (Beer Sheba, far south) are reaching the remote areas that brigade activists call the "Israeli depth," creating a sense that no place in Israel is safe, just as Israel threatens all of Palestine. The performance of martyrdom operations in these two cities in particular—both Palestinian cities depopulated in 1948 and now inhabited exclusively by Jews—has a particular resonance.

The Political Strategy of Martyrdom

A common theme among Palestinian politicians and academics is that ethical considersations aside, martyrdom operations performed by Palestinian factions are causing severe political damage to the Palestinian cause by harming Palestinians' international standing at a time when international pressure on Israel is most needed. In other words, Palestinian politicians who are invested in the political program of establishing a Palestinian state in the West Bank and Gaza and their supporters see martyrdom operations as an act that spoils their efforts rather than reinforces it. Unlike coercion politics, according to this reasoning, martyrdom operations reinforce arguments that Israel would jeopardize its own security if it withdrew from the West Bank and Gaza and allowed for Palestinian independence. Palestinian politicians and negotiators rely greatly on international politics to pressure Israel; hence they are in constant need to demonstrate legitimacy of Palestinian demands. Martyrdom operations against Israeli civilians severely harm the standing of Palestinian politicians in the international arena.

I took up these issues with the activists and group leaders whom

I interviewed. I further discussed with them what political objectives they saw themselves serving by engaging in this form of violence. As for how these operations discredit Palestinians before the international community, Sheikh Omar replied: "We do not need a certificate of good conduct from anyone. This is our land and it is our right to continue a struggle until we restore our rights in it. They [the international community] see the daily crimes Israel commits and consider it self-defense. Why are [the Israelis] permitted self-defense and the Palestinian people not? The Palestinian people's self-defense is seen as terrorism. Regrettably, they only see from the Israeli point of view." Hasan's reaction:

> The world is not going to benefit us. It did not benefit us during peace or during war. The Palestinian people understand that this world has become shameless, is a rude and careless world, and it is under the control of Israeli media. We are not going to be the hostage of the world's public opinion. There is a trend to avoid worrying about how the world views us and rather worry about how we are going to protect ourselves and achieve our rights. Israeli people started thinking: Why are they in Gaza? And they will think: Why are they in the West Bank? In Palestine? There is an opposite migration within Israel, the settlers are moving toward Israel. Yes, there is an increase in radicalization and an increase in hatred, but [the radicalization and hatred] is also an increase in the probability of [the Israeli] inability to continue here. The Israeli radicalization is not a matter that really concerns us that much. Who isn't radical in Israel or in Israel's history? This violence started during Barak's government, the liberal government. Settlements, checkpoints, all started with liberal governments and they were no different during right-wing governments. What is clear is that Sharon's government was elected to achieve security for Israel and it did not bring security to Israel.

As these statements indicate, there is an increased lack of faith and trust in the "world community" as normally represented by the United Nations (UN), other global agencies, and powers like the United States, the European Union, and Russia in their treatment of the Palestinian question. The UN is in some sense held responsible in that it called for the partition of Palestine in 1947 in the first place, gave international legitimacy to the state of Israel, and did not protect the collective political rights or individual rights of the Palestinians. In short, the international community as represented by these agencies and powers has not been impartial toward the people of Palestine. Further, the respect that these global institutions used to enjoy is fading in the "new world order" dominated by the United States. Palestinians see the new world order as signifying the collapse of a morally bankrupt world system. As Hasan puts it: "this world has become shameless, is a rude and careless world."

The statement from Hasan implies that the resistance has been reconceptualized so as to challenge the Zionist project as a whole, its martyrdom operations aimed at destabilizing Israel. Hasan sees that Palestinians are not any worse off as a result of their martyrdom operations, since Israel has always been applying policies of settlement and land confiscation, denial of Palestinian rights, and harassment of Palestinian populations. The martyrdom operations radicalize and corrode Israeli society, which increases the chances for Israel's defeat. At least in Hamas, there is an awareness of the discursive, mimetic effect of Palestinian violence on Israeli society, as discussed in chapter 3. Hasan further states:

> Reality tells that Israel is increasing in its radicalization and there is a new wall, there is an increase in the troops on the ground but also settlement building before this *intifada*, [the expansion] was going on uninterrupted and was burning on slow fire. I believe this *intifada* contributed to advancing the Palestinian nationalist program. It limited the spread of Israeli settlements and there is a bleeding of Israeli society and it pushed the Israeli to think about the question of the feasibility of their existence here. Even this separation wall is a sort of set back for Israel. They see this land as theirs. This is the "Land of Israel." Regardless of how small or large the size that they fenced with this wall, and they got out of, [the Israeli] excluded himself from it, withdrew from it, and is now withdrawing from Gaza. All of this was caused by the resistance and, in particular, these operations.

Hamas and Zionism have very similar yet diametrically opposed programs. Zionism seeks to establish a Jewish homeland in Palestine, or the "Land of Israel," and Hamas seeks to establish a Palestinian Arab Muslim state in Palestine. The so-called Israeli disengagement plan that started under Sharon's leadership is a plan of separating and isolating Palestinian communities by erecting fences, walls, and roadblocks that confine Palestinians' movements to small areas and limit their interactions with Israelis and the outside world. These measures have led to a process of "othering" that at the same time reduces the relationship between Palestinians and Israelis to one of war. This organization of difference, coupled with relations of war, legitimizes the annihilation of Palestinians within Israeli publics.[16] But the organization of difference works in two ways. By reducing Palestinians' relations with Israelis to one of war, it also legitimizes the annihilation of Israelis within Palestinian communities. Hamas and Islamic Jihad too want to reduce the relationship of Palestinians with Israelis to one of war. The more Israelis are separate from Palestinians, the more the "othering" process works with Palestinians as well. It is precisely at this point where the political programs of the state of Israel and Hamas meet. Hamas and Jihad seek to defeat any Palestinian program that would be willing to normalize Israel in Palestine. The increased realization among Palestinians that the Zionist state has been implementing nothing but expansionist policies has moved them more and more toward programs that challenge the Zionist project as a whole.

Add to these exclusive programs the corruption and bankruptcy of the "pragmatic" program, represented by the two-state solution, suffered at the hands of Oslo when the most intensified Israeli state expansion scheme was taking place under the banner of peace and reconciliation. The advocates of a Palestinian state in the West Bank and Gaza refer to it as *al-mashrua' al-watani al-filistini* (the Palestinian nationalist project). Their usual argument against martyrdom operations is that they interfere with the negotiation process and thus the nationalist project. When I asked Hasan why some Palestinians see martyrdom operations as standing in the way of the Palestinian nationalist project, he replied: "What is the nationalist project? For these people it's a matter of economic investment. The Palestinian high interests cannot be represented by corrupt people like this. The solution lies in dissolving this so-called authority and the 1,000 thieves that are called 'the Nationalist Project.' These are a strain on the nationalist project. And there are those who criticize the operations because of their fear of the level of support these operations are gaining and in turn the level of support the organizers of these operations get. Israel is an entity that destroys your society, in all of its social forms; they come and organize boys and girls through *'amaliyyat al-isqat* (corruption operations).[17] How do you want us to live with this entity?" The attempt at state expansion under the banner of peace and resolution can only help to move opinions toward programs that are diametrically opposed to Israel's very existence. The characterization of the Palestinian Authority as the "1,000 thieves" that call themselves the "nationalist project" is part of the dark reality brought on by Israel and Oslo: any well-intended, open-minded forces in Palestine that seek a common future for Palestinians and Israelis will be discredited. In addition, the abusive Israeli practices of harassment and corruption—such as recruiting Palestinian kids as informants to the Israeli secret service—tamper with the fabric of Palestinian society and create a fundamental cultural barrier between Palestinians and Israelis.

On the other hand, lack of hope for resolution does not automatically mean that the Palestinians would surrender. In fact, one of the political objectives of martyrdom operations is precisely that they would not allow Israel to win. Throughout the Oslo process Israel was seeking a declaration of the "end of the conflict," in Ehud Barak's famous words. Martyrdom operations were successful in that the end of the conflict is nowhere in sight. It would have been more accurate for Pape to title his book "Dying to Not Let You Win" instead of "Dying to Win." Israel can only win if it can conclude the conflict on its terms. So far all attempts at concluding the conflict by guaranteeing Palestinian surrender have failed, even though many military victories have been gained by Israel. As Anwar states: "The overall strategy [of the resistance] is the liberation. However, we realize that [martyrdom operation] will not liberate Palestine. But it is an expression of no surrender to the reality and for the [Palestinian] cause to remain alive in our memory and [the Israelis'] memory." This statement is essential to gaining a political understanding of the application of these operations as an "expression of no surrender." Contrary to Pape's theory of coercion, the forces that organize martyrdom operations do not believe it is feasible to forge a political settlement with Israel now. The minute there is hope of a genuine negotiated settlement, the application of martyrdom strategies will become inappropriate. The organizers' political goal, while they are at disadvantage in the power scale, is not to let a powerful Israel conclude the conflict and accomplish its objective of reconfiguring Palestine into Israel. As such, strategies of martyrdom remain in the framework of resistance.

Hamas does not have a problem building a Palestinian state on any part of Palestine, no matter how small, as long as doing so does not entail recognition of Israel's entitlement to the remainder of Palestine. As Hasan communicated above, the Israeli disengagement plan is considered a win for Hamas and other forces who have similar programs because Israel withdraws from parts of Palestine without agreements, and that is what Hamas seeks. Palestinians are fully aware that they are at a disadvantage in the power scale, but there is an amazing belief among Palestinians that they will prevail in the end. Hasan shares in this sentiment: "Al mabni 'ala khata' fahuwa khata' (what's founded on wrong is wrong) [an Arabic proverb].[18] We will leave it to future generations. What will not happen here is what has happened with the British in Australia or Canada. The Palestinian culture and the subject of religion are enormous things that will stand in the way of all these proposals being laid out. The resolution is for them to go back or this struggle will continue." These sentiments represent a strong belief among Palestinians that the Israeli programs will most certainly always face. It is the belief that the Palestinian cause cannot be liquidated and the Palestinians cannot become a minority in their own homeland as the Native Americans and Tasmanians did. The reference to culture and religion is a reference to rootedness, sacrifice, and religious practices that hold a community together in the face of the destructive tactics of colonial state expansion.

Another dimension in the political strategy of martyrdom rests on the widespread view among Palestinians and Arabs alike that if Israel is left unchecked, it will act on its expansionist ambitions beyond Palestine in the region. There is a pattern of Israeli territorial expansion and retreat in its short history. Israel occupied the Egyptian Sinai peninsula for six years and southern Lebanon for twenty years, and it has occupied the Syrian Golan Heights for the last forty years. One political achievement that organizers attribute to martyrdom strategies is that they have limited Israel's capacity to conduct further expansions in the region. Hasan asks: "Until when is the Palestinian going to continue to be denied family gatherings? Continue to be dispersed by geographical fragmentation and continue to be denied from the dream of statehood? These kinds of martyrdom operations even scare the wider Zionist project. Their dreams of expansion to Jordan and Lebanon are shattered because they are forced to work in the Palestinian areas and to concentrate on the land of Palestine. This wide spread of the organized military within

Israel and the West Bank, the whole Israeli military machine now occupied in protecting their entity and they no longer can even think of expansion."[19]

This dimension of Hamas's strategy of martyrdom addresses regional and global political objectives. Regionally, these operations not only limit Israel's capacity to expand but also mobilize popular movements in the Arab world to support the Palestinians and pressure their local regimes. Furthermore, the regional instability caused by martyrdom operations exerts pressure on global agencies and powers with interests in the region to be more actively involved. Anwar remarks: "We say the message is that we are a people under occupation and this people seeks liberation. And there is a message to the West and to the Americans, in particular, through these operations that there will not be an investment or a politically stable situation in the Middle East that allows for investment or the simplest of economic investment as long as we have a problem. As long as these operations exist, there is instability in the Middle East region and the Arab and Islamic region as a whole. There is also a message to the Arab nation to give an example for them to follow so we gain their support for complete liberation. This operation proves that no one is weak." Hamas activists believe that the "West" is guided by its material economic interests in formulating its policies as opposed to the cultural ideas that normally drive and motivate national liberation groups. The political stability in the region is a subject that concerns global powers and global economies. Most industrialized nations are compelled to factor the Palestinian-Israeli conflict into their energy policies because of the extent of oil reserves in the Middle East and the impact that the conflict has on the region. Accordingly, having the ability to stir up regional instability where global powers like the United States, the European Union, and the G8 have material interests creates a medium through which small groups can engage the global power structure and global economies. This medium is a dialogue through the performance of violence. It is also a medium for dialogue with Israeli society at large and world Zionism—in contrast to the more limited engagement with Israeli state agents that would be achieved through conventional military action. The strategies of coercion that are employed here go beyond the "enemy" and extend to publics and communities that support the resistance regionally and abroad. This process alters the power configuration. With multiple forces and publics directly engaged in the conflict, the state's actions, policies, strategies, and historical narratives are being checked and judged by different viewers.

Power cannot only be measured through military might. Israel has the military might and could militarily beat the Palestinians in the short run, but it does not have the power to conclude the conflict in the long run. Martyrdom operations project a fear that spreads over Israeli communities and to the Zionist movement as a whole, and they are therefore a source of power for the groups that use them. They also motivate other small oppositional groups in the region. Hamzi has noted that "the martyrdom operation occupies a much wider media space than the conventional operation." Attracting the media to these performances excites actors because that widens the political impact of the performances and the power reach of the actors. In this regard, the media become co-producers of the violent acts, altering the form of violence by paying more attention to some than to others (Allen and Seton 1999).

Anwar explained that Hamas at first executed military operations against Israeli targets with the objective of asserting the presence of Hamas in the playing field. He described Hamas's strategy during the first intifada as allowing any cell that could organize an attack to carry it out. This seems to be the strategy of Islamic Jihad now. Islamic Jihad hardly has an organized presence. Every cell that the group organizes seeks to conduct operations against Israeli targets, and at all times Israeli forces seek to assassinate their members. For Hamas it outgrew this strategy. The group has a wide presence in organization and at the popular level. Its strategies have advanced from asserting the presence of Hamas to entering the political sphere in order to achieve political outcomes from the resistance. Both Anwar, the military leader, and Sheikh Omar, the political leader, espoused a new policy to scale back the performance of martyrdom and coordinate it with political activism. Anwar stated that "the operation has now become a tactic, not a strategy." This shift amounts to a repositioning of the role that Hamas plans to play in the Palestinian-Israeli playing field. Sheikh Omar criticized the PA for negotiating with Israel, because it does so in isolation of the resistance:

> The struggle cannot be built on disorder. There is a political objective. The rifle plants and the politics harvest. When do we plant, when do we harvest, and how? The Palestinians are resisting, this is planting. There are those who

object to the planting, represented by the appointed Palestinian leadership, through dialog, cessations, and agreements with the Israeli side. This was an infertile and mock harvest for the Palestinians.[20]

There cannot be mockery on the political negotiating side that makes a mockery of the people's rights and puts it in a foggy position that threatens its loss. We want to coordinate the rhythm, the rhythm of the resistance. There are various methods to throw out the occupation, both tracks [resistance and politics] have to be in harmony. What is required from all active in the settlement activities [i.e. the negotiators] is to review their calculation and to line up with the beat of the resistance because this is the way to get rid of the occupation.

This analysis further demonstrates Hamas's new thinking with regard to political involvement, especially given that I conducted these interviews shortly after the assassination of Hamas's top two leaders, Sheikh Ahmad Yassin and Dr. Abdel Azziz Al-Rantisi. That Hamas is still expressing such ideas after the assassination of its top leaders indicates that political engagement is a fully formulated and developed strategy of the organization. Using performance terminology to refer to the resistance—"the rhythm of the resistance" and "the beat of the resistance" —and linking the performance of violence to political objectives and the processes of achieving those objectives indicate that Hamas is ready to enter the political sphere and reconfigure martyrdom operations as elements of a political strategy rather than cultural assertions.

Shifting the Battlefields

Martyrdom operations in their military, political, and cultural dimension are moving the Palestinian battle with Israel from the physical battlefield, where Palestinians are at a disadvantage, to the conceptual battlefield of identity and rootedness. Particularly in public spaces, martyrdom operations effectively target the Israeli civil order itself. It is difficult to see how the political goals of Palestinian martyrdom can be formulated if we conduct political analysis in isolation from the cultural assertions associated with this form of violence. Martyrdom as a cultural performance not only mediates social processes among Palestinians by asserting their identity and rootedness but also takes the conflict from the military to the cultural sphere. Whitehead's notion of violence as a cultural performance is a useful tool for helping us understand the cultural space occupied by the violent act and the social processes mediated by its application. What my research adds to this framework is an explanation of how the performance is integrated into material political processes.

The process of shifting the battle from the physical to the conceptual field is achieved primarily by targeting the civil order of the expanding "enemy" state. There is an important difference between suicide operations performed against military targets—such as those of Hezbollah against the Israeli, American, and French armies in the early 1980s, of the Liberation Tigers of Tamil Elam (LTTE) against political leaders in Sri Lanka, and of the Kurdistan Workers Party (PKK) against the Turkish military—and operations carried out by the Palestinian resistance, mostly in civil public spaces in Israel. In fact, responses and reactions to different operations show that operations against military checkpoints and other military targets have less impact and attract much less media attention than operations carried out in public places. With military targets the operation loses potency and some of the cultural meanings conveyed to the communities of the victims as well as the communities of perpetrators in the cultural imaginary. By losing those meanings the operation is less likely to affect wide cultural spheres and spaces. In contrast, operations performed in public spaces against civilian targets affect a much wider space, society at large, and for a much longer time where the threat looms. The terror inflicted on society through these forms of violence represents a form of violence in the imaginary, after Whitehead (2004) and Hinton (2004), that permeates Israeli society and beyond into the Zionist movement. All the political analyses of suicide bombing offered thus far, by scholars and military strategists alike, lump together suicide bombing against military targets and civilian targets, overlooking the significant differences between these two kinds of operations (Bloom 2005; Khosrokhavar 2005; Pape 2005; Shay 2003; Reuter 2004).

Drawing on the analysis by Michel Foucault (1995) of the *Composition of Forces* in seventeenth- and eighteenth-century Europe, I make use of the understanding provided by Foucault of the positioning of the soldier in the battleground. Even though Foucault analyzes strategies of military domination and not tactics of resistance, the insights provided by his analysis are useful in understanding the value of the individual soldier in the battleground. Foucault points out that the value of the soldier lies in the space he occupies. This is precisely what sets the martyrdom operation in civil public spaces apart from conventional military operations. The Palestinian martyrdom operation extends the sphere of action over greater space, well beyond the physical space where it takes place. It affects Israeli society at large, multiple cultural spaces in Palestine and Israel, and communities connected to Palestinians and Israelis regionally and globally. These operations are not merely in retaliation against Israeli army practices, nor do they communicate with the Israeli army per se. They represent a means of dialogue and engagement with Israeli society and the Zionist movement and its supporters. The martyrdom operations question state policies, society's obligations, and individual responsibilities toward a state's actions and policies. They question the state's historical narrative, strategies, and choices for the future. These social and political dynamics are initiated and stirred up through the application of a violence that disturbs the normalcy, the perceived peace, and the constitutionalized civil order.

Certainly strategies of martyrdom as a form of violence in public spaces cannot be fully understood without factoring in the subject of legitimacy. However, the legitimacy in itself is an important element in the power configuration. Although there is no ambiguity in the illegitimacy of violence against civilians in public spaces of the sort carried out in Palestinian martyrdom operations, because these acts of violence mimic the violence of the state, questions arise as to the legitimacy of the state's actions. By making the state's violence visible through the application of mimetic violence against the publics that support the state, the acting groups level the political ground and apply pressure to hold the state accountable to moral standards similar to those applied to members of the opposition and the resistance.

In my interview with Marwan of El-Funoun al-Sha'abiya Dance Troup, which illustrates the resistance through music, dance, and images that express the complexities of Palestinians' lives and their encounter with Israel and the world order, Marwan commented on the message of the resistance scenes:

> The world receives the Palestinian messages in a negative form and they only see the body parts of the other side. They do not ask about the reasons behind this work. The show starts with the bodies. The screen shows the

bodies without the context of the story. The world is responsible for those reasons. The world is responsible for supporting the methods of obliteration. The world is asking why the Palestinian is doing this, when he is supposed to be doing that. Memory is important. If the memory disappears, the entitlement to rights disappears. We have institutions with five thousand years of memories. We are historical from the moment of birth. The world needs to know my history, all of it. We are under occupation, not in a normal state. So there are not normal practices such as martyrdom operations. Why is it asked from one side to be a saint, human, and the other to let go of its dignity? The free is he who refuses other forms of living and insists on living free. You are a slave, not free, as you enslave others. The side that has to prove its freedom is the side that practices enslavement of others. The Palestinian side has no [ethical] problem.

Israeli strategists find themselves in increasingly challenging positions and are baffled that even as Palestinians are engaged in the most violent attacks against Israeli civilians in the history of the conflict, they are gaining international public support (Bloom 2005). In the conceptual field of culturally asserted identity and rootedness, and entitlements to those cultural ideas and social processes, Palestinians have an advantage over Israelis. They are local and indigenous, anciently rooted as opposed to Israelis who are foreign and newcomers.[21] As a newly constructed political entity that has not yet achieved regional acceptance in its place, Israel remains vulnerable in the conceptual field. This vulnerability threatens the legitimacy and viability of the state before the publics that make it and sustain it. At the height of the sustained campaign of martyrdom operations carried out by Palestinian groups against Israeli civilian targets in the spring of 2002 (almost an operation every day), Prime Minister Sharon appeared in the American media several times stating that Israel was the Jewish ancestral homeland. This assertion of Israel's legitimacy was made necessary by the martyrdom operations in public spaces, which took the battle to the identity level and the cultural sphere.

The strategies of martyrdom became the strategies of the resistance as a whole after the Oslo process effectively demonstrated to Palestinians that Israel was not interested in anything other than Palestinian containment and Israeli expansion. It is too early to judge the impact of these strategies on the groups that sponsor them. It also remains to be seen to what extent they will address or realize the political aspirations of Palestinians. One thing is clear, however: Palestinians are not "missing out" on any offer, despite what the American media continue to reiterate. On the contrary, the martyrdom strategies have put an end to a process through which Israel hoped to empower a Palestinian arm that would control the Palestinian population and enable Israel to maintain its expansion and conclude the conflict. The Oslo process, which held promises for Israel and false hopes for the Palestinians, is now history. This does not mean that Palestinians are any closer to their political aspirations, but preventing Israel from concluding the conflict on its own terms represents a persistence of Palestinian nationhood and of the Palestinian entitlement to Palestine.

CHAPTER SEVEN

Conclusion

ANTHROPOLOGY OF VIOLENCE

The performance of martyrdom in Palestine shows how violence may become a logical, meaningful, and intelligible practice. The meanings attached to and generated by the performance of violence may construct certain violent practices to become a significant aspect of people's lives. In fact, martyrdom in Palestine shows that these meanings can even substitute for human life entirely. In my endeavor to understand martyrdom practices in Palestine and the violence associated with martyrdom performances against Israeli targets, I found that the cultural meanings associated with these acts of violence are fundamental to their practice. I learned that their cultural meanings are entangled with their political goals and are prominent in the system of motivations for individuals, groups, and community support. Furthermore, examining and analyzing the cultural ideas expressed through acts of martyrdom provides a close analysis of how the practice of violence figures into the political calculus and insights toward understanding the position of violence in the cultural order.

However, explorations of these performances of violence, their poetic and cultural conceptions, and the new meanings emerging from these poetics do not in any way suggest that the violence manifests specific cultural forms in Palestinian culture. Rather, these acts are generated along the violent encounter with an expanding "modern" state, the violent insertion of political arrangements, and the promotion and dissemination of global cultural ideas of "modernity" according to "development" schemes. Throughout my analyses of martyrdom in Palestine it is very clear that the violence against Israeli targets through the performance of martyrdom operations in Israeli public sites is closely linked to Israeli state violence and the global dynamics of "modernity," cultural hegemony, and the "new world order." I have been careful to bring attention to how violence is enacted as a "cultural performance" (Whitehead 2002) with an intended audience, by means of which the violence becomes a medium to construct and alter cultural relationships between individuals, groups, nations, and global power structures. The exploration of martyrdom in Palestine that I present further demonstrates how violent performances have become a medium for constructing cultural relationships between human lives and their environment and between human lives and divine life. Ethnographic analyses of violence show that violence plays a significant role in human lives.

The performance of violence may be the ultimate medium for constructing and affecting these cultural relations, but rarely is violence the only medium or the final medium for achieving these effects. To fully understand the ideas that make the application of violence culturally appropriate and legitimate, I focused my study on the anthropology of experience, so that individuals are not separate from the social analysis, and experiences are not separate from cultural representations (Klienman, Lock, and Das 1997; Turner and Bruner 1986). Acts, ideas, experiences, and representations cannot be treated in separate realms, nor can they be fully understood separately from each other. Hence the bodily practices, cultural forces, and individual and shared cultural ideas are integral components of human existence. The experience, collective and individual, as lived and conceived from the daily dynamic of the Palestinian encounter with Israel shapes the form of violence. Thus performing violence cannot be only seen through the political instrumental calculus. Its very instrumentality is rather contingent on the performance's capacity to amplify the cultural force of violence through its cultural conceptions. I have intended to show how variations in the aesthetics in the performances of similar acts of violence result in variations in their effects and cultural conceptions in multiple spheres.

My purpose in providing an understanding of the cultural meanings of violence is not intended to lessen the cruelty that violence projects on its victims. Rather these understandings provide us with the tools necessary to develop appropriate and effective responses to violence. In this regard, we have to give equal attention to victims and perpetrators, as the subjectivities of both parties are integral to the act. The act of martyrdom has become widespread in Palestine because it provides cultural meanings to Palestinians and can enter the imaginations of Israelis, Jews, Arabs, Muslims, and international observers. The killing of the Palestinian martyr who performs the martyrdom operation along with the killing of his or her Israeli victims, killings celebrated by individuals, groups, and communities, does not represent a psychological pathology but rather a cultural expression of how violence is conceived and culturally understood, in this specific cultural context in the historic moment of its performance.

Martyrdom constructs a cultural discourse of sociocultural significance. This discourse speaks directly to the relations of Palestinians to Palestine, the Divine, Israeli victims and the Israeli state, the Arab region, Zionist support abroad, and international power structures and publics. The force of martyrdom does not lie only in the pronounced and vivid physical harm suffered by Israeli victims but more importantly in the ways martyrdom reconfigures Palestine in the Palestinian imaginary, asserts Palestinian peoplehood and rootedness in Palestine, recalls history, and reconstructs pre–colonial occupation Palestine, thereby suggesting the fragility of Israel and its institution and constitutions in Palestine.

These theoretical considerations have weighed heavily on my analyses of martyrdom in Palestine. I have not intended to simply engage in criticism of outsiders' attempts to provide understandings of the logic of "suicide bombings," but rather engage some of these contributions from an anthropological perspective by pointing out the cultural complexities associated with the performance of violence and showing how the anthropological understandings lie at the heart of, and are central to, its political analysis. That said, I went the extra length required to provide an anthropology of violence by making sure not to limit my analyses to narrow theoretical paradigms. My study of violence in Palestine is grounded in the recognition that cultural formation and transformation in a community is a very fluid and complex process. Such a process is shaped by a wide spectrum of intercommunity relations; other local, regional, and transregional encounters and exchanges; communities' relations to their place in an ever-changing environment; ideas, beliefs, rituals, and so on; and the historical context of all these relations. Understanding the act of violence as a cultural practice calls for a great deal of extra work to understand its cultural context. If anthropology is to deliver on its promises of providing understandings of distant cultures, then anthropologists cannot afford to approach their inquiries from a narrow theoretical focus. Doing so would barely scratch the surface of their often complex cultural questions and provide texts that are distinguished from the work of other disciplines only by a cultural relativism for which anthropology is often criticized. To provide anthropological analyses that stand apart from narrow political, sociological, or psychological analyses, ethnographers must be doing what anthropology is, studying human practices in their entirety, looking at their many dimensions, viewing them from different angles, and examining the multiple forces that shape them and the multiple voices that express and represent them.

To provide an anthropological understanding of the application of political violence in Palestine I conducted a multi-tier anthropological study. I developed this approach in reflexive engagement with my field research. This multi-tier study provides an account of the multiple dimensions that are relevant to my inquiry into the practice of martyrdom in the context of the Palestinian-Israeli conflict. To grasp the cultural formations in present-day Palestine requires a deep understanding of histories, "prescriptive" and "critical" events as well as the cultural "generative schemes" they have produced, and the current dynamics of the encounter. The study further required competence in understanding signs, symbols, and systems of meanings in rituals and performances where they are applied and manipulated. I have been careful to demonstrate that the different theoretical paradigms relevant to the questions raised are not independent schemes of cultural formation and transformation that independently relate to the human acts I am studying but rather integral components of the same cultural process and the same construction of the acts that are at the center of my study.

Another implication of this study for anthropology lies in how this research demonstrates the centrality of the performance of violence as a cultural expression to the cultural order as a whole. Anthropology has often preferred to confine violence to the pathology of individual actors, and has been resistant to see the collective cultural expressions and conceptions generated by the violence of individuals. Some attention has been given to how state violence mimics the violence of nonstate actors but still fails to see violence as a means of cultural exchange through which cultural relations are mediated. A few ethnographies of violence have demonstrated how the cultural conceptions of violent acts are used to amplify and extend their force into cultural spheres and how these acts of violence generate shared idioms of meanings. The most enlightening of these are an exceptional ethnography by Whitehead (2002) of the practice of Kanaima among Amerindians of the highlands of Guyana and an ethnography by Hinton (2005) of the Cambodian genocide. My research builds on this scholarship on the subject of violence.

My research closely examines the cultural schemes generated along the encounter with external forces and cultural ideas, and their transformations across time. I provide a close look at the cultural representations of the performance of violence to illuminate the oppositions, analogies, and homologies integrated into the performance. By providing a historicized understanding of generative cultural schemes and cultural representations, we can see the extent of the polarizations generated by the performance of the violent act. These polarizations, created by oppositions, analogies, and homologies, generate poetics that give the acts of violence new and shared meanings, a process through which the application of violence generates a cultural force that extends its application to diverse cultural spheres. These poetics and their cultural conceptions provide otherwise unavailable means for mediating social processes.

These capacities of violence not only make the application of violence intelligible but also demonstrate how violence represents a form of cultural expression and exchange through which cultural ideas are formulated and communicated, and cultural relations are constructed, negotiated, defined, and redefined. Thus to fully understand the cultural practices of the people we study, anthropology must recognize the centrality of violence in the cultural order and the working of society.

Anthropology of Martyrdom in Palestine

In my research I analyzed the performance of martyrdom in Palestine as a form of resistance in the context of state expansion. The bulk of the literature on "suicide terrorism" focuses on the political goals and instrumentalities of this form of violence. However, the most careful polit-ical analysis does not necessarily provide a full understanding, particu-larly because this form of violence is mediated through local cultural representations and knowledge. Most political analysis into suicide ter-rorism focuses on the targets of the act and fails to consider the killing of the performer that is integral to the performance. Palestinian acts against Israeli targets through the performance of martyrdom or suicide bombings contain two kinds of violence. The first is the sacrifice of Palestinian bodies in Palestinian places, and the second is violence against Israeli publics in these places. The sacrifice expresses rooted-ness, Palestinian identity, and independence, while the violence against Israeli publics destabilizes Israel as the source of denial of Palestinian identity and rootedness in Palestine.

By analyzing the generative cultural schemes and cultural representa-tion of martyrdom operations in Palestine, I have demonstrated how the bodily practice of sacrificing Palestinians' bodies and violence applied against the "enemy" in the same act mediate cultural ideas such as uprooting and rootedness, fragmentation and unity, confinement and freedom, domination and independence. These social processes are me-diated through the cultural conceptions that are produced by the poetics of martyrdom in Palestine. I have given examples of how the poetics of martyrdom in Palestine create unconfined life for Palestinians, unseg-mented Palestinian peoplehood, and unfragmented and united Palestine in the Palestinian cultural imaginary. These cultural conceptions are also created in opposition to Palestinians' ontological conditions of confine-ment, fragmentation, encapsulation, displacement, uprooting, and po-litical domination. Thus the performances of sacrifice and their cultural representations recreate pre-occupation Palestine, free and naturalized in its Palestinian setting and characteristics. Furthermore, the partici-pants' taking of their own lives further asserts agency, self-reliance, and control. For Palestinians in particular these conceptions mediate long-sought independence. In its construction, application, and conceptions the performance of martyrdom in Palestine intensifies polarizations be-tween ontological conditions and political aspirations, giving rise to a system of motivations for individuals and groups.

I began my study by exploring Palestinian history and how it is inter-twined in constructing and constantly transforming Palestinian cultural identity and representations. I looked particularly at the historical narratives (histories) that are modes of consciousness for the Palestinians, as well as "prescriptive" and "critical" events that have generated cultural schemes within Palestinian society and across their encounter with Israel. By exploring the junctures of histories and historicities in Palestine I sought to historicize the Palestinian cultural present. An examination of the junctures of histories and historicities in Palestine demonstrates that Palestinians have mostly asserted their history of heroism over their losses in their confrontations with colonial powers, Israel in particular. These political attitudes and the historical consciousness of Palestinians continue to inform the Palestinian public's positions in relation to Israel and the future of Palestine. Through this rehearsal of history I also sought to present an image of pre-occupation Palestine that is alive in Palestinian memory and cultural consciousness. I further demonstrated the emergence of land as an object of sacrifice through the generative cultural schemes produced by the history of the encounter with Israel.

I then examined why Palestinians have consistently taken the rocky road, asserting heroism over the catastrophe, by exploring other cultural processes associated with the historical encounter and how these processes form knowledge, influence people's thinking of their environment, and define identities in relation to that environment. The most vivid expression in Palestinian cultural production emerging from an ethnographic reading in Palestine is the theme of rootedness and Palestinians' conceptions of land and place. Examining the history of Palestinian representation in the land of Palestine, Palestinians' ideas about land and how these ideas are reduced to symbols, and the transformation of these symbols across time provides us with a deeper understanding of Palestinian cultural representations in land, as well as an opportunity to appreciate the experiences that Palestinians have when they incorporate these symbols back into their performances. Here we see how Palestinians are engaged in representing peoplehood and nationhood in their environment across time.[1] These explorations demonstrate how symbolic meanings emerge, are articulated, and are transformed in Palestinian communities to assert a sense of community and rootedness in resistance to exclusion, encapsulation, expulsion, denial, and erasing. Such assessments are crucial to understanding and appreciating cultural performances in which these signs and symbols are integrated and provide a window into people's cultural conceptions generated by the poetics of cultural representations and performances. The semiotic analysis and understanding of symbolic meanings is important but not sufficient to understanding the degree to which these symbols are embodied in human lives. By exploring how these semiotics are manipulated—and how they affect communities over time—we have a view of the space that these symbols occupy in the lives of Palestinians.

These symbolic meanings, through their constant performances, further attach Palestinians to the land of Palestine in the absence of physical access to most of it. Furthermore, exploring these performances demonstrates how the land is more extensively configured as Palestine in the Palestinian cultural imaginary than it has ever been, even though much of it has been reconfigured by Israelis in ways foreign to Palestinians. Today we have a better-articulated and better-asserted sense of Palestinian nationhood that is substantiated in a more acculturated land of Palestine. This deep and historicized understanding of signs and symbols is necessary to fully appreciate their use in the cultural representation of the acts and performances of martyrdom and the violence associated with them. Analyzing the poetics of symbolic performance provides us with solid ground for assessing the impact of these symbolic meanings on the lives of the communities and for assessing how they can be integrated into material processes and how they inform and motivate actions.

I have extended my historical cultural analysis into the particulars of colonial state expansion schemes and Palestinian encounters with the state, global agencies, and globalized cultural ideas. The Palestinian issue and the Palestinian-Israeli conflict have been a site of active international diplomacy for nearly a century. The diplomacy has always been accompanied by state expansion schemes. Exploring this history has demonstrated how Israel, with the aid of global agencies, powers, and global media, has persistently presented state expansion schemes as "peace" proposals. Thus to see where these agencies fit in relation to the production of violence, it is important to gain an accurate understanding of the state expansion schemes and the roles of global agencies of development and aid, and of the media.

I have applied and built on the concept of Ferguson and Whitehead (2001) of a "tribal zone" representing the "physical and conceptual space" affected by cultural contact through state expansion. These explorations make visible the episodic, symbiotic, and mimetic nature of the encounter, one that produces a hybrid culture of conflict in which enemies exist in oppositional yet intimate relationships. The encounter itself constitutes a shared historical legacy between the expanding state and the subjects of expansion, and contains mimetic meanings produced by opposition and conflict. Within the tribal zone I sought a historical assessment of the cultural impact that the colonial contact has had on Palestinian indigenous communities and their intercommunity relations. I explored the social transformations associated with colonial contact and the reconfiguration of political and spatial boundaries as well as processes of militarization, resistance, and rebellion. The resulting ethnographic accounts demonstrate how contact with the expanding state creates and modifies political grouping. By providing details on the wider consequences of the encounter with colonial expansion and the transformation of sociopolitical formations, I showed how new forms of tribalization or localized cult formations emerge in Palestinian society.

In these explorations it became apparent how the ideological construction of Zionism as a form of Jewish nationalism that is politically preeminent in the state of Israel creates a state identity that is highly exclusive of non-Jewish populations in the spaces to which the state expands and over which it attempts to inscribe itself. Israeli identity constructions have led Israel to continually seek to incorporate territories into the state and keep their indigenous populations at the periphery of the state system. In response, Palestinian groups developed Palestinian martyrdom operations as a means of resisting state expansion and asserting Palestinian identity and rootedness. Palestinian groups have also used martyrdom operations to exact retaliation, to make historical references, and to articulate cultural concepts of sacrifice.

The analyses of state expansion further reveal the role of international media and international development agencies in the production of local violence. The media present understandings of the conflict that inform the composition of outside interventions, while also affecting the violence itself. Hence the media representation is part and parcel of the violence produced in acts of martyrdom. The media have also promoted Israel's state expansion schemes as peace processes while concealing the details of political agreements and constraints embodied in these agreements that make the Palestinian Authority (PA) into a mere agent of Israel's expansion. As for the international development agencies, by providing relief services to alleviate some of the disastrous outcomes of Israel's state expansion and its associated violence, they not only help pacify the resistance but also make local communities more dependent on the agencies. Furthermore, these global agencies disseminate cultural concepts of "modernity" and foreign cultural ideas that develop a local social class of cultural hybridization. This hybridization of local groups creates "vertical polarization" between the new local élites that work with international agencies and the further marginalized social classes that have become more indigenized by the exclusions and fragmentations of state expansion (Friedman 2003). These processes have contributed to the production of violence in resistance to hybridization and a resurgence of local traditions in resistance to a modernity that stifles cultural distinctiveness.

To understand the conflict and the processes it generates that produce the violence, I have closely examined the link between the external and internal forces producing it. The ethnography presented here moves beyond the cultural representation of the present to examine the generative processes that are constantly forming and transforming current cultural ideas, formations, and representations. By viewing the details of Palestinians' daily life in Palestine and the nature of their encounter with Israel, I provide a window into how the dynamics of the encounter influence people's thinking and decision making on the practicalities of everyday life. These dynamics transform cultural ideas and social patterns and generate social processes that influence individual and group behavior, motivate their actions, and alter their beliefs. To understand the martyrdom and the violent practices associated with its performance, I have sought to provide an understanding of the overarching meanings associated with the practice, the generation and formulation of those meanings as well as what motivates them. Hence my ethnography is anchored in an anthropology of experience that goes beyond cultural representations by viewing cultural forms from a cosmological and ontological point of view (Kapferer 1988). The exploration of experience that I have presented here extends the conception of experience beyond living episodes to the multifaceted range of experiences lived through myriad cultural performances (Turner and Bruner 1986). Within this analysis we can further appreciate the violent practice itself and its position in negotiating and navigating the cultural order.

The description of everyday life in Palestine presented here also demonstrates how the encounter with Israel is a prominent part of Palestinians' texture of life. I have sought to demonstrate the extent of isolation, fragmentation, confinement, encapsulation, domination, and violence to which Palestinians are subjected in order to realize the magnitude of the polarizations between the ontological conditions and aspirations that are created in the cultural representation of acts of resistance. The isolation, fragmentation, and constant threat of violence that Palestinians are forced to live under reconfigure Palestinian society in fundamental ways. Furthermore, I have explored how the loss of ability to navigate one's own space and the constant presence of fear resulting from the physical and imaginary violence projected by the state of Israel lead people toward ideologies and thoughts that provide certainty and reassert cultural ideas. Under these sociopolitical conditions, cultural performances that provide a means for mediating social processes become intelligible, popular acts. The performance of martyrdom includes self-sacrifice in culturally constructed Palestinian places from which Palestinians are excluded as well as retaliatory violence, along with the dynamics of an encounter that is overloaded with state violence. These acts create a site with aspirations and entitlements on one side and confinements, sufferings, and denials on the other. In the poetics of the performance, individuals and groups generate collective cultural conceptions within which homologies are fused, which leads to the mediation of the contested or denied social processes. I gave examples of cultural representations of acts of martyrdom where such polarizations and fusions are created. In the process a naturalized, free, unbounded Palestine is created in the cultural representations, the image connected to the act of sacrifice through which sacrificed Palestinians' body parts create parts of the Palestinian environment through a homologic relationship. As Palestinians sacrifice themselves for Palestine, Palestine is recreated and its cultural characteristics become alive. These dynamics make the performance of self-sacrifice in the martyrdom operation, and its violence against others, into an intelligent act that motivates individuals and groups and is meaningful to the community at large.

The cultural processes associated with and generated by the performance of these martyrdom missions construct a cultural discourse within which a pattern of motivation to carry them through has emerged in Palestine. An individual may be motivated by a variety of reasons based on his or her personal history. However, it is the discourse of martyrdom in Palestine, blending personal experience with local knowledge and cultural ideas, that generates the system of motivation. This system exists in relation to mimetic encounters with Israel and oppositions to its policies, in addition to cultural conceptions of Palestine and political aspirations; the result is that the performance of martyrdom generates poetics rich in sensory meanings and political goals. My exploration of the life histories of some of the mission carriers demonstrates how individual experiences motivate the martyrdom mission within a cultural discourse that melds personal experiences with cultural ideas. These explorations demonstrate how martyrdom missions in Palestine have a fully developed cultural form beyond the political goals of the organizing groups and the motivations and experiences of the individual actors. The martyrdom missions gained popularity through the multiple articulations that accompany their application in the broader Palestinian cultural discourse of resistance, sensory meanings embedded in the aesthetics of their performance, and the nature of the encounter with the state of Israel and the ways these operations mimic Israeli state violence. The conceptions of these "poetics of violence"—the effects of the semiotic performances over time—give the violence the capacity to mediate social processes, thereby making its performance an intelligible act (Whitehead 2002; Whitehead 2004).

Once this motivation system is fully developed, it becomes real for everyone who lives in the cultural dynamic where this cultural discourse takes place, as the individual becomes socially integrated into it and the cultural representations of the experiences of others cease to be separate from experiencing. Within the cultural discourse of martyrdom the life of the martyr is further articulated and illuminated through the impact of the sacrificial performance. Martyrdom becomes a form of living in and by death. It becomes a form of living preferable to the crippled present life. Conceptualized as such, death would become something not feared but something to compete for, a form of living that is more meaningful than Palestinians' actual lives. In this context, death is about living, not dying. To die is to live. The sacrifice of the body and its *concentration* through the performance of this form of violence against the backdrop of the encounter with Israel and its histories and landscape, senses, and conceptions makes a concentration of the *sacrificer*, here the social person performing the sacrifice (Hubert and Mauss 1964). Thus the social person is made an icon through the sacrifice of the body.

This concentration of the martyr icon is further extended to the community at large through its representation. The representations assert the iconic image of the martyr carrier and motivate future participants. Within this discourse the conceptual space that the martyr's life occupies is much wider than the physical and social space the person occupies in life. It is primarily this social life of the martyr that is constructed in the cultural discourse of martyrdom that makes death through sacrifice something to aspire to. Furthermore, these martyrs become immortalized in the representations and poetics that these representations produce. By extension, the Palestinian *people*, whom these icons signify, become immortalized. Hence the immortalization of martyrs' physical fusion in the land of Palestine through the "blood covenant" of sacrifice becomes an immortalization of Palestinian peoplehood and the rootedness of the Palestinian nation in the land of Palestine.

Martyrdom mediates conditions of social suffering and is also a ritual directly connected to the creation of an alternative life. The overwhelming suffering of Palestinians, combined with a discourse of negligence, silence, complacency, and complicity in the conditions of suffering, makes the world uninhabitable. The cultural meanings associated with martyrdom and sacrifice for the land, the people, and the Divine make more life in the loss of life. Hence the loss of life through a mission of martyrdom is *dying to live*. The representations presented exemplify sacrifice as a ritual sequence connected to patterns of creation (Lincoln 1991). The dismembered parts of the sacrificed martyrs recreate Palestine. These ideas are conceived of through homologic relations according to which different parts of Palestine are created by corresponding pieces of sacrificed martyrs' bodies. This relationship is conceived through the breakdown of the human body and their mapping onto the place for which the human body is sacrificed, Palestine. The martyr's blood becomes water, streams, and rivers that nourish the fields. The martyr's flesh becomes soil where plants grow. The martyr's tears become oceans and seas. The martyr's bones become mountains that hold Palestine together. Through these homologies the human life of the martyr is transformed into the life of Palestine and, by extension, the Palestinian people.

These cultural meanings attached to the act of martyrdom motivate individuals and groups to carry them through and enable the acts of martyrdom to be integrated into political and military strategies. That the Palestinian civil order is ruined through Israeli state violence makes meaningful the terror projected on Israeli publics through the violence of martyrdom operations, in that the operations challenge the normalcy of Israelis' lives even as they mimic Israel's violence toward Palestinians. The political strategies of martyrdom seek to mimic Israeli state violence by projecting on Israeli publics a terror that challenges the legitimacy and normalcy of Israel's civil order, an order built on the destruction and constant deformation of the Palestinian civil order. These processes make the application of this form of violence appropriate in the collective Palestinian conceptions.

The strategy of martyrdom, and the violence applied against civilians in particular, represent a strategy of challenging state legitimacy and questioning the global political order. Martyrdom operations challenge the "internationally" established rules of engagement as enshrined in international human rights, international law, and global agencies' frames of reference by bringing the battlefield into new sites in the public spaces. Doing so brings attention to the pattern of using these international tools unequally, based on political power. These martyrdom strategies seek to challenge Israeli state legitimacy and also to challenge the legitimacy of the global order and its international legal and moral codes.

The strategy of moving the battle to nonconventional sites and the performance of nonconventional violence extend the force of violence into wider conceptual fields. They move the confrontation away from one between, on one side, the state and its security apparatuses and, on the other side, opposition and resistance groups. In its place is a confrontation in which multiple forces are engaged from both societies of the fighting forces, their wider alliances, and distanced observers in the conceptual battleground. Transforming the battle one waged primarily in the conceptual fields and the identity level broadens the engagement of civil societies, giving more weight to the moral elements in the struggle and reasserting the cultural dimensions of the conflict. Expanding states and the societies supporting them that become targets of martyrdom strategies are then compelled to fight their battles culturally in the conceptual fields and not just militarily in the physical fields, where they have an edge. This reconfiguration of the battleground leads to a reconfiguration of the power structure. These capacities produced by acts of violence that target civilians make their application logical and intelligent for the groups that sponsor them. In my view this strategy comes with no guarantees of positive results or positive engagements on the part of new forces and publics that are brought into the conflict spheres. But it certainly reconfigures the battlefield in composition and in the form of engagements. Furthermore, by making the state's violence visible through the application of mimetic violence against the society of the state system, the acting groups level the political playing field and apply pressure to hold the state accountable to moral standards similar to those expected of oppositions and resistance.

Directions for the Future

I have provided an ethnographic explanation and understanding of the cultural and political forces that make violent martyrdom meaningful and culturally appropriate for the communities and groups that practice it. All the strategies of martyrdom presented rest on the premise that the violence and the societal support for it are a form of resistance to oppressive state practices and global politics. As long as the oppositional groups and the local societies that support them hold the higher moral ground, these strategies are intelligible to individuals and groups, and hence they are bound to increase and intensify. Thus all effective responses to strategies of martyrdom will depend on the morality of states and their actions.

I also demonstrate that the state's violence, which often has been greater and more catastrophic than that of the resistance, does not necessarily derail the resistance but rather fuels it and makes its performance of violence more culturally valid. I further demonstrate the state's interest in a continued level of violence or threatened violence against its citizenry and alliances as a way of maintaining unity. Thus in developing appropriate responses to violence, we must focus on societal strategies: we must not leave the task of developing responses to the state alone, since it helped to bring about the violence in the first place and may have an interest in perpetuating it. Second, to develop an effective response to violence that is primarily a form of cultural assertion, we need to pay equal attention to all the cultural and political forces that are participants in the production of violence, including not only the perpetrators' groups but a range of political and cultural agencies of both societies that are in conflict, as well as global agencies.

The performance of violence in "civil" public sites is an explicit assertion that political conflicts are between societies in their cultural and social entirety and not just between armies and resistance groups. The key to an effective response is not to rally behind the calls of states and global agencies to respect the organization of conflicts, war, and violence, but rather to demand that state and global agencies pursue moral conduct and thus challenge the morality of the performers of violence. States and global agencies have been invested in organizing conflicts that conform to specific sites, such as organized armies, and demand that resistance groups bring their contestations to those sites. This form of violence, unlike warfare, seeks to challenge states and the global order's authority to dictate the rules of engagement. A good starting point in developing alternative response strategies may be to think of how we can challenge the moral and political authority of the groups that perform this kind of violence by questioning the morality of the political and regulatory systems and the Israeli state policies and practices to which the violence is a response.

As demonstrated in my research, Palestinian cultural identity and rootedness in Palestine is a prominent aspect of the Palestinian social being.
The performance of martyrdom operations is closely linked to these cultural assertions. One way of thinking about alternative responses to this kind of violence would be to think of means by which these legitimate social processes can be expressed and mediated. What alternatives can be created for expressing cultural identity, rootedness, and senses of place and space so that these social processes can be experienced and mediated? How can we lessen the gap between Palestinians' conditions on the ground and their aspirations for freedom, independence, and sense of home? We will find that many of the sources of meaning for the performance of violence can be undermined if the Israeli state's policies change in ways that open new ways for Palestinians to experience the

social processes that are mediated through the performance of the violent act.

The Palestinian example explored here demonstrates that punishing or liquidating actors and groups pursued by the state does not necessarily remove the cultural sources of conflict or end the violence. Many Palestinian resistance groups that were active in the 1960s no longer exist. Others active in the 1970s and 1980s no longer exist. Still others changed their forms of resistance through history. But one constant is the resistance. The only thing that the state's "counter-resistance" strategies accomplish is to recirculate the groups' destructions and formations. However, the form of resistance chosen by the new groups is informed by the histories of their predecessors, and the resistance is increasingly vehement. The total demise of an active group will not end the violence as long as the cultural source of violence persists. Any serious effort to diminish this form of violence must address the social processes that make its performance appropriate from the performer's perspective. The most prominent of these processes is a recognition of Palestinian cultural identity in Palestine and an opening of the physical space for Palestinians to realize Palestine in Palestinian cultural characteristics.

The current Israeli political dynamics in Palestine, which rest on separating Palestinians and Israelis through the "disengagement plan," is a process that further intensifies the violence and threatens more violent confrontations between the two societies. The separation between the two groups reduces the relationship between them to that of war. These processes of organizing difference help the state of Israel to legitimize to its citizenry policies of continuous war, containment, and isolation against the Palestinians and to maintain the power needed to continue these policies. At the same time, the separation physically isolates Palestinians from places to which they are strongly connected and in which they are rooted. This geographic separation of Palestinians will continue to be a source of violence, as Palestinians strive for a conceptual rootedness and the maintenance of Palestine in the cultural imaginary in the absence of physical access. Hence the most promising approach for reducing the violence is to move the political process in directions that would open spaces for alternative exchanges between Palestinians and Israelis, restore access of Palestinians to their landscape, break down physical barriers, and afford Palestinians space in which to experience their rootedness. In this book I have analyzed the social processes mediated among Palestinians through the performance of violence: rootedness, cultural identity, independence, and freedom. The key to appropriate responses to martyrdom and the violence associated with its performance is not to suppress these legitimate social processes but to open alternative avenues for their mediation.

The Newspaper at a Glance on a "Normal" Day in
Palestine Al-Hayat, 23 April 2004

Main headlines:

Bulldozing Lands in Dir El-Balah, Attacking Mosque in Yatta,
Arrests in Hebron and Bethlehem

Nine Citizen Martyrs in Qalqilya, Tulkarem, and Beit Lahi,
Among Them Two Young Girls and One Boy

The Destruction of 20 Houses in Rafah and the Occupation
Inflicts Wide Destruction in the North of Gaza

Sharon: "The American Support We Got Is an Unprecedented
Historical Accomplishment for Israel"

Subtitles:

The arrests of four citizens in the town of Al-Khader and Bethlehem

The assassination of three activists among them the local leader of
Al-Aqsa Martyrs Brigades in Tulkarem Camp

The attack on a mosque in Yatta and the arrest of 10 youths in Hebron
A child wounded in a settler attack on citizens' houses in Hebron

Two young girls killed and 20 citizens wounded by the occupation
in Beit Lahi

The destruction of handicapped rehabilitation center and
the number killed in two days rises to 14

The destruction of 20 homes and three citizens during an
incursion in *Rafah*

An incursion into *Al-Barakeh* area and the bulldozing of
20 dunums* of farm land in *Dir El-Balah*

Al-Nada area, Gaza is threatened by the occupation terror

Shabak (Israel Secret Service) reveals that the three Palestinian youths arrested in Nazareth have no relation to the charged killing of the Israeli

* One dunum is 1000m².

CHAPTER ONE Introduction

1. In 1968 Israel launched its first military offensive in the Jordanian Al-Karameh valley against the newly organized Palestinian armed resistance, the Palestine National Liberation Movement (Fatah) and the Popular Front for the Liberation of Palestine (PFLP). Reports from the Al-Karameh battle described Palestinian fighters strapping themselves with explosives and throwing themselves at Israeli tanks, and Palestinian fighters firing rocket-propelled grenades at virtually point-blank range. The Israeli military, having suffered an unanticipated level of casualties and loss of tanks and armored vehicles, was forced to withdraw. This was the first Arab victory against the Israeli army, which had recently (in 1967) scored a major victory against the armies of Egypt, Syria, and Jordan.

2. In Islam a *shahid* is someone who has died while fighting a Muslim's war. Dying in the cause of spreading Islam's message is referred to as *al-mawtu fi sabili allah* (the death in the path for God) and the death is considered *shahadah* (martyrdom). Among the cognates of the term are *shahada* (witnessed) and *istashhada* (the main pillar of Islam of the *shahadatayn*). The *shahadatayn* are the declarations that there is no God but Allah and that Muhammad is his messenger. Pronouncing the shahadatayn is enough for a person to be considered Muslim.

3. Interview with Anwar, a leader in the Izzideen al-Qassam Brigades, Jenin, January 2005.

4. These Palestinian cities were mostly depopulated of their Palestinian inhabitants in 1948 and subsequently populated by Israelis. Palestinian inhabitants of East Jerusalem remained in the city, but Jerusalem as a whole remains out of reach for the majority of Palestinians. I elaborate on the significance of these places throughout the book.

5. The interviews were conducted with more than one person. Normally in the interview I would talk with the father, the mother, and sometimes siblings.

6. This category included leaders in the brigades of Hamas (Islamic), Fatah (secular), and the P F L P (Marxist), as well as members of these brigades.

7. This category includes what Palestinian activist communities refer to as *musayyisseen* (political cadres). These are activists affiliated with certain active groups who serve as intermediaries between on the one hand the political leadership and resistance groups and on the other hand the general public. They play a significant role in situating the act of resistance in the political and cultural context.

8. Interview with one of the top political leaders of Hamas in Palestine.

9. The category includes activists who organize and participate in demonstrations, such as those who attack the Israeli army with stones when they enter Palestinian towns. For two of the activists who were under the age of eighteen, I conducted the interviews after obtaining permission from their parents, and in the presence of at least one of the parents.

10. Women twenty-five to forty-five years old who were active in the making of the cultural discourse of the resistance.

11. Activists who focused on issues related to Palestinian refugees, such as the right of return, refugees' integration in or exclusion from the political process, and their role in the "development" programs of N G O s.

12. Families whose homes have been taken by the Israeli army for use as a base of operations while soldiers conduct undercover operations in the city, during which the family members are kept as hostages.

13. Cultural performers and producers who are independent of organized groups.

14. Among those interviewed were traditional farmers knowledgeable about land tenure systems who worked their lands.

15. This interview included a Palestinian scholar who has been following the development of Islamic groups in the Palestinian resistance.

CHAPTER TWO   Histories and Historicities in Palestine

1. A *hamula* is an extended family or nonnomadic tribe. Villages in Palestine normally consist of a few hamulas; some hamulas can spread over a few villages.

2. Marj Ibin 'Amer is the central fertile plain in Palestine, between Nazareth and Jenin, that has historically been regarded by Palestinians as the breadbasket of Palestine (Al-Dabbagh 1972).

3. A working animal was an ox or mule, rarely a horse.

4. Interview, Othman, Jenin, January 2004.

5. *Al-marba'aniyya* is the winter period that begins about 20 December and extends until the end of January.

6. Zer'in, a Palestinian village in the central Marj Ibin 'Amer Plain, was demolished by Israel in 1948.

7. Al-qaq is a perennial plant.

8. These techniques of demarcation are still common in rural Palestine today.

9. Interview, Othman, January 2004.

10. Ibid.

11. Interview, Faisal, February 2004.

12. Interview with Ismael, Berqin, October 2004.

13. Khalidi (1997) reports two incidents of confrontation between the *fellahin* and the new Jewish settlers over land eviction, one in the Tabaria area in the village of Sejera in 1907, the lands of which were sold by the Sursuq family in Beirut, and one in the village of Al-Foula in central Marj Ibin 'Amer in 1909, site of the present-day Israeli town of Afula. The confrontations resulted in the death of one Jewish settler and two Palestinian fellahin in 1907, and two Jewish settlers in 1909.

14. Many instances of dispossession resulted in confrontation between the fellahin land owners and the British authorities. Akram Za'iter (Za'iter 1980), who was among the organizers of the revolution of 1936, reports in his diary: "On January 30th, 1935 I received a letter from Haifa that the Arabs were kicked out of Al-Harthiya lands near Haifa. The land is about 12,000 dunums and farmed by the Zebaidat extended family that consists of nearly 60 farming families. The Jewish company claimed that it had purchased it from Iskander Sursuq in Beirut. When the land register came along with the police to execute the court order of evacuating the Zebaidat family they resisted the evacuation and Saad Mohammed Ali was killed and fell as *Shahid* defending his land."

15. From *al-hasad al-jihadi al-usboui' likatae'b al-qassam* (Weekly Harvest of the Qassam Brigades Struggle), 5 February 2004.

16. My translation from the Arabic.

17. In Arabic culture the horn represents corruption, rudeness, and carelessness. A person who is openly corrupt and does not care may be described as *mqarrin*, meaning that he has horns.

18. The *munazara* is a poetry contest between poets or popular poets of *zajal*. The zajal is a folkloric singing contest in which the poets improvise poetry spontaneously.

19. In the fall of 1935 Palestinians were furious over the news that a shipment supposedly of cement from Belgium to a Jewish company in Tel Aviv turned out to be a huge shipment of rifles, machine guns, and ammunition. Jews were permitted to carry arms and train on "their" settlements, while it was illegal for Palestinians, other than those working for the English police, to bear arms under the British administration (Za'iter 1980).

20. Palestinian activists often cite historical events from these sources in their statements and historical references.

21. Misha'al refers to a Palestinian farmer who resisted during the British Mandate and became a symbol of resistance and sacrifice among Palestinians. Songs are sung in his name.

22. Salman Abu Sitta, a Palestinian engineer, printed a map of Palestine locating all the destroyed Palestinian villages and providing information about massacres and refugee populations. He also wrote a paper on Israeli demographics in which he argued that most of the rural areas were scarcely populated and that there was room to accommodate returning Palestinian refugees. This paper became a historical document to Palestinian activists and was treated almost like a land deed.

23. Interview with Iyad, a singer from Jenin Refugee Camp, December 2004. Explanations added.

24. The cities of Akka (Acre), Haifa, Jaffa, Safad, Tiberias, Bissan (Bet Shaen), Bir As-Sabea' (Beer Sheba), Al-Lod, Al-Ramla, Khedara (Hedara), and Al-Majdal (Ashqalon).

25. New Israel evacuated nine Palestinian villages in 1949 and thirteen villages in 1956, and depopulated the coastal city of Al-Majdal in the south by trucking its nine thousand Palestinian inhabitants into the Gaza Strip in 1951. Some Palestinian Bedouin tribes were forced out of the Negev desert into Jordan in 1959 (Al-Dabbagh, 1971; Jiryis 1973). New Israel further confiscated approximately 70 percent of the properties belonging to residents of the remaining Palestinian villages that were not depopulated or destroyed (Jiryis 1973).

26. The ID card was and still is the Israeli occupation's main tool of control. The Israeli army often takes the ID cards of Palestinian youths, who are then asked to wait by the side of the road. The wait can last a few hours, a day, or overnight. Palestinians are effectively immobilized as long as the ID card is in the hands of the army. Anyone who abandons the site and leaves without his or her ID card would be placed on the wanted list and therefore subject to arrest at any time, or, these days, at risk of being killed by the Israeli army.

27. Begin was the Israeli prime minister at the time.

28. The makhsum tayyar is a surprise Israeli army checkpoint. This is not one of the normal stationed checkpoints, which people know about and can circumvent. In some trips we would encounter half a dozen of these temporary checkpoints between Ramallah and Jenin in addition to the permanent ones.

29. Interview with Madi, Nablus, February 2004.

30. Interview with Majdi, Jenin Refugee Camp, December 2004.

CHAPTER THREE   State Expansion

1. *Rawabet al-qura* is a program initiated by Israel under which the West Bank and Gaza were organized into regional village councils staffed by Palestinian figures friendly to Israel and some informants and collaborators with Israel.

2. *Al-hukm al-thati*, proposed to the Palestinians under the Israel-Egypt peace treaty brokered by President Jimmy Carter, provided that the Palestinians would have control over municipal administrative affairs in their communities, but that the communities would remain under the Israeli state system.

3. *Al-idara al-madaniyeh* is a project attempted by Israel during the early 1980s under which Israel changed the name of *al-hukm al-'askari* (the military authority) to *al-idara al-madaniyya* (the civil administration). There were no noticeable changes in the rules apart from changes in titles and appearances. *Al-hakem al-'askari* (the military governor) of the city became *ra'is al-idara al-madaniyya* (the civil administrator), *maqar al-hukm al-a'askari* (the military headquarters) of the city became *markaz al-idara al-madaniyya* (the civil administration center), the legend at the top of Palestinian ID cards was changed from *qiyadat jaysh al-difa'a al-isra'ili* (leadership of the Israeli Defense Army) to *al-idara al-madaniyya li mantiqat yahouda wa al-samera* (Civil Administration for Judea and Samaria Region), and some of the Israeli army officers started wearing civilian clothes in the headquarters. Judea and Samaria are the Hebrew names that Israel uses to refer to the Palestinian territories in the West Bank.

4. *Al-taqasum al-wazifi* is a project of civil administration that Israel attempted to implement in the West Bank and Gaza in cooperation with King Hussein of Jordan in 1985–86. The project was aimed at establishing local municipal administrative governments tied to Jordan while Israel maintained control of territories, security, and natural resources. Similar ideas are now being reintroduced by Israel.

5. Article I, the *Agreement in Preparatory Transfer of Powers and Responsibilities between Israel and the PLO*, August 29, 1994, Avalon project at Yale Law School.

6. During its administration of the West Bank, Israel maintained some of the Jordanian laws that had been in effect in these territories before its occupation. Some of these laws were also maintained under Oslo.

7. Article IX, *Oslo Declaration of Principles*, 1994, Avalon project at Yale Law School.

8. Article VII, the *Agreement in Preparatory Transfer of Powers and Responsibilities between Israel and the PLO*, August 29, 1994, Avalon project at Yale Law School.

9. Article IX, the *Agreement in Preparatory Transfer of Powers and Responsibilities between Israel and the PLO*, August 29, 1994, Avalon project at Yale Law School.

10. Article V, *Agreement on Preparatory Transfer of Power and Responsibilities between Israel and the PLO*, August 29, 1994 states: "The Palestinian Authority will con-

tinue to employ Palestinian Civil Administration employees currently employed in the offices included in each Sphere."

11. Bet Eil is the Israeli headquarters of the West Bank and Gaza administration north of Ramallah. The administration headquarters is the same center that has directed Israel's army activities and policies during the occupation of the West Bank territories since 1967.

12. Al-irtibat al-madani is the department in the PA through which Israel passes on its instructions and lays out details to the PA at the regional and local levels of the extent of its authority. Al-irtibat al-madani handles a number of issues like individuals' permits to Israel, failed border crossings, reports of persons taken prisoner by Israel, and attempts to get an ambulance through a checkpoint.

13. Both towns are originally Palestinian. Afula was the Palestinian village Al-Foula, site of the first confrontation between Palestinian farmers and Jewish immigrants over land dispossession in 1909 (Khalidi 1997). Khedara was the Palestinian town of Al-Khedayra, which had its Palestinian population displaced in 1948 and was fully occupied by Jewish settlers.

14. Statement by the Political Bureau, Islamic Resistance Movement (Hamas), 16 April 1994 (Hroub 2000).

15. Ibid.

16. Interview with Zaki, Jenin, December 2004.

17. Interview with Kamal, Al-Aqsa Martyrs Brigades, Jenin, January 2005.

18. *Israel-Palestine Liberation Organization Agreement, 1993*, Avalon project at Yale Law School, http://www.yale.edu/lawweb/avalon/mideast/isrplo.htm.

19. *Agreement on Preparatory Transfer of Powers and Responsibilities between Israel and the PLO*, August 29, 1994, Avalon project at Yale Law School, http://www.yale .edu/lawweb/avalon/mideast/transfer_powers.htm.

20. Among these new groups were the national and international networks of the Popular Committees for the Defense of the Right of Return in Palestine, the Higher Committee for the Defense of the Right of Return in Jordan, A'idun (returning) in Syria and Lebanon, the Association for the Defense of the Rights of the Internally Displaced in Shafa 'Amer in Palestinian communities in Israel, the Palestine Right to Return Coalition, and *al-awda* (the return) in Europe and North America, as well as research and resource centers dedicated to the right of return and refugee issues like the Alternative Resource Center for Palestinian Residency and Refugee Rights *Badil* (the alternative) in Bethlehem-Palestine, the Arab Resource Center *al-jana* (the harvest) in Lebanon, and the Palestine Return Center (PRC) in London.

21. Interview with Dr. Iyad Barghouthi, Ramallah, January 2005.

22. Interview with Kamal, an Al-Aqsa Martyrs Brigades leader, Jenin, January 2005.

23. The stolen cars are Israeli cars, provided by suppliers in large numbers.

Many of the overt brigades' members drive them around. The Israeli Shabak (the active Israeli undercover units in Palestine) also use them to target some of the brigade members by sending stolen cars set up with explosives.

24. One of the main weapons and ammunition dealers in the area is involved in the Al-Aqsa Martyrs Brigades and has been engaged in similar activities since the first intifada and the *al-fahad al-aswad* (Black Panthers) period. Some are suspicious of his survival in militarized activism over such a long period of time since he is not undercover.

25. Interview with Hamzi, leader of the Al-Aqsa Martyrs Brigades in Jenin, January 2004.

26. Interview with Reda, member of the Al-Aqsa Martyrs Brigades in Jenin, October 2003.

27. Ibid.

28. Interview with Shalabi, a Fatah cadre in Jenin, October 2003.

29. Interview with Anwar, a leader of the Izzideen Martyrs Brigades, Jenin, January 2005.

30. *Haram* is the forbidden according to the Islamic *shari'a* (religious law). The term is also often used to refer to any cruel act.

31. Interview with Salim, a political cadre of Hamas in Jenin, May 2004.

32. *Fiqih* is the field of religious interpretation in Islam.

33. *Takfir* is the declaration of Muslim individuals or groups as *kuffar* (infidels).

34. Interview with Marwan, El-Funoun El-Sha'abiya Dance Troup, Jerusalem, December 2004.

35. *Zakat* is the taxation on income that a Muslim is obliged to pay according to the Shari'a code. Hamas set up a program to collect zakat money from Palestinians in Palestine, but mainly it collects money for relief efforts from Palestinians in exile. Hamas distributes these funds to the needy through the Zakat Committees according to the religious code. The effects of this distribution are noticed by the community, and no charges of theft or corruption have been made against Hamas's institutions.

36. The Imam is the religious sheikh who leads the prayer at the Mosque and delivers the Friday sermon.

37. Interview with Dr. Iyad Barghouthi, Ramallah, January 2005. The *mahsoubiyeh* is a form of institutional corruption under which promotions, allocations, and appointments are decided based on personal connections; the term also refers to the cults of personalities that this sort of corruption produces.

CHAPTER FOUR   The Carrier

1. Interview with Suleiman Mansour, Jerusalem, January 2005.

2. Normally what the shops are playing is the audio material that is selling at

the time. Samples represent the general mood of the market; these days the audio sampling seems to respond to the need to make sense of the surrounding environment. Some of the audio shops would be playing the latest Arabic pop music in a matter of weeks in a relaxed political environment.

3. The randomness of the Israelis' intrusions into the city—when they surround it, close it, or enter it—makes for an enormous sense of uncertainty and anxiety that changes people's movements and temperament in the market.

4. See reports on mental health conditions in the Gaza area produced by Gaza Community Mental Health Program at www.gmcmhp.net.

5. "Not allowing it to affect you" refers to psychological trauma. However, enduring violence for extended periods does affect people culturally in fundamental ways, as explored here.

6. Awsaj is a local wildflower that sprouts in the Palestinian landscape in the springtime.

7. A new Italian film entitled Private by Saverio Costanzo (2005) presents an excellent visual, artistic depiction of these experiences.

8. Interview with Salem's family, Jenin, October 2003.

9. Interview with Ahlam, Jenin, October 2003.

10. During my research in Jenin a driver was shot dead on the access road to the settlement of Ganim. The driver was not from the area and did not realize he was on a settlement road when he was shot by the patrolling Israeli army vehicle.

11. Hannoun is the poppy flower which Palestinians believe takes its red color from martyrs' blood. See chapter 2.

12. Sheikh Izzideen Al-Qassam was a Palestinian leader of the revolution against the British in 1936 who died fighting in the Jenin area. He is the hero for whom Hamas's military wing is named. See more details in chapter 2.

13. Yahia Ayyash is the Hamas leader known as "the Engineer" who first started the martyrdom operations in the Palestinian resistance.

14. Hasan al-Banna is the Egyptian founder of the Muslim Brotherhood movement. Hamas represents the Palestinian branch of the organization. The movement is strong in Jordan and Egypt.

15. For most Palestinians in Palestine the Star of David is a symbol of Zionism. It is often used in Palestinian posters to denote Zionist colonialism in Palestine. However, most of these depictions illustrate Israeli army brutality against Palestinians, and the symbol has evolved to signify aggression rather than colonialism more generally.

16. Qassam is a reference to the Izzideen al-Qassam Brigades, Hamas's military wing.

17. Al-liwa is a flag that signifies the quest.

18. "Set me up" here is a call to be set up as a "suicide bomber" on a self-sacrifice mission.

19. Zakariya Zbaideh is the leader of Al-Aqsa Martyrs Brigades, Fatah's military wing, that is also involved in sending martyrdom operations. I chose not to use a pseudonym here because he is a known figure and naming him here does not reveal any new information.

20. The *istishhadiyeen* (singular *istishhadi*) are those who go on *'amaliyyat istishhadiyya* (martyrdom operations).

21. *Zaghareed* is a high-pitched type of yodeling normally done by women at celebrations, and signifies a key moment in an event—for example, when the groom enters the party, or the groom places the ring on the bride's finger, or the bride enters her new husband's house, or a mother hears of her son's or daughter's success in graduation from school.

22. The reference to tearing down the Al-Aqsa mosque builds on Palestinian worries about Israeli plans, models, and debates concerning the possible re-erecting of the Jewish temple mount on the site of Al-Aqsa mosque in Jerusalem. Details of the debate in Israeli society are explored in Abu El Haj (2001), *Facts on the Ground.*

23. The phrase "blood is beating, looking forward to blooming flowers" is in reference to the *shaqiq* or *hannoun* flower, the red flower that covers much of the landscape in Palestine during the spring (see note 12 to chapter 4, above). The blood is pushing people to become martyrs and refers to those who are ready to go on sacrifice operations, eager to have their blood bloom out of the land of Palestine in the next season.

24. The phrase "beneath you" refers to a tunnel that the Israelis have dug under Al-Aqsa mosque; attempts to open it in 1996 sparked protests at which hundreds died. The phrase also refers to Israeli archeological digs that are taking place under Al-Aqsa mosque, compromising the stability of the mosque structures.

25. *Ababil* are birds described in a Qur'anic story. In the story the birds carry balls of fire and drop them on the invading Abrahha Al-Ashram army, successfully pushing it back and preventing Al-Ka'aba, the Muslims' holiest shrine in Mecca, from being destroyed.

26. All Palestinian factions that have a military wing call it "Brigades." When they speak of brigades they are referring to the military wings of the factions that emerged in the recent intifada and practiced the martyrdom operation.

27. Saraya is the military wing of Islamic Jihad and Qassam is the military wing of Hamas.

CHAPTER FIVE Dying to Live

1. This thought was expressed to me by Hasan (a Hamas activist) in an interview, Ramallah, March 2004. The argument was also confirmed by members of Al-Aqsa Martyrs Brigades in subsequent interviews.

2. Interview with Kamal, Jenin, January 2005.

3. Interview with Shalabi, Jenin, October 2003.

4. In the traditional naming of parents the *abu* (father of) or *um* (mother of) would be followed by the first name of the eldest son.

5. These years mark the beginnings of the labor migration to the Gulf states as the oil industry created new job opportunities there.

6. *Nai'meh* is finely crushed stone used to prepare concrete.

7. *Jableh* is the concrete mix, which then was mixed by hand using a hoe.

8. A dunum is 1,000 square meters.

9. Al-Fahad al-Aswad, a splinter of Fatah that was born toward the end of the first intifada, carried out armed raids on Israeli targets. Mainly it set up ambushes for Israeli army vehicles and interrogated and killed Palestinians suspected of collaborating with Israel. The group was critical of the Fatah political leadership.

10. The *Mukhtar* is like the mayor of a village.

11. *Omra* is the process of visiting Mecca and conducting most of the Haj rituals and prayer during times of the year other than the Haj time.

12. The cars that Eyad used were stolen cars from Israel, which are available in abundance in the Jenin area (see note 23 to chapter 3, above). The stolen cars are used by both the Palestinian resistance and the Israeli army. Reportedly many wanted members of resistance factions have been killed when they were sold a stolen car with a bomb in it that the Israeli Shabak remotely set off when the wanted person was in the car.

13. *Niyyaluh* is an expression of envy: "How lucky he is to get what he has got." In this case it refers to martyrdom.

14. These results have changed in the last two decades because of the tightening grip of occupation, economic setbacks for the average family, Israeli restrictions on Palestinian movements in and out of Palestine, and the inability of most graduates to find jobs. Now certificates are valued mainly for the social status that they bring.

15. Jerusalem Media and Communication Center, 2003.

16. *Pomila* is a large citrus fruit, larger than a grapefruit.

17. The *'asha'* is the last call for prayers for the day, about two hours past dusk.

18. This is an Israeli army practice: a soldier cocks a gun when walking into a bus to show that the gun is empty. The organizers have followed the procedures of the Israeli army in detail so that the carrier is not exposed.

19. Saraya al-Quds is the name of the Islamic Jihad military wing that set up the mission.

20. Ragheb's family name.

21. Khayber was a battle in early Islam at which the Prophet Mohammed's army fought the Jews of Khayber in southern Arabia.

22. Sila is the village where Ragheb comes from.

23. *Sanabel* are wheat stalks.

24. Interview with Abu Hanadi, December 2004.

25. Bissan is one of eleven Palestinian cities that were depopulated of Palestinians by Jewish militias in 1948, were later settled by Jewish immigrants, and are now predominantly Israeli cities.

26. See note 22 to chapter 4, above.

27. Interview with Um Hanadi, December 2004.

28. Interview with Kamal, Jenin, January 2005.

29. *Al-Haqa'iq*, 9 October 2003.

30. *Al-Hayat*, 17 October 2003.

31. Felicia Langer is an Israeli lawyer who used to defend Palestinian prisoners before Israeli military courts in the 1970s and 1980s. She no longer lives in Israel.

32. *Al-Hayat*, 10 October 2003.

33. *Tartil* is the act of reading the Qur'an. The Islamic tradition of reading the Qur'an out loud calls for all to listen. The tartil refers to the voice of the Qur'anic reading in the midst of silence and calmness.

34. *Muslim Palestine Journal*, November 2003.

35. *Al-Safir*, Beirut, 25 October 2003.

36. BBC News, www.newsvote.bbc.co.uk, 17 January 2004.

37. Ibid.

38. BBC News, *Art Attack under Press Spotlight*, www.newsvote.bbc.co.uk, 19 January 2004.

39. The Nakba refers to the loss of Palestine in 1948, the establishment of Israel, and the associated displacements and dispossessions endured by the Palestinians.

40. The Marj Ibin 'Amer Plains are the main fertile area in Palestine between Haifa, Jenin, and Nazareth (see note 2 to chapter 2, above). These fields are historically known as the breadbasket of Palestine and were seized by Jewish militias in 1948.

41. Interview with Suleiman Mansour, Jerusalem, January 2005.

42. The key emerged as a symbol of memory and struggle for the return, as most Palestinian refugees kept the keys to the homes that they left behind in Palestine in 1948. See Abufarha (2008) for a full analysis of key symbolism.

43. *Iqal*, a part of the Palestinian traditional male headdress (the black ring that keeps the *hatta* in place), is a symbol of manhood and assertion.

44. *Mawwal* is a Palestinian folkloric singing style through which the improviser makes an argument or claim, recounts a proverb, or tells a story.

45. Interview with Marwan of El-Funoun El-Sha'abiya, December 2004.

CHAPTER SIX The Strategies and Politics of Martyrdom

1. Hanadi Jaradat, who executed a "spectacular" operation in the Israeli beachfront restaurant in Haifa, had not only asked to be sent on a mission but even threatened the local leader of Islamic Jihad in Jenin that if he did not send her she would attack the checkpoint while armed only with a knife. There are indications that she rather than the organization chose her target. This possibility is borne out by the differences between successive accounts of her mission that circulated in Jenin: the mission was said first to have been carried out in or near a hospital in Haifa, then at a Maxim restaurant in Haifa. Finally, it was reported that Hanadi made it to the vicinity of the hospital and bought chocolate from a store in the area before executing her mission at Maxim.

2. Interviews with Shalabi, a Fatah activist in Jenin, October 2003, and with Tawalbeh's father, Jenin, December 2004.

3. The assertion was printed on the book jacket.

4. For example, Pape characterized the Palestinian faction Fatah as a "socialist movement" (17) when it is closer to being the Palestinian republican party. The rich in Palestine have mainly supported Fatah, and the political leaders of Fatah have historically been major Palestinian capitalists. Ahmed Qreia', the Palestinian negotiator in Oslo and signatory to the treaty, considered the second-ranking man in Fatah after Mahmoud Abbas, runs major trade and construction companies. One of his companies is accused of importing cement from Egypt to sell to the Israeli companies who are building the wall. The third in rank, Nabil Shaath, owns multiple large companies that operate in Egypt and Gaza. The minister of national economy appointed by the PA and Fatah, Maher Al-Masri, is a Palestinian millionaire who made his fortune in the Gulf states. The new minister of national economy, Mazin Sinnoqrut, is Ramallah's leading businessman, running several successful businesses nationally in Palestine in addition to import-export companies. Fatah has historically been associated with the prestigious families of Nablus, Ramallah, Jerusalem, and Hebron, which hold tremendous influence within the movement.

5. Emphasis added.

6. Emphasis added.

7. The "offshore balancing" strategy is what the United States had been pursuing all along in the region before the Gulf War: supporting local state dictatorships while maintaining the capability to rapidly deploy American forces in the region if any of the regimes became unstable.

8. Interview with Sami, a leader in the Abu Ali Mustafa Brigades, Jenin, January 2005.

9. Hatta, also called kuffiyya, is the Palestinian traditional headdress that became a symbol of resistance worn by Palestinian fighters and activists. Fatah

activists wore the black and white hatta while PFLP activists wore the red and white *hatta* (an allusion to communism). Farmers in the region wore both kinds of hatta.

10. Interview with Salim, Jenin, May 2004.

11. There are two Eid holidays in the Islamic calendar. Eid al-Fitter (the Feast of Breaking the Fast of Ramadan), also called al-Eid al-Saghir (the Minor Feast), falls on the first of Shawwal in the Hijri Islamic calendar. Eid al-Adha (the Feast of Sacrifice), also called al-Eid al-Kabir (the Major Feast), falls on the 10th of Zu'lhijja in the Hijri Islamic calendar, the day when the pilgrims at the Haj in Mecca slaughter a *dhahiya* (sacrificial animal), normally a sheep or goat of mature size. A third of the dhahiya is distributed to the immediate family of the sacrificer, one third to relatives of the sacrificer, and one third to the poor and needy in the community. This was the Major Eid (Eid al-Adha).

12. This statement is in reference to the number of Palestinians killed by the Israeli army when Palestinians protested Sharon's break into Al-Aqsa Mosque square.

13. In a "no escape" operation members of the faction enter Israel for a shooting raid on Israeli targets, assuming that their mission will end in martyrdom.

14. Interview with Anwar, Izzideen Al-Qassam Martyrs Brigades leader, Jenin, January 2005.

15. Interview with Anwar, Jenin, January 2005.

16. Here I am building on Hinton's analysis of the Cambodian genocide (Hinton 2004).

17. 'Amaliyyat al-isqat (operations of corruption) are pitiful psychological and social embarrassment traps that Israelis set up for Palestinian youths to induce them to become informants for the Israeli secret service. The photos depicting the torture and sexual abuse of Iraqi prisoners in the Abu Ghraib prison by Lynndie England and others are examples of how Americans follow Israeli tactics of isqat (corruption). One potent threat leveled against prisoners is that photographs of their mistreatment will be circulated throughout the community. For example, Israeli Shen Bet agents will typically lure a boy or a girl to meet with a Shen Bet officer or Palestinian collaborator, then take a photograph of the meeting and threaten to publicize it if the youth does not cooperate. Many other tactics are used to entrap and corrupt Palestinian youths, who become hostage to the process. Palestinian factions have still not allowed a clear way of self-redemption for these victims.

18. The proverb here refers to the foundation of Israel.

19. Interview with Hasan, Palestine, May 2004.

20. Interview with Sheikh Omar, Palestine, December 2004.

21. Although Israel and Zionists have always claimed that Israel is the "an-

cestral homeland," this claim is based on an ideological construction and not a shared historical experience, unlike the collective experience of rootedness of the Palestinians. The "ancestral" notion remains vague because of the uncertainty as to which period of a social group's history determines ancestry.

CHAPTER SEVEN Conclusion

1. I analyze these cultural dynamics in depth in "Land of Symbols: Cactus, Poppies, Orange and Olive Trees in Palestine" (2008).

BIBLIOGRAPHY

Abu-Amr, Ziad. 1994. *Islamic Fundamentalism in the West Bank and Gaza: Muslim Brotherhood and Islamic Jihad.* Bloomington: Indiana University Press.

Abu El-Haj, Nadia. 2001. *Facts on the Ground: Archeological Practice and Territorial Self-fashioning in Israeli Society.* Chicago: University of Chicago Press.

Abufarha, Nasser. 2008. "Land of Symbols: Cactus, Poppies, Orange and Olive Trees in Palestine." *Identities: Global Studies in Culture and Power* 15, no. 3, 343–68.

Abu-Saad, Ismael. 2004. "Epilogue: Reflections on Race and Racism in Contemporary Israeli Society: 'Wishing the Barbarian Away.'" *Social Identities* 10, no. 2, 293–99.

Al Dabbagh, Mustafa. 1970–73. *Biladuna Filistin* [Our homeland Palestine]. Beirut: Dar at-Tali'a.

Al Kayali, Abdelwahhab. 1978. *Tarikh Filistin al-Hadith* [Modern History of Palestine]. Beirut: Dar al-Tali'a.

Al Qasm, Ahmed Mahmoud Mohammed. 2003a. *Al-abtal al-istishhadiyyoun wa al-irhab al-israeli* [The martyrous heroes and the Israeli terror]. Ramallah.

———. 2003b. *Ash-shuhada' al-atfal fi intifadat al-aqsa* [The Child Martyrs in al-Aqsa Intifada]. Bethlehem: Dar al-Bayan.

———. 2002. *Shuhada' intifadat il-aqsa* [Martyrs of the al-Aqsa Intifada]. Ramallah: As-Said.

Al Tal, Abdullah. 1959. *Karithat filistin: muthakarat Abdullah at-Tal, Qa'id ma'arakat al-Quds* [The catastrophe of Palestine: Memoirs of Abdullah al-Tal, the commander of the Jerusalem battle]. Cairo: Dar al-Qalam.

Allen, Tim, and Jean Seoton, eds. 1999. *The Media of Conflict: War Reporting and Representations of Ethnic Violence.* New York: Zed.

Alloush, Naji. 1970. *Munaqashat hawla al-thawra al-filistiniya* [Discussions around the Palestinian Revolution]. Beirut: Dar al-Tali'a.

Almog, Oz. 2000. *The Sabra: The Creation of the New Jew.* Berkeley: University of California Press.

Anderson, Benedict. 1991 [1983]. *Imagined Communities: Reflections on the Origin and Spread of Nationalism.* New York: Verso.

Andoni, Lamis. 1997. "Searching for Answers: Gaza's Suicide Bombers." *Journal of Palestine Studies* 26, no. 4, 33–45.

Andriolo, Karen. 2002. "Murder by Suicide: Episodes from Muslim History." *American Anthropologist* 104, no. 3, 736–42.

Appadurai, Arjun. 1996. *Modernity at Large: Cultural Dimensions of Globalization.* Minneapolis: University of Minnesota Press.

Applied Research Institute. 2000. *An Atlas of Palestine.* Jerusalem: Applied Research Institute.

Apter, David E., ed. 1997. *The Legitimization of Violence.* New York: New York University Press.

Aruri, Naseer. 1995. *The Obstruction of Peace: U.S., Israel and the Palestinians.* Monroe, Minn.: Common Courage.

Atran, Scott. 2004. "Mishandling Suicide Terrorism." *Washington Quarterly* 27, no. 3, 67–90.

———. 2003. "Genesis of Suicide Terrorism." *Science,* 7 March, 1534–39.

Azam, Jean-Paul. 2005. "Suicide-Bombings as Inter-generational Investment." *Public Choice* 122, 177–98.

Bergen, Peter L. 2002. *Holy War, Inc.: Inside the Secret World of Osama bin Laden.* New York: Simon and Schuster.

Bloom, Mia. 2005. *Dying to Kill: The Allure of Suicide Terror.* New York: Columbia University Press.

Boullata, Kamal. 2001. "'Asim Abu Shaqra': The Artist's Eye and the Cactus Tree." *Journal of Palestine Studies* 30, no. 4, 68–82.

Bourdieu, Pierre. 1977. *Outline of a Theory of Practice.* Trans. Richard Nice. Cambridge: Cambridge University Press.

Casey, Edward S. 1996. *The Fate of Place: A Philosophical History.* Berkeley: University of California Press.

Conner, Walker. 1978. "A Nation Is a Nation, Is a State, Is an Ethnic Group . . ." *Nationalism,* ed. John Hutchinson and Anthony D. Smith. Oxford: Oxford University Press.

Cormier, Loretta. 2003. "Decolonizing History: Ritual Transformation of the Past among the Guagá of Eastern Amazonia." *Histories and Historicities in Amazonia,* ed. Neil Whitehead. Lincoln: University of Nebraska Press.

Dabbagh, Nadia Taysir. 2005. *Suicide in Palestine: Narratives of Despair.* Northampton, Mass.: Olive Branch.

Das, Veena. 1997. "Language and Body: Transactions in the Construction of Pain." *Social Suffering,* ed. Arthur Kleinman, Veena Das, and Margaret Lock. Berkeley: University of California Press.

———. 1995. *Critical Events: An Anthropological Perspective on Contemporary India.* Oxford: Oxford University Press.

Davis, Joyce M. 2003. *Martyrs: Innocence, Vengeance, and Despair in the Middle East.* New York: Palgrave Macmillan.

De Jong, Jan. 2005. "The End of the Two-State Solution: A Geo-political Analysis." *Palestinian-Israeli Impasse: Exploring Alternative Solutions to the Palestine-Israel Conflict*, ed. Mahdi Abdul Hadi. Jerusalem: PASSIA.

Dorraj, Manochehr. 1997. "Symbolic and Utilitarian Political Value of a Tradition: Martyrdom in the Iranian Political Culture." *Review of Politics* 59, 489–521.

El-Haddad, Laila. 2005. "Israeli Sonic Booms Terrorizing Gaza." Aljazzira.net, 26 December.

El-Sarraj, Eyad. 2002. "Suicide Bombers: Dignity, Despair, and the Need for Hope." *Journal of Palestine Studies* 31, no. 4, 71–76.

Emerson, R. M., R. I. Fretz, and L. L. Shaw. 1995. *Writing Ethnographic Fieldnotes.* Chicago: University of Chicago Press.

Falah, Ghazi-Walid. 2005. "The Geopolitics of 'Enclavisation' and the Demise of the Two-State Solution to the Israeli-Palestinian Conflict." *Third World Quarterly* 26, no. 8, 1–32.

———. 1993. *Al-jalil wa mukhatatat at-tahwid* [The Galilee and Judaization Schemes]. Beirut: Institute of Palestine Studies.

———. 1983. *The role of British Administration in the Sedentarization of the Bedouin Tribes in Northern Palestine.* Durham: Center of Middle East and Islamic Studies, University of Durham.

Fein, Helen. 1979. *Accounting for Genocide: National Responses and Jewish Victimization during the Holocaust.* New York: Free Press.

Feld, Steven, and Keith H. Basso, eds. 1996. *Senses of Place.* Santa Fe: School of American Research Press.

Fenlon, James V. 1998. *Culturicide, Resistance, and Survival of the Lakota ("Sioux Nation").* New York: Garland.

Ferguson, R. Brian. 1995. *Yanomami Warfare: A Political History.* Santa Fe: School of American Research Press.

———. 1997. "Violence and War in Prehistory." *Troubled Times: Violence and Warfare in the Past*, ed. D. L. Martin and D. W. Frayer, 321–55. Langhorne, Penn.: Gordon and Breach.

———. 2003. *The State, Identity and Violence: Political Disintegration in the Post–Cold War World.* London: Routledge.

Ferguson, R. Brian, and Neil L. Whitehead, eds. 2001. *War in the Tribal Zone: Expanding States and Indigenous Warfare.* Santa Fe: School of American Research Press.

Foucault, Michel. 1995 [1977]. *Discipline and Punish*, trans. Alan Sheridan. New York: Vintage.

Fox, Richard G., and Barbara J. King. 2002. *Anthropology beyond Culture.* New York: Berg.

Friedman, Jonathan, ed. 2003. *Globalization, the State, and Violence.* New York: Alta Mira.

Gambill, Gary C. 1998. "The Balance of Terror: War by Other Means in Contemporary Middle East." *Journal of Palestine Studies* 28, no. 1, 51–66.

Geertz, Clifford. 1996. Afterword, *Senses of Place*, ed. Steven Feld and Keith H. Basso. Santa Fe: School of American Research Press.

Gordon, Haim, Rivca Gordon, and Taher Shriteh. 2003. *Beyond Intifada: Narratives of Freedom Fighters in the Gaza Strip*. Westport, Conn.: Praeger.

Gowers, A., and T. Walker. 1992. *Behind the Myth: Yasser Arafat and the Palestinian Revolution*. New York: Olive Branch.

Gray, A. Z. 1876. *The Land and the Life: Sketches and Studies in Palestine*. New York: A. D. F. Randolph.

Green, Alberto Ravinell Whitney. 1975. *The Role of Human Sacrifice in the Ancient Near East*. Missoula, Mont.: Scholars.

Guyatt, Nicholas. 1998. *The Absence of Peace: Understanding the Israeli-Palestinian Conflict*. New York, Zed Books.

Hafez, Mohammed M. 2003. *Why Muslims Rebel: Repression and Resistance in the Islamic World*. Boulder: Lynne Rienner.

Hasso, Frances S. 2005. "Discursive and Political Deployments by/of the 2002 Palestinian Women Suicide Bombers/Martyrs." *Feminist Review* 81, 23–51.

Hazony, Y. 2000. *The Jewish State: The Struggle for Israel's Soul*. New York: Basic.

Heacock, Roger. 2004. "Palestinians: The Land and the Law: An Inverse Relationship." *Journal of International Affairs* 57, no. 2, 151–65.

Herbst, Jeffrey. 1990. "War and the State in Africa." *International Security* 14, no. 4, 117–39.

Herzfeld, Michael. 1997. *Cultural Intimacy: Social Poetics in the Nation-State*. New York: Routledge.

Hinton, Alex. 2004. "The Poetics of Genocidal Practice: Violence under the Khmer Rouge." *Violence: School of American Research Advanced Seminar Series*, ed. Neil L. Whitehead. Santa Fe: School of American Research Press.

———. 2005. *Why Did They Kill?: Cambodia in the Shadow of Genocide*. Berkeley: University of California Press.

Hirsch, Eric, and Michael O'Hanlon, eds. 1995. *The Anthropology of Landscape: Perspectives on Space and Place*. Oxford: Clarendon.

Hroub, Khaled. 2000. *Hamas, Political Thought and Practice*. Washington: Institute of Palestine Studies.

Hubert, Henry, and Marcel Mauss. 1964. *Sacrifice: Its Nature and Function*, trans. W. D. Halls. London: Cohen and West.

Jean-Klein, Iris. 2000. "Mothercraft, Statecraft, and Subjectivity in the Palestinian Intifada." *American Ethnologist* 27, no. 1, 100–127.

Jenin New Center for Studies and Information. 2003. *Ash-sheikh al-janaral: qissat jihad qa'id malhamat mukhayam Jenin ash-shahid Mahmoud Tawalbeh* [The general sheikh: The story of the struggle of the leader of the Jenin camp battle, martyr Mahmoud Tawalbeh].

Jiryis, S. 1973. Al-Arab fi Israel [The Arabs in Israel]. Beirut: Center for Palestine Studies.

Juergensmeyer, Mark. 2000. Terror in the Mind of God: The Global Rise of Religious Violence. Berkeley: University of California Press.

Kadi, Leila S. 1969. Basic Political Documents of the Armed Palestinian Resistance Movement. Beirut: Palestine Liberation Organization Research Center.

Kaomea, Julie. 2003. "Dilemmas of an Indigenous Academic: A Native Hawaiian Story." Decolonizing Research in Cross-Cultural Contexts: Critical Personal Narratives, ed. Kagendo Mutua and Beth Blue Swadener, 34–52.

Kapferer, Bruce. 1988. Legends of People, Myths of State: Violence, Intolerance, and Political Culture in Sri Lanka and Australia. Washington: Smithsonian Institution Press.

——. 1997. The Feast of the Sorcerer: Practices of Consciousness and Power. Chicago: University of Chicago Press.

Kelly, John D., and Martha Kaplan. 2001. Represented Communities: Fiji and World Decolonization. Chicago: University of Chicago Press.

Khalidi, Rashid. 1997. Palestinian Identity: The Construction of Modern National Consciousness. New York: Columbia University Press.

Khalidi, Walid. 1992. All That Remains: The Palestinian Villages Occupied and Depopulated by Israel in 1948. Washington: Institute for Palestine Studies.

——. 1984. Before Their Diaspora. Washington: Institute for Palestine Studies.

Khashan, Hilal. 2003. "Collective Palestinian Frustration and Suicide Bombings." Third World Quarterly 24, no. 6, 1049–67.

Khosrokhavar, Farhad. 2005. Suicide Bombers: Allah's New Martyrs, trans. David Macey. Ann Arbor: Pluto.

Kimmerling, Baruch, and Joel S. Migdal. 2003. The Palestinian People: A History. Cambridge: Harvard University Press.

Kleinman, Arthur, Veena Das, and Margaret Lock, eds. 1997. Social Suffering. Berkeley: University of California Press.

Klieman, Aharon. 2000. Compromising Palestine: A Guide to Final Status Negotiations. New York: Columbia University Press.

Lincoln, Bruce. 1991. Death, War, and Sacrifice: Studies in Ideology and Practice. Chicago: University of Chicago Press.

Low, Setha M., and Denise Lawrence-Zúniga, eds. 2003. The Anthropology of Space and Place: Locating Culture. Malden, Mass.: Blackwell.

Malkki, Liisa H. 1995. Purity and Exile: Violence, Memory, and National Cosmology among Hutu Refugees in Tanzania. Chicago: University of Chicago Press.

Mamdani, Mahmood. 2001. When Victims Become Killers: Colonialism, Nativism, and the Genocide in Rwanda. Princeton: Princeton University Press.

Maren, Michael. 1997. *The Road to Hell: The Ravaging Effects of Foreign Aid and International Charity.* New York: Free Press.

Margalit, Avishai. 2003. "The Suicide Bombers." *New York Review of Books,* 16 January.

Marqus, George. 1998. *Ethnography through Thick and Thin.* Princeton: Princeton University Press.

Marx, Emmanuel, and Avschalom Shamueli. 1984. *The Changing Bedouin.* New Brunswick, N.J.: Transaction.

Mauss, Marcel. 1990. *The Gift, the Form and Reason for Exchange in Archaic Societies,* trans. W. D. Halls. New York: W. W. Norton.

Merari, Ariel. "The Readiness to Kill and Die: Suicidal Terrorism in the Middle East." *Origins of Terrorism,* ed. Walter Reich. Baltimore: Johns Hopkins University Press.

Mishal, Shaul, and Avraham Sela. 2000. *The Palestinian Hamas: Vision, Violence, and Coexistence.* New York: Columbia University Press.

Morris, Benny. 1987. *The Birth of the Palestinian Refugee Problem, 1947–1949.* Cambridge: Cambridge University Press.

——. 1990. *1948 and After: Israel and the Palestinians.* Oxford: Clarendon.

Moser, Caroline O. N., and Fiona C. Clark, eds. 2001. *Victims, Perpetrators or Actors? Gender, Armed Conflict and Political Violence.* London: Zed.

Myers, Fred R. 1991. *Pintupi Country, Pintupi Self: Sentiment, Place, and Politics among Western Desert Aboriginies.* Berkeley: University of California Press.

Narayan, Kirin. 1993. "How Native Is a 'Native' Anthropologist?" *American Anthropologist* 95, no. 3, 671–86.

Nasir, Tania Tamari. 2002. *Spring Is Here: Embroidered Flowers of the Palestinian Spring.* Jerusalem: Institute for Jerusalem Studies.

Nordstrom, Carolyn. 2004. "The Tomorrow of Violence." *Violence: School of American Research Advanced Seminar Series,* ed. Neil L. Whitehead. Santa Fe: School of American Research Press.

Nordstrom, Carolyn, and Antonius C. G. M. Robben, eds. 1995. *Fieldwork under Fire: Contemporary Studies of Violence and Survival.* Berkeley: University of California Press.

Ohnuki-Tierney, Emiko. 2002. *Kamikaze, Cherry Blossoms, and Nationalisms: The Militarization of Aesthetics in Japanese History.* Chicago: University of Chicago Press.

——. 2001. "Historicization of the Culture Concept." *History and Anthropology* 12, no. 3, 213–54.

——. 1993. *Rice as Self: Japanese Identities through Time.* Princeton: Princeton University Press.

——. 1987. *The Monkey as Mirror: Symbolic Transformations in Japanese History and Ritual.* Princeton: Princeton University Press.

Oliver, Anne Marie, and Paul Steinberg. 2005. *The Road to Martyr's Square: A Journey into the World of Suicide Bombers.* New York: Oxford University Press.

Palestinian Academic Society for the Study of International Affairs (PASSIA). 2002. *The Palestine Question in Maps: 1878–2002.* Jerusalem: PASSIA.

Pape, Robert A. 2005. *Dying to Win: The Strategic Logic of Suicide Terrorism.* New York: Random House.

Pappe, Ilan. 1992. *Making the Arab-Israeli Conflict.* London: Tauris.

——. 2004. *A History of Modern Palestine: One Land, Two Peoples.* Cambridge: Cambridge University Press.

Peteet, Julie M. 1994. "Male Gender Rituals of Resistance in the Palestinian Intifada: A Culture of Violence." *American Ethnologist* 21, no. 1, 31–49.

——. 1991. *Gender in Crisis: Women and the Palestinian Resistance Movement.* New York: Columbia University Press.

Quigley, John. 1990. *Palestine and Israel: A Challenge to Justice.* Durham: Duke University Press.

Reuter, Christoph. 2004. *My Life Is a Weapon: A Modern History of Suicide Bombing,* trans. Helena Ragg-Kirkby. Princeton: Princeton University Press.

Riches, David, ed. 1986. *The Anthropology of Violence.* New York: Basil Blackwell.

Ritchie, Donald A. 2003. *Doing Oral History: A Practical Guide.* Oxford: Oxford University Press.

Rosenfeld, Maya. 2004. *Confronting the Occupation: Work, Education and Political Activism of Palestinian Families in a Refugee Camp.* Stanford: Stanford University Press.

Saez, Lawrence. 2000. "Sri Lanka in 2000: The Politics of Despair." *Asian Survey* 41, no. 1, 116–21.

Sahlins, Marshall D. 1976. *Culture and Practical Reason.* Chicago: University of Chicago Press.

——. 1985. *Islands of History.* Chicago: University of Chicago Press.

Said, Edward. 1993. *Culture and Imperialism.* London: Chatto and Windus.

——. 2000. *The End of the Peace Process: Oslo and After.* New York: Pantheon.

Schama, Simon. 1995. *Landscape and Memory.* New York: Alfred A. Knopf.

Scott, James C. 1985. *Weapons of the Weak: Everyday Forms of Peasant Resistance.* New Haven: Yale University Press.

——. 1998. *Seeing like a State: How Certain Schemes to Improve the Human Condition Have Failed.* New Haven: Yale University Press.

Shaw, R. Paul, and Yuwa Wong. 1989. *Genetic Seeds of Warfare: Evolution, Nationalism, and Latriotism.* Winchester, Mass.: Unwin Hyman.

Shay, Shaul. 2004. *The Shahids: Islam and Suicide Attacks,* trans. Rachel Lieberman. New Brunswick, N.J.: Transaction.

Shoufani, Elias. 1978. *Ash-sharia at-taswiyya al-israeliyya, 1967/1978: Dirasa taw-*

thiqiyya naqdiyya [The Israeli (political) settlement projects, 1967/1978: A critical documentary study]. Beirut: Institute of Palestine Studies.

Simmons, A. John. 2001. *Justification and Legitimacy: Essays on Rights and Obligations.* Cambridge: Cambridge University Press.

Skocpol, Theda. 1985. "Bringing the State Back In: Strategies of Analysis in Current Research." *Bringing the State Back In*, ed. Peter Evans, Dietrich Rueschemeyer, and Theda Skocpol. Cambridge: Cambridge University Press.

———. 1981. *The Ethnic Revival.* Cambridge: Cambridge University Press.

Smith, L. T. 1999. *Decolonizing Methodologies: Research and Indigenous Peoples.* London: Zed.

Stein, Rebecca L., and Ted Swedenburg, eds. 2005. *Palestine, Israel, and the Politics of Popular Culture.* Durham: Duke University Press.

Stewert, Pamela, and Andrew Strathern. 2004. *Witchcraft, Sorcery, Rumors, and Gossip.* Cambridge: Cambridge University Press.

———. 1999. *Reflections on Violence.* Cambridge: Cambridge University Press.

Swedenburg, Ted. 1995a. "Prisoners of Love: With Genet in the Palestinian Field." *Fieldwork under Fire: Contemporary Studies of Violence and Survival*, ed. Carolyn Nordstrom and Antonius C. G. M. Robben. Berkeley: University of California Press.

———. 1995b. *Memories of Revolt: The 1936–1939 Rebellion and the Palestinian National Past.* Minneapolis: University of Minnesota Press.

Tambiah, Stanley J. 1996. *Leveling Crowds: Ethnonationalist Conflicts and Collective Violence in South Asia.* Berkeley: University of California Press.

Taussig, Michael. 1987. *Shamanism, Colonialism, and the Wild Man.* Chicago: University of Chicago Press.

———. 1997. *The Magic of the State.* New York: Routledge.

Taylor, Christopher C. 2004. "Deadly Images: King Sacrifice, President Habyarimana, and the Iconography of Pre-genocidal Rwandan Political Literature." *Violence: School of American Research Advanced Seminar Series*, ed. Neil L. Whitehead. Santa Fe: School of American Research Press.

———. 1999. *Sacrifice as Terror: The Rwandan Genocide of 1994.* Oxford: Berg.

Turner, Victor. 1967. *The Forest of Symbols: Aspects of Ndembu Ritual.* Ithaca: Cornell University Press.

Turner, Victor, and Edward M. Bruner. 1986. *Anthropology of Experience.* Urbana: University of Illinois Press.

Twitchell, James B. 1989. *Preposterous Violence: Fables of Aggression in Modern Culture.* Oxford: Oxford University Press.

Valeri, Valerio. 1985. *Kingship and Sacrifice: Ritual and Society in Ancient Hawaii.* Chicago: University of Chicago Press.

Van den Berghe, Pierre L., ed. 1990. *State Violence and Ethnicity.* Niwot: University of Colorado Press.

Victor, Barbara. 2003. *Army of Roses: Inside the World of Palestinian Women Suicide Bombers*. Emmaus, Penn.: Rodale.

Vidal, Sylvia M. 2003. "The Arawak-Speaking Groups of Northwestern Amazonia: Amerindian Cartography as a Way of Preserving and Interpreting the Past." *Histories and Historicities in Amazonia*, ed. Neil Whitehead. Lincoln: University of Nebraska Press.

Walzer, Michael. 2004. *Arguing about War*. New Haven: Yale University Press.

Weiner, James. 1991. *The Empty Place: Poetry, Space, and Being among the Foi of Papua New Guinea*. Bloomington: University of Indiana Press.

White, Luise. *Speaking with Vampires: Rumor and History in Colonial Africa*. Berkeley: University of California Press.

Whitehead, Neil L., ed. 2004. *Violence*. School of American Research Advanced Seminar Series. Santa Fe: School of American Research Press.

———. 2003. *Histories and Historicities in Amazonia*. Lincoln: University of Nebraska Press.

———. 2002. *Dark Shamans: Kanaima and the Poetics of Violent Death*. Durham: Duke University Press.

———. 2001. "Tribes Make States and States Make Tribes: Warfare and the Creation of Colonial Tribes and States in Northeastern South America." *War in the Tribal Zone: Expanding States and Indigenous Warfare*, ed. R. Brian Ferguson and Neil L. Whitehead, eds. Santa Fe: School of American Research Press.

Wolf, Eric. 1999. *Envisioning Power: Ideologies of Dominance and Crisis*. Berkeley: University of California Press.

Wright, J. W., Jr., ed. 2002. *Structural Flaws in the Middle East Peace Process*. New York: Palgrave.

Yiftachel, Oren. 1999. " 'Ethnocracy': The Politics of Judaizing Israel/Palestine." *Constellation: An International Journal of Critical and Democratic Theory* 6, 364–90.

Z'aiter, Akram. 1980. *Yomiyyat Akram Za'ter: Al-haraka al-wataniyya al-filistiniyya, 1935–1939* [The diary of Akram Za'ter: The Palestinian nationalist movement, 1935–1939]. Beirut: Muwassasat ad-dirasat al-filistiniyya [Institute of Palestine Studies].

Zertal, I. (1998). *From Catastrophe to Power: Holocaust Survivors and the Emergence of Israel*. Berkeley: University of California Press.

INDEX

Abbas, Mahmoud, 85, 86, 254
Abbasid, 126
Abdelshafi, Haidar, 63, 74
AbrarY, 161
absentee landlords, 3, 34
Abu 'Aisheh, Dareen, 135–37
Abu Ali Mustafa Brigades, 71, 72,
    194, 196, 197, 202, 254
Abu 'Arraj, 82
Abu Dhabi, 142
Abu el-'Asal, Murad, 145
Abu Sitta, Salman, 39
access roads, 113, 114, 250
Administration of Civil Coordination
    Department (al-irtibat al-madani),
    67, 248
aesthetics, 2, 3, 18, 69, 135, 136, 139,
    157, 166, 176, 188, 189, 223, 233
Afghanistan, 4
afterlife, 77, 139, 152
Afula, 8, 67–70, 124, 125, 137, 245,
    248
agency, 3, 15, 16, 185, 190, 227
Agreement on Preparatory Transfer of
    Powers and Responsibilities, 65
'A'idun (Returning), 248
Akhras, Ayat Al-, 135, 136
Akka (Acre), 28, 170, 180, 246
Ali, Mohammed Saad, 245
alloformic Palestine, 14, 168, 169
Almong, Zai'v, 165

Alternative Resource Center for Pales-
    tinian Residency and Refugee
    Rights (Badil), 248
'amaliyyat istishhadiyya, 2, 7, 18, 61,
    70, 251
Amarneh, Ammar, 67, 68
American University of Beirut, 42
'ammal, 30
Amn Al-Wiqa'i, Al- (Palestinian Pre-
    ventive Security), 189
'Anabta, 144
analogies, 6, 226
Aqsa Intifada, Al-, 1, 7, 12, 18, 71, 81,
    82, 83, 85, 86, 87, 100, 106, 121,
    134, 178. See also intifada
Aqsa Martyrs Brigades, Al-, 71, 81, 82,
    83, 85, 86, 87, 122, 125, 136, 137,
    138, 165, 195, 196, 197, 200, 202,
    248, 249, 251
Aqsa Mosque, Al-, 74, 77, 124, 129,
    130, 131, 204, 251, 255
Arab-American University, 102
Arabia, 166, 252
Arab League, 135
Arab Resource Center al-jana, 248
Arab Summit, 135
Arafat, Yasser, 42, 54, 68, 85, 87, 135
archives, 112
ardh as-sahil, 30
ardh mushajjara, 30
'Arraba, 143

'Arraba Junction, 147
Ashdod, 70, 207
'Ashiqin, Al-, 44
Ashqalon, 246. *See also* Al-Majdal
Ashram, Al-, 251
Asmar, Ashraf al-, 146
Asqalan Jail, 144
assassination, 20, 87, 121, 122, 125–27, 131, 144, 146, 148, 161, 162, 187, 190, 192, 193, 194, 197, 217
Assassins, 187
Association for the Defense of the Rights of the Internally Displaced, 248
audience, 9, 10, 16, 55, 100, 126, 166, 179, 180
Australia, 214
awda, al- (return), 248
Ayyash, Yahia, 121, 250

Babylon, 171
Badil, 248
Baker, James, 63
Banna, Hassan Al-, 121, 250
Barak, Ehud, 210, 213
Barakeh, Al-, 242
Barghouthi, Iyad, 81, 95, 96, 249
Barghouthi, Marwan, 134
Bedouins, 29, 31, 35–36, 246
Beer Sheba, 246. *See also* Bir As-Sabea'
Begin, Menachem, 54, 246
Beirut, 36, 42, 49, 135, 177, 245
Beirut Summit, 136
Beit Lahi, 241
Belgium, 245
Berqin, 101–2, 104, 158
Bet Eil, 67, 248
Bethlehem, 75, 94, 157, 241
Bet Shaen, 246. *See also* Bissan
Bin Laden, Osama, 90, 191
Bir As-Sabea', 209, 246
Birzeit, 113
Bissan, 13, 33, 160, 246, 253

Black Panthers (al-Fahad al-Aswad), 143, 249, 252
blockade, 1
Bosnia, 4
Bride of Haifa, 165
Bride of Jenin, 173, 174
Bride of Palestine, 125, 165, 166
Britain, 5, 9, 26, 188, 214
British Mandate, 35, 246
Bush, George W., 11, 63, 170, 171

Cairo, 36, 42
California, 116
Camp David, 75–76
Canada, 214
carrier, 8, 17–18, 69–70, 97–100, 135, 138, 139, 141, 154, 155, 188, 189, 190, 205, 208, 233, 234, 249
Carter, Jimmy, 247
cartography, 27
catastrophe (al-Nakba), 41, 71, 75, 177, 228, 253
Celts, 14, 168
certificate, 147, 148, 149, 150
Chechnya, 188, 191
checkpoints, 1, 20, 58, 64, 67, 81, 93, 104, 106, 112, 114–21, 165, 172, 173, 182, 184, 197–200, 208, 210, 218, 246, 248, 254
Chicago, 116
Christians, 8, 28, 106
Civil Administration (al-idara al-madaniyya), 50, 63–65, 247
civil disobedience, 60
civilians, 4, 10, 171, 188, 218, 220, 236
civil order, 87, 171, 217–19, 235
civil society, 235
closure, 51, 100–101, 104, 109, 114
colonial powers, 228
combatants, 189
communism, 91–92, 106, 255
concentration, 151, 185, 233, 234
confinement, 1, 3, 20, 107, 111, 114,

120, 157, 167, 173, 181–84, 227, 232

containment, 9, 137, 183, 220, 238

cosmological conditions, 88, 132, 185, 231

counterinsurgency, 192

critical event, 28, 37, 51, 74, 75, 225, 228

cross-border operations, 8, 42, 187

cult formation, 87, 88, 96

cultural conception, 3, 6, 13, 14, 23, 45, 121, 164, 181, 184, 187, 226, 229

cultural construction, 29, 31

cultural imaginary, 3, 14, 20, 44, 120, 159, 164, 169, 184, 218, 227, 229, 238

cultural order, 2, 16, 104, 106, 171, 179, 225, 231

cultural processes, 34, 39, 41, 43, 100, 108, 138, 188, 228, 232

cultural production, 20, 38, 43, 78, 152

cultural representation, 2, 3, 6, 14, 26, 28, 38, 44, 47, 78, 100, 114, 120, 131–33, 139, 140, 177, 179, 181, 183, 184, 186, 226–29, 231–33

cultural schemes, 2, 6, 225–28

curfew, 60, 84, 100–101, 110, 185, 207

Damascus, 36

Damun, 75

Declaration of Principles, 64, 66

Deir Yassin, 167

demolition, 20, 99, 147, 175, 193

development, 23, 80, 91, 93, 222, 229, 244, 231

DFLP (Democratic Front for the Liberation of Palestine), 91–92, 106, 134, 194, 196

diplomacy, 49, 62

Dir El-Balah, 241, 242

disengagement plan, 238

displacement, 3, 69, 120, 167, 168, 227, 253

divinity, 12, 13, 15, 46–47, 139, 152, 163, 164, 174, 185, 222, 224, 234

Dome of the Rock, 121. See also Aqsa Mosque, Al-

donor agencies, 91–92, 95

education, 27, 64, 65, 91

Egypt, 42, 49, 72

encapsulation, 3, 64, 66–67, 72, 83–84, 87–88, 95, 99, 157, 184, 194, 227, 228, 232

engagement, 7, 21, 114, 136, 146, 174, 188, 195, 197, 205, 215, 217, 219, 225, 235, 236

England, Lynndie, 255

ethnic cleansing, 40–41, 99, 112

ethnography, 4, 6, 17, 18, 21, 38, 51, 56, 58–59, 97, 100, 108, 204, 225–26, 231

Europe, 4, 12, 33, 75, 84, 248

European Union, 211, 215

exile, 120, 177, 178, 180, 184, 249

Expressen, 176

Fahad al-Aswad, Al- (Black Panthers), 143, 249, 252

fardh, 70

Fatah, 7, 18, 42–43, 71, 78–79, 81–82, 85–88, 92, 123–24, 134–38, 141, 144, 190, 195–97, 202, 205, 206, 243, 244, 249, 251, 252, 254

feddan, 29–31

Feiler, Dror, 175

Feiler, Ganilla Skold, 176

fellahin, 28–29, 31, 33–34, 36, 245

fida' (sacrifice), 2, 3, 6, 8, 9, 12–16, 22, 44–47, 56, 69, 70, 72, 78, 120–21, 123, 129, 131–37, 139, 141, 142, 149, 151–53, 157–59, 162, 164, 166, 168–72, 174, 175, 178, 184–86, 189, 193, 207, 214, 227–34, 245, 251, 255

fida'i (sacrificer), 7, 8, 10, 13–15, 43–
   48, 70, 77, 121, 128, 130
fieldwork, 6, 7, 16, 100, 109, 116, 197,
   200
Foula, Al-, 245, 248. *See also* Afula
fragmentation, 1, 3, 9, 12, 16, 83, 88,
   93, 95, 105, 132, 157, 159, 184, 214,
   227, 231, 232
freedom, 1, 3, 9, 23, 65, 85, 120, 128–
   29, 131, 157, 162, 168, 173, 183,
   227, 237, 239
French army, 218
Funoun, El- (Palestinian Popular
   Dance Troupe), 177–79, 182, 219,
   249, 253

G-8, 115
Galilee, 28, 51, 66
Ganim settlement, 250
Gaza, 9, 124, 129–30, 146, 168, 173–
   75, 194, 203, 241, 242, 250, 254
global agency, 189, 210, 215, 229,
   235, 237
globalization, 2, 15, 185, 190, 192
global powers, 9, 23, 126, 173, 191,
   222, 229
global system, 17, 171
Golan Heights, 214
grassroots, 82, 92, 134
Gulf War, 254

Habash, George, 42
Habibi, Emile, 100
habitus, 140, 172
Haifa, 13, 36–37, 47, 137, 153, 154,
   159, 161, 165–67, 170, 177, 180,
   205, 208, 209, 215, 245, 246, 248,
   249, 250, 251, 253, 254
Hamas (Harakat al-Muqawama al-
   Islamiyya; Islamic Resistance
   Movement), 7, 8, 10, 18, 37, 49, 61,
   67–72, 76–77, 79–80, 82, 87–91,
   95–96, 122–31, 137, 144, 146, 194–

97, 202, 203, 205, 206, 211–13,
   216, 217, 244
Hammurabi Code, 170, 171
hamula, 29, 244
hannoun, 48, 117, 250, 251
Harakat al-Jihad al-Islami (Islamic
   Jihad), 7, 18, 49, 72, 76–77, 80, 82,
   88–89, 95, 124, 137, 140–42, 144–
   47, 157, 161, 165, 166, 175, 190,
   194, 195, 202, 205, 212, 216, 254
Harakat al-Muqawama al-Islamiyya.
   See Hamas
Harakat al-Taharur al-Watani al-
   Filistini, 7
Harthiya, Al-, 161, 245, 253
Hasanain, Muhammed, 146
hatta, 34, 254
Hebrew University, 114
Hebron (Al-Khalil), 28, 68–69, 130,
   157, 173, 174, 241, 254
Hebron massacre, 69
Hedara, 246
hero, 11, 40, 56, 60, 77, 102, 121, 159
heroism, 9, 10, 15, 40, 56, 58–60, 77,
   126, 156, 158, 174, 177, 228
Hewara checkpoint, 115
Hezbollah, 218
Hiba Daraghmeh, 137
Higher Committee for the Defense of
   the Right of Return in Jordan, 248
historical narrative, 38–40, 50, 216,
   219, 228
historicity, 22, 39, 40, 228, 244
historiography, 27
Hizb al-Tahrir al-Islami (Islamic Liberation Party), 80
homeland, 8, 12, 41, 69–70, 107, 113,
   115, 127–28, 130–31, 167, 169, 183,
   184, 190, 211, 214, 220, 256
homologies, 6, 14, 45, 168, 226, 232,
   234–35
honor, 34, 44, 48, 139, 147

hukm al-thati, Al-, 247
human rights, 66, 235
Hussein, King, 63, 247
hybridization, 94

Ibrahimi Mosque, Al-, 68–69
icons, 3, 8, 10, 17, 43–44, 77–78, 102,
    126, 151, 154, 157, 175, 185, 234
idara al-madaniyya, Al- (Civil Admin-
    istration), 50, 63–65, 247
identification cards, 53, 55, 57–58,
    60, 93, 110, 115–16, 199, 246, 247
ideology, 10, 70, 78–79, 106, 132, 144,
    232
Idris, Wafa, 135, 136
imaginary, 20, 77, 105–7, 132, 175,
    206, 224, 232; imagination, 10, 70,
    195, 224. See also cultural imaginary
incorporation, 63–64, 66, 72–74
independence, 3, 16, 23, 69, 74–75,
    77, 120, 185, 227, 237, 238
Indo-Europeans, 14, 168
Indonesia, 5
Innab, 116
international aid, 94
international community, 9, 10, 41,
    61, 78, 93
international law, 10
international order, 3, 9, 10
intifada, 8, 9, 10, 22, 56–57, 60–63,
    68, 73–77, 79, 86, 90–91, 102,
    104–5, 113, 126, 136, 145, 148, 161,
    175, 177, 194, 196, 202, 211, 216,
    249, 251, 252. See also Aqsa Intif-
    ada, Al-
Iran, 80
Iraq, 4, 91
irtibat al-madani, al- (Administration
    of Civil Coordination Department),
    67, 248
Islam, 7, 8, 10, 15, 49, 61, 70, 76, 79–
    81, 88, 95, 102, 121, 125–26, 128,
    130, 134–35, 144, 150, 152, 172,

174, 191, 194–96, 243–44, 249,
    253, 255
Islamic Jihad, 7, 18, 49, 72, 76–77,
    80, 82, 88–89, 95, 124, 137, 140–
    42, 144–47, 157, 161, 165, 166, 175,
    190, 194, 195, 202, 205, 212, 216,
    254
Islamic Liberation Party, 80
Islamic Resistance Movement. See
    Hamas
Islamic Revolution, 80
isolation, 1, 12, 83, 93, 95, 99, 106,
    132, 157, 159, 182, 184, 216, 217,
    232, 238
Israeli air force, 105
Israeli army, 1, 5, 8, 40, 42–43, 50–
    52, 55–60, 67, 74, 93, 100–101,
    103, 106–18
Israeli navy, 165
Israeli Secret Service (Shabak), 145,
    165, 242, 249, 252, 255
istishhadi, 8–11, 13–19, 22, 67, 70,
    76–78, 88, 127, 131, 134–35, 140,
    141, 150–51, 183, 184, 185, 195,
    202, 207, 251
Izzideen al-Qassam Martyrs Brigades,
    10, 34, 196, 201, 203, 243, 249, 255

Jabaa', 143
Jabha al-Shaa'biyya li-Tahrir Filistin
    (Popular Front for the Liberation of
    Palestine), 7, 18, 42–43, 63, 72,
    78–82, 88, 91–92, 106, 124, 134,
    160, 194, 195, 197, 202, 243, 244,
    255
Jaffa, 28, 167, 170, 246
Jalama, al-, 1, 30, 82, 121, 200, 201
Jalama checkpoint, 82
Japan, 191
Jaradat, Hanadi, 159–76, 254
Jaradat, Ragheb, 147–59
Jarash University, 160
Jazeera, al-, 8

Jenin, 1, 12, 21, 51, 54, 58, 67, 83, 85–
    86, 101, 103, 107, 109, 113, 115–24,
    137, 138, 141, 143, 145–47, 153,
    155–58, 160, 161, 173, 174, 194,
    197–202, 243, 244, 246, 248–50,
    252–55; battle in, 40, 152, 189;
    massacre in, 40, 183; refugee camp
    in, 40, 59, 82, 87–88
Jericho, 73, 180
Jerusalem, 13, 28 35, 42, 64, 74, 76–
    77, 93, 99–100, 114–15, 135, 136,
    153, 174, 177, 180, 188, 209, 243,
    249, 22, 254
Jerusalem Battalions, 202
Jewish immigrants, 75, 114, 248, 253
Jewish militias, 74, 160, 253
Jewish National Fund, 28, 33
Jewish nationalism, 72, 97, 99, 230
Jewish Zealots, 187
jihad, 70, 128–29, 163, 195
Jihad, Al- (Islamic Jihad), 7, 18, 49,
    72, 76–77, 80, 82, 88–89, 95, 124,
    137, 140–42, 144–47, 157, 161, 165,
    166, 175, 190, 194, 195, 202, 205,
    212, 216, 254
Jnaid jail, 144
Jordan, 8, 26, 41–43, 63, 72, 75, 160,
    161, 166, 187, 214, 243, 246–48,
    250
Jordanian Royal Guard, 43
Jordan River, 42, 45
Jordan Valley, 28, 114, 160
Judea, 247

Ka'aba, Al-, 251
Kabul, 75
Kamikaze, 188, 189
Kanafani, Ghassan, 38
Karameh, Al-, 7, 8, 42–44, 243
Khalifi, Marcel, 106
Kharita al-Haykaliyya, Al- (Skeleton
    Map), 66–67
Khayber, 252

Khedara, 8, 67–70, 146, 246, 248
Kirkuk Junction, 146
Knesset, 144, 194
kuffiyya, 34, 254
Kufor Rai'i, 142, 143

Land Day, 51
land dispossession, 29, 31, 33–35, 51,
    66, 79, 178, 211, 245, 248, 253
land register, 31, 245
landscape, 26, 34, 100, 113–15, 119–
    20, 132, 140, 158, 159, 164, 166,
    168, 172, 177, 184, 186, 234, 238,
    250, 251
Land Settlement Ordinance, 36
land tenure, 21, 244
land use, 66–67
Langer, Felicia, 169, 253
Lebanese resistance, 188
Lebanon, 166, 187, 188, 191, 214, 248
Legislative Council, 65
legitimacy, 4, 5, 7, 137, 207, 210, 219,
    220, 235
liberation, 8, 80, 126, 128, 174, 187,
    213, 215
life history, 2, 18, 23, 140, 141, 233
Likud, 68
local knowledge, 15, 69, 71–72, 108–
    9, 138
Lod, Al-, 246
London, 171, 248
LTTE (Liberation Tigers of Tamil
    Elam), 188, 218

macrocosm, 168, 169
Madrid, 61, 64, 73
Majdal, Al-, 167, 246
Mansour, Suleiman, 98–100, 177,
    178, 249, 253
marba'aniyya, al-, 30, 244
Marj ibn 'Amer, 29, 36, 177, 244, 245,
    253
Marxism, 8, 134, 195, 244

Masri, Maher Al-, 31, 254
Masri, Zafer Al-, 63
massacre, 68–69, 157, 168, 183, 246
Mecca, 144, 252, 251, 255
media, 11, 16, 19, 39, 43, 66, 70, 74,
    76, 136, 137, 152, 153, 160, 176,
    177, 207, 210, 216, 218, 220, 221,
    229, 230, 252
mediation, 4, 6, 7, 71, 72, 239
Mediterranean Sea, 160
Megiddo Junction, 146
microcosm, 168, 169
Middle East Peace Conference, 63
modernity, 2, 80, 94, 181, 222, 223,
    231; modernization, 193
Mofaz, 169, 172
Mohammed, Prophet, 80, 252
Morocco, 5
motivation, 3, 5, 6, 10, 11, 15, 26, 71, 72,
    138–40, 152, 164, 186, 188, 227, 233
Mount of Olives, 114
Muslim Brotherhood Society (Jama'at
    al-Ukhwan al-Muslimeen), 49, 79–
    80
Mu'tasem, 145

Nablus, 59, 113, 115–17, 143–45, 157,
    246, 254
Nakba, Al- (catastrophe), 41, 71, 75,
    177, 228, 253
Nasab, 31
narrative, 25, 26, 112–13, 115, 126
nationalism, 11, 49, 84
National Resistance Brigades, 196
nationhood, 56, 221, 228, 229
Native Americans, 214
Nawab, Muzaffer Al-, 34
Negev, 28
Netanyahu, Benjamin, 68, 74
New World Order, 9, 171, 211, 223
NGOs, 81, 92–95, 200, 244
Nile River, 166
no escape operation, 187, 188, 205, 255

noncombatant, 8, 189
normalcy, 3, 16, 158, 159, 170, 171,
    219, 235
North America, 4, 75,248
Nusseibeh, Sarri, 39

occupation, 9, 12, 15, 20, 49–51, 55,
    60, 62–63, 65–66, 69, 79–80, 83,
    111, 164, 185, 191, 206, 215, 217,
    220, 224, 241, 242, 246–48, 252
Oman, 166
ontology, 15, 104; ontological condi-
    tions, 3, 6, 23, 88, 120–21, 132–33,
    157, 167, 182, 184, 186, 227, 231,
    232; ontological order, 16
oppositions, 6, 219, 226, 233, 235,
    236
oral history, 26
Oslo accords, 20, 22, 39, 64, 66–68,
    71–77, 79, 82, 86, 136, 141, 144,
    177, 178, 206, 212, 213, 220, 221,
    247, 254
Ottomans, 31

PA (Palestinian Authority), 20, 64–
    67, 74, 79–91, 93, 95, 135–37, 144,
    213, 216, 231, 247, 248, 254
Palestine Liberation Organization
    (PLO), 8, 43–44, 48–50, 63–64,
    68, 73–74, 76–82, 91, 96, 134, 144,
    247, 248
Palestine Return Center (PRC), 248
Palestine Right to Return Coalition,
    248
Palestinian Authority (PA), 20, 64–
    67, 74, 79–91, 93, 95, 135–37, 144,
    213, 216, 231, 247, 248, 254
Palestinian Legislative Council, 65
Palestinian National Liberation Move-
    ment (Fatah), 7, 18, 42–43, 71, 78–
    79, 81–82, 85–88, 92, 123–24, 134–
    38, 141, 144, 190, 195–97, 202, 205,
    206, 243, 244, 249, 251, 252, 254

Palestinian Red Crescent Society, 63
peace process, 20, 22, 23, 39, 49, 61–62, 66, 68, 73–78, 81, 141, 195
peoplehood, 3, 16, 45, 157, 181, 184, 185, 227, 228, 234
People's Party, 91
Peres, Shimon, 68
Persia, 187
Persian Gulf, 142, 252, 254
Persians, 14, 168
PFLP (Popular Front for the Liberation of Palestine), 7, 18, 42–43, 63, 72, 78–82, 88, 91–92, 106, 124, 134, 160, 194, 195, 197, 202, 243, 244, 255
PKK (Kurdistan Workers Party), 188, 218
place, 13, 15–18, 24, 31, 67, 71, 95, 100, 115, 158, 171, 181–86, 193, 197, 218, 220, 227, 228, 232, 235, 243
PLO (Palestine Liberation Organization), 8, 43–44, 48–50, 63–64, 68, 73–74, 76–82, 91, 96, 134, 144, 247, 248
poetics, 2, 3, 6, 13, 14, 26, 43, 47, 70, 72, 107, 120, 140, 151, 152, 154, 156, 157, 168, 169, 183, 186, 226, 229, 232, 233, 234
polarization, 3, 14, 23, 71–71, 93, 132–33, 154, 157, 168, 169, 179, 183, 184, 226, 227, 231, 232
political processes, 4, 45, 50
poppy, 47, 167, 183, 250, 256
Popular Committees for the Defense of the Right of Return in Palestine, 248
Popular Front for the Liberation of Palestine (PFLP), 7, 18, 42–43, 63, 72, 78–82, 88, 91–92, 106, 124, 134, 160, 194, 195, 197, 202, 243, 244, 255

prescriptive event, 28, 33, 41, 43, 225, 228
publics, 3, 9, 10, 19, 70, 73, 84, 195, 206, 207, 212, 215, 220, 224, 227, 228, 235, 236

Qabatiya, 82, 102, 104, 165
Qaeda, Al-, 188, 190
Qalandia, 143
Qalandia Technical Institute, 142
qaq, al-, 30, 245
qa'qur, 30
Qassam, 124, 127, 130
Qassam, Ahmed Al-, 121
Qassam, Izzideen Al-, 37, 250
Qassam Martyrs Brigades, Al-, 197, 251, 255
Qreia', Ahmed, 254
Quds, Al- (Jerusalem), 13, 28 35, 42, 64, 74, 76–77, 93, 99–100, 114–15, 135, 136, 153, 174, 177, 180, 188, 209, 243, 249, 22, 254
Quds University, Al-, 39

Rabin, Yitzhak, 60, 68–69
Radio Monte Carlo, 154
Rafah, 174, 175;
raids, 20, 22, 37, 44–45, 82, 252, 255
Ramallah, 58, 92–94, 113, 115, 117, 127, 130, 139, 201, 246, 248, 249, 251, 254
Ramla, Al-, 246
Rantisi, Abdel Aziz Al-, 89, 126–28, 130, 217
rawabet al-qura (Village League), 63
reconfiguration, 15, 62, 40–41, 115, 131, 169, 184, 236
Red Cross, 144
refugee camps, 41, 43–44, 49, 75, 78, 84, 104, 126, 175, 202; Jenin Camp, 40, 59, 82, 87–88; Rafah Camp, 241, 242; Tulkarem Camp, 241

refugees, 22, 37, 74–75, 83, 178, 244, 246, 253

religion, 17, 70, 79, 124, 126, 130, 132, 155, 163, 214

representation, 17, 18, 20, 25, 27, 34, 47, 61, 63, 74, 109, 114–15, 120, 144, 151, 168, 173, 183, 228, 230, 231, 233, 234

resistance groups. See DFLP; Fatah; Hamas; Islamic Jihad; PFLP

Revolution of 1936, 37, 79, 245

right of return, 39–40, 44, 72, 75–76, 85, 178, 184, 244, 248

ritual, 14, 15 151, 166, 168, 173, 224, 225, 234

roadblocks, 64, 114, 116, 169, 182, 206, 211

Romans, 119, 188

Russia, 188, 210

Sabra and Shatila, 75

sacredness, 13, 46, 48

Safad, 13, 209, 246

Salem, 161

Samaria, 247

Sammoudi, Hamzi Al-, 146

Saraya (military wing of Islamic Jihad), 124, 130, 251, 252

Saudi Arabia, 135, 136, 190, 192

Sawalha, Eyad, 143

Scythians, 14, 168

Sea of Galilee, 207

secularism, 7, 8, 49, 61, 71, 134, 139, 152, 195, 244

Security Council, 169, 170

Sejera, 245

self-determination, 63

self-reliance, 3, 9, 15, 44, 78, 227

self-sacrifice, 6, 7, 8, 10, 18, 70, 187, 188, 232, 250

semantics, 70

semiotics, 6, 69, 140, 188, 229, 233

sensory meanings, 159, 164, 168

settlements, 32, 33, 42, 49–50, 64, 66, 69, 82, 79, 113, 114, 136, 184, 209, 210, 211, 217, 245, 248, 250

Shaath, Nabil, 254

Shabak, 145, 165, 242, 249, 252, 255

Shafa 'Amer, 248

shahada (witness), 10, 243

shahadah (certificate of martyrdom), 147, 148, 149, 150, 243

shahid, 37, 59–60, 70, 77–78

Shahid Abu Jihad College, 144

shaqiq, 48

shari'a (Islamic law), 81

Sharm el Sheikh, 196

Sharon, Ariel, 11, 77, 124, 130, 169–72, 203, 204, 210, 211, 255

Shehadeh, Salah, 146, 203

Shin Bet, 255

Shiqaqi, Khalil, 39

shuhada', 8

Shuhada, Al-, 102, 104

siege, 49, 51–52, 157, 173, 181

Sila al-Harthiya, Al-, 161, 245, 253

Sinai, 214

Sinnoqrut, Mazin, 254

sinsileh, 101

Six-Day War, 62

social processes, 3, 4, 7, 15, 26, 44, 51, 139, 140, 176, 183, 220, 226, 227, 231, 232, 237–39

Soviet bloc, 48

Soviet Union, 68, 80, 91, 190

Spain, 5

Sri Lanka, 188, 191, 218

state building, 74

state expansion, 20, 22, 23, 50, 62, 66–67, 78–79, 84, 88, 115, 131–32, 181, 190–94, 206, 212, 214, 226, 229, 230, 247

statehood, 63, 85, 214

Stockholm, 175

Stockholm Museum of Antiquities, 175

struggle, 10, 40–41, 49–50, 69, 77, 81, 85, 88, 95, 99, 123, 125, 128, 130, 135, 155, 178, 182, 195, 204, 210, 214, 235, 253

suicide, 1, 2, 4, 5, 6, 8, 11, 12, 13, 68, 76, 84, 124, 137–39, 187–92, 218, 224, 226–27, 250

Sursuq, Isqandar, 245

symbols, 20, 44, 179, 183, 225, 228, 229, 256

Syria, 41–42, 49, 75, 166, 187, 243, 248

Tabaria, 33

tabu, 31

takfir, 90, 249

tanzim, 82, 85, 87

Taqasum al-Wazifi, Al-, 247

Taqatqeh, 'Andaleeb, 135

target, 2, 8, 10, 11, 18, 42, 50, 55, 89, 125, 134, 171, 185, 188, 189, 192, 207–9, 216, 218, 220, 222, 227, 235, 236, 249, 252, 254

Tasmanians, 214

Tawalbeh, Mahmoud, 189, 190, 254

Taybeh, 145

Tel Aviv, 11, 117, 125, 146, 205, 245

Tel Aviv University, 139

torture, 53–54, 66, 143, 255

Toubasi, Shadi Al-, 47

tribalization, 86, 88–90, 194, 230

tribal zone, 62, 229, 230

Tulkarem, 117, 125, 145, 241

Tunisia, 49

Turkey, 188, 191

Ukraine, 153

Umayyad, 126

Unified National Leadership of the Uprising (Al-Qiyada Al-Wataniyya Al-Muwahada), 60

United Arab Emirates, 166

United Kingdom, 75

United Nations (UN), 41, 75, 93–94, 155, 210; Security Council, 169, 170

United States, 5, 9, 39, 57, 61, 63, 76, 80, 88–90, 102, 135, 188, 190, 192, 193, 210, 215, 254

unity, 1, 3, 12, 16, 84–86, 105, 125, 157, 159, 164, 168, 184, 186, 227, 236

university, 42, 50–51, 60–61, 63, 102, 114–16, 118–19, 139, 147–50, 160, 161, 200, 201, 252

University of Cairo, 42

University of Wisconsin, 115

uprooting, 3, 99, 120, 159, 167, 175, 227

Value Added Tax (VAT), 65

victim, 4, 9, 13 –15, 46, 54–55, 78, 105, 111–12, 135, 165, 168, 176, 183, 204, 218, 223, 224, 255

Village League (rawabet al-qura), 63

violence: mimetic, 3, 72, 155, 158, 171, 172, 175, 185, 219, 235, 236; nonstate, 155, 158; political, 1, 2, 7, 94, 225; state, 2, 17, 18, 72, 131, 139, 157, 159, 171, 172, 192, 219, 223, 226, 232, 233, 235, 236

Voice of Palestine, 44, 51, 52

Wadi Birqin, 47

wafer, 30

wall, 157, 167, 172, 184, 193, 211, 254

War on Terror, 11

wasem, 30

Woods and Forest Ordinance, 35

Yalon, 169

Yamoun, 82

Yassin, Ahmed, 121–26, 128, 217

Yatta, 241

Yemen, 49

Zakarneh, Ra'id, 67

Zbaideh, Zakariya, 82, 85, 125, 251

Zbuba, 165

Zer'in, 30, 160, 245

Zion, 158

Zionism, 9–10, 28, 37, 68, 77, 84,
97–98, 112, 126, 165, 182, 203, 211–
16, 218, 219, 224, 230, 250, 255

NASSER ABUFARHA RECENTLY RECEIVED HIS PH.D.

IN ANTHROPOLOGY FROM THE UNIVERSITY OF

WISCONSIN, MADISON.

Library of Congress Cataloging-in-Publication Data
Abufarha, Nasser, 1964–
The making of a human bomb : an ethnography of Palestinian resistance /
Nasser Abufarha.
p. cm.—(The cultures and practice of violence series)
Includes bibliographical references and index.
ISBN 978-0-8223-4428-5 (cloth : alk. paper)
ISBN 978-0-8223-4439-1 (pbk. : alk. paper)
1. Suicide bombers—Palestine. 2. Suicide bombings—Palestine.
3. Arab-Israeli conflict—1993– 4. Political violence—Palestine. I. Title.
II. Series: Cultures and practice of violence series.
HV6433.P25A28 2009
956.9405—dc22   2009006501